Samsung®
Galaxy S®6

FOR

DUMMIES®

A Wiley Brand

Samsung® Galaxy S®6

FOR DUMMIES®
A Wiley Brand

by Bill Hughes

Samsung® Galaxy S®6 For Dummies®

Published by: John Wiley & Sons, Inc., 111 River Street, Hoboken, NJ 07030-5774, www.wiley.com

Copyright © 2015 by John Wiley & Sons, Inc., Hoboken, New Jersey

Published simultaneously in Canada

No part of this publication may be reproduced, stored in a retrieval system or transmitted in any form or by any means, electronic, mechanical, photocopying, recording, scanning or otherwise, except as permitted under Sections 107 or 108 of the 1976 United States Copyright Act, without the prior written permission of the Publisher. Requests to the Publisher for permission should be addressed to the Permissions Department, John Wiley & Sons, Inc., 111 River Street, Hoboken, NJ 07030, (201) 748-6011, fax (201) 748-6008, or online at http://www.wiley.com/go/permissions.

Trademarks: Wiley, For Dummies, the Dummies Man logo, Dummies.com, Making Everything Easier, and related trade dress are trademarks or registered trademarks of John Wiley & Sons, Inc. and may not be used without written permission. Samsung and Galaxy S are registered trademarks of Samsung Electronics Co. Ltd. All other trademarks are the property of their respective owners. John Wiley & Sons, Inc. is not associated with any product or vendor mentioned in this book.

For general information on our other products and services, please contact our Customer Care Department within the U.S. at 877-762-2974, outside the U.S. at 317-572-3993, or fax 317-572-4002. For technical support, please visit www.wiley.com/techsupport.

Wiley publishes in a variety of print and electronic formats and by print-on-demand. Some material included with standard print versions of this book may not be included in e-books or in print-on-demand. If this book refers to media such as a CD or DVD that is not included in the version you purchased, you may download this material at http://booksupport.wiley.com. For more information about Wiley products, visit www.wiley.com.

Library of Congress Control Number: 2015941962

ISBN 978-1-119-12060-5 (pbk); ISBN 978-1-119-12064-3 (ebk); ISBN 978-1-119-12062-9 (ebk)

Manufactured in the United States of America

10 9 8 7 6 5 4 3 2 1

Contents at a Glance

Table of Contents

Introduction

. . . .

*T*he Samsung Galaxy S6 and S6 Edge are powerful smartphones, perhaps the most powerful mobile phones ever sold. As of the publication of this book, the Galaxy S6s are the standard against which all other Android-based phones are measured.

Each cellular carrier offers a slightly customized version of the Galaxy S6 line-up. Some phones from cellular carriers come out of the box with pre-loaded applications, games, or files. Some come with accessories, such as a corded headset; others don't. This book doesn't dwell on these kinds of differences.

Although the name for each network is different, these phones are largely the same (at least one marketing person at each cellular carrier is cringing as you read this). This similarity allows me to write this book in a way that covers the common capabilities. I will simply refer to the phone as the Galaxy S6 unless there is a relevant difference worth mentioning from this point on.

At a more core level, these phones are built for high-speed wireless communications. The cellular carriers have spent kajillions upgrading their networks to offer more coverage and better data speeds than their competition. Again, this book doesn't dwell on these differences in network technology because they don't really make much difference (again, at least one engineering person at each cellular carrier is cringing as you read this).

I assume that you already have a Galaxy S6, and I just hope that you have good coverage where you spend more of your time with your phone. If so, you'll be fine. If not, you need to switch to another network; otherwise the experience with your phone will be frustrating. I would advise you to return your phone to that carrier and buy your Galaxy S6 at another cellular carrier. As long as you have good cellular data coverage, owning a Samsung Galaxy S6 will be an exciting experience!

First, in much the same way that different brands of PCs are all based on the Microsoft Windows operating system, all Galaxy S phones use the Google Android platform. The good news is that the Android platform has proven to be widely popular, even more successful than Google originally expected when it first announced Android in November 2007. More people are using Android-based phones and more third parties are writing applications. This is good news because it offers you more options for applications (more on this in Chapter 8 on the Play Store, where you buy applications).

In addition, all Galaxy S6 phones use a powerful graphics processor, employ Samsung's Super AMOLED touchscreen, and are covered in Corning's Gorilla Glass. The superior screen experience differentiates this product line from other Android phones. Because of these enhanced capabilities, you can navigate around the screen with multi-touch screen gestures instead of the hierarchical menus found on lesser Android phones. Plus, the videos look stunning from many angles.

Smartphones are getting smarter all the time, and the Galaxy S6 is one of the smartest. However, just because you've used a smartphone in the past doesn't mean you should expect to use your new Galaxy S6 without a bit of guidance.

You may not be familiar with using a multi-touch screen, and your new phone offers a lot of capabilities that you may or may not be familiar with. It would be unfortunate to find out from a kid in the neighborhood that the phone you've been carrying around for several months could solve a problem you've been having because you were never told that the solution was in your pocket the whole time.

In fact, Samsung is proud of the usability of its entire Galaxy lineup — and proud that the user's manual is really just a "quickstart" guide. You can find lots of instructions on the web. However, you have to know what you don't know to get what you want unless you plan to view every tutorial.

That's where this book comes in. This book is a hands-on guide to getting the most out of your Galaxy S6.

About This Book

This book is a reference — you don't have to read it from beginning to end to get all you need out of it. The information is clearly organized and easy to access. You don't need thick glasses to understand this book. This book helps you figure out what you want to do — and then tells you how to do it in plain English.

I don't use many conventions in this book, but here are a few you should know about:

  ✔ Whenever I introduce a new term, I put it in *italics* and define it shortly thereafter.

- I use **bold** for the action parts of numbered steps, so you can easily see what you're supposed to do.

- I use `monofont` for web addresses and e-mail addresses, so they stand out from the surrounding text. If you're reading this as an e-book, these links are live and clickable. **Note:** When this book was printed, some web addresses may have needed to break across two lines of text. If that happened, rest assured that we haven't put in any extra characters (such as hyphens) to indicate the break. So, when using one of these web addresses, just type in exactly what you see in this book, pretending that the line break doesn't exist.

What You're Not to Read

I think you'll find every last word of this book scintillating, but I may be a little biased. The truth is, you don't have to read:

- **Sidebars:** Sidebars are those gray boxes throughout the book. They're interesting, but not essential to the topic at hand, so if you're short on time (or you only want the information you absolutely need), you can skip them.

- **Text marked with the Technical Stuff icon:** For more on this icon, see the "Icons Used in This Book" section, later in this Introduction.

Foolish Assumptions

You know what they say about assuming, so I don't do much of it in this book. But I do make a few assumptions about you:

- **You have a Galaxy S6 phone.** You may be thinking about buying a Galaxy S6 phone, but my money's on your already owning one. After all, getting your hands on the phone is the best part!

- **You're not totally new to mobile phones.** You know that your Galaxy S6 is capable of doing more than the average phone, and you're eager to find out what your phone can do.

- **You've used a computer.** You don't have to be a computer expert, but you at least know how to check your e-mail and surf the web.

How This Book Is Organized

The 18 chapters in this book are divided into six parts. Here's what you can find in each part.

Part I: Getting Started with the Samsung Galaxy S6

The first part of this book gets you familiar with the basic capabilities of your Galaxy S6 phone. Chapters 1 and 2 are an introduction to everything from turning it on and off, to understanding cellular billing, to managing battery life.

Part II: Communications

In this part, I walk you through the basic capabilities of the Galaxy S6 for communicating with voice, texts, and e-mail. Chapter 3 is about making calls. Chapter 4 covers what you need to know about texting. Chapter 5 covers e-mailing, and Chapter 6 explores how the phone works with your Contacts database.

Part III: Live on the Internet: Going Mobile

This part is all about the Internet — how to access it from your Galaxy S6 phone. I also introduce you to the Play Store, where you can trick out your phone with more apps.

Part IV: Entertainment Applications

An important use for many smartphone owners involves entertainment. Chapter 9 covers the impressive picture-taking capabilities of your phone, but really only covers some of the capabilities. Chapter 10 looks at the impressive gaming capabilities; Chapter 11 explores navigating to all the fun places you can go in the real world; and Chapter 12 walks you through playing music and video on your phone.

Part V: Productivity Applications

In this part, I cover the capabilities of the Galaxy S6 smartphone that make you more productive at home and work.

Part VI: The Part of Tens

This wouldn't be a *For Dummies* book without a Part of Tens. In this book, the Part of Tens covers ten ways to customize the phone to make it truly your own, how to keep your information safe, and ten capabilities to look for in future releases.

Icons Used in This Book

Throughout this book, I used *icons* (little pictures in the margin) to draw your attention to various types of information. Here's a key to what those icons mean:

This whole book is like one big series of tips. When I share especially useful tips and tricks, I mark them with the Tip icon.

This book is a reference, which means you don't have to commit it to memory — there is no test at the end. But once in a while, I do tell you things that are so important that I think you should remember them, and when I do, I mark them with the Remember icon.

Whenever you may do something that could cause a major headache, I warn you with the, er, Warning icon.

These sections provide a little more information than is necessary to use your phone. The hope is that these sections convey extra knowledge to help you understand what is going on when things go wrong, or at least differently than you might have expected.

Beyond the Book

This book has more great online extras. To access the book's online cheat sheet, go to www.dummies.com/cheatsheet/samsunggalaxys6. To read articles about the Samsung Galaxy S6, go to www.dummies.com/extras/samsunggalaxys6.

Occasionally, we have updates to our technology books. If this book does have technical updates, they will be posted at www.dummies.com/extras/samsunggalaxyS6.

Where to Go from Here

You don't have to read this book from cover to cover. You can skip around as you like. For example, if you need the basics on calling, texting, and e-mailing, turn to Part II. To discover more about photos, games, and apps, go to Part IV. To find out about the phone's calendar functions or about using the Microsoft Office, turn to Part V.

Many readers are already somewhat familiar with smartphones, and won't need the basic information found in Parts I and II. A reasonably astute mobile phone user can figure out how to use the phone, text, and data capabilities. Parts I and II are not for those readers. For them I recommend skipping ahead to the chapters in Parts III through VI.

Former iPhone users, on the other hand, are a special case (first, welcome to the world of Android!). The reality is that the iPhone and Galaxy S series have very similar capabilities, but these functions are just done in slightly different ways and emphasize different approaches to the similar problems. iPhone users, don't worry if you find that this book spends a fair amount of time explaining capabilities with which you're familiar. You can read through those chapters quickly, focus on the *how* instead of the description of *what,* and bypass potential frustration.

Current Samsung Galaxy S5 users are also a special case. The Samsung Galaxy S6 is very similar to the Galaxy S5 in many ways. Galaxy S6 operates mostly like the S5, but has improvements in usability, power consumption, and performance. If you're comfortable with the Galaxy S5, and now have a Galaxy S6, Chapters 15 and beyond would be of interest to you.

Part I

Getting Started with the Samsung Galaxy S6

 Visit www.dummies.com/extras/samsunggalaxys6 for great Dummies content online.

In this part. . .

- ✐ Review the capabilities of mobile phones and what sets smartphones apart
- ✐ Navigate your Galaxy S6 for the first time
- ✐ Turn off your phone and manage sleep mode
- ✐ Make sense of cellular billing

Exploring What You Can Do with Your Phone

. . . .

In This Chapter

▶ Reviewing the basic capabilities of just about any mobile phone

▶ Understanding what sets smartphones apart

▶ Mapping out what makes Samsung Galaxy S6 phones so cool

▶ Making sense of cellular billing

. . . .

Whether you want just the basics from a mobile phone (make and take phone calls, customize your ringtone, take some pictures, maybe use a Bluetooth headset) or you want your phone to be always by your side (a tool for multiple uses throughout your day), you can make that happen. In this chapter, I outline all the things your Samsung Galaxy S6 can do — from the basics to what makes Galaxy S6 phones different from the rest.

Discovering the Basics of Your Phone

All mobile phones on the market today include basic functions, and even some entry-level phones are a little more sophisticated. Of course, Samsung includes all basic functions on the Galaxy S6 model. In addition to making and taking calls (see Chapter 3) and sending and receiving texts (see Chapter 4), the Galaxy S6 sports the following basic features:

✔ **16MP digital camera:** This resolution is more than enough for posting good-quality images on the Internet and even having 8" x 10" prints made.

✔ **Ringtones:** You can replace the standard ringtone with custom ringtones that you download to your phone. You also can specify different rings for different numbers.

- **Bluetooth:** The Galaxy S6 phone supports stereo and standard Bluetooth devices. (See Chapter 3 for more on Bluetooth.)

- **High-resolution screen:** The Galaxy S6 phone offers one of the highest-resolution touchscreens on the market (2560 × 1440 pixels).

- **Capacitive touchscreen:** The Galaxy S6 phone offers a very slick touch-screen that's sensitive enough to allow you to interact with the screen accurately, but not so sensitive that it's hard to manage. In addition, it has an optional setting that steps up the sensitivity in case you want to use your phone while wearing gloves!

Taking Your Phone to the Next Level: The Smartphone Features

In addition to the basic capabilities of any entry-level phone, the Galaxy S6, which is based on the popular Android platform for mobile devices, has capabilities associated with other smartphones, such as the Apple iPhone and the phones based on the Windows Phone 8 operating system:

- **Internet access:** Access websites through a web browser on your phone.

- **Photos:** The Galaxy S6 comes with a very intelligent camera that has millions of combinations of settings, filters, and resolutions, and also has the capability to manage photos.

- **Wireless e-mail:** Send and receive e-mail from your phone.

- **Multimedia:** Play music and videos on your phone.

- **Contact Manager:** The Galaxy S6 lets you take shortcuts that save you from having to enter someone's ten-digit number each time you want to call or text a friend. In fact, the Contact Manager can track all the numbers that an individual might have, store an e-mail address and photo for the person, and synchronize with the program you use for managing contacts on both your personal and work PCs!

- **Digital camcorder:** The Galaxy S6 comes with a built-in digital cam-corder that records live video at a resolution that you can set, including UHD (ultra-high definition, which is just now becoming available on the newest televisions).

- **Mapping and directions:** The Galaxy S6 uses GPS (Global Positioning System) in your phone to tell you where you are, find local services that you need, and give you directions to where you want to go.

✓ **Fitness information:** The Galaxy S6 automatically tracks important health information within the phone and with external sensors.

✓ **Business applications:** The Galaxy S6 can keep you productive while you're away from the office.

I go into each of these capabilities in greater detail in the following sections.

Internet access

Until a few years ago, the only way to access the Internet when you were away from a desk was with a laptop. Smartphones are a great alternative to laptops because they're small, convenient, and ready to launch their web browsers right away. Even more important, when you have a smartphone, you can access the Internet wherever you are — whether Wi-Fi is available or not.

The drawback to smartphones, however, is that their screen size is smaller than that of even the most basic laptop. On the Galaxy S6 phone, you can use the standard version of a website if you want. You can pinch and stretch your way to get the information you want. (See Chapter 2 for more information on pinching and stretching. For more information on accessing the Internet from your Galaxy S6 phone, turn to Chapter 7.)

To make things a bit easier, many popular websites offer an easier-to-use app that you can download and install on your phone. This is discussed in detail in Chapter 8. Essentially the website reformats the information from the site so that it's easier to read and navigate in the mobile environment. Figure 1-1 compares a regular website with the app version of that website.

Photos

The image application on your phone helps you use the digital camera on your Galaxy S6 phone to its full potential. (It would almost make sense to call the Samsung Galaxy S6 a smartcamera with a built-in phone!)

Studies have found that mobile phone users tend to snap a bunch of pictures within the first month of phone usage. After that, the photos sit on the phone (instead of being downloaded to a computer), and the picture-taking rate drops dramatically.

The Galaxy S6 image management application is different. You can integrate your camera images into your home photo library, as well as photo-sharing sites such as Picasa and Flickr, with minimal effort.

For more on how to use the Photo applications, turn to Chapter 9.

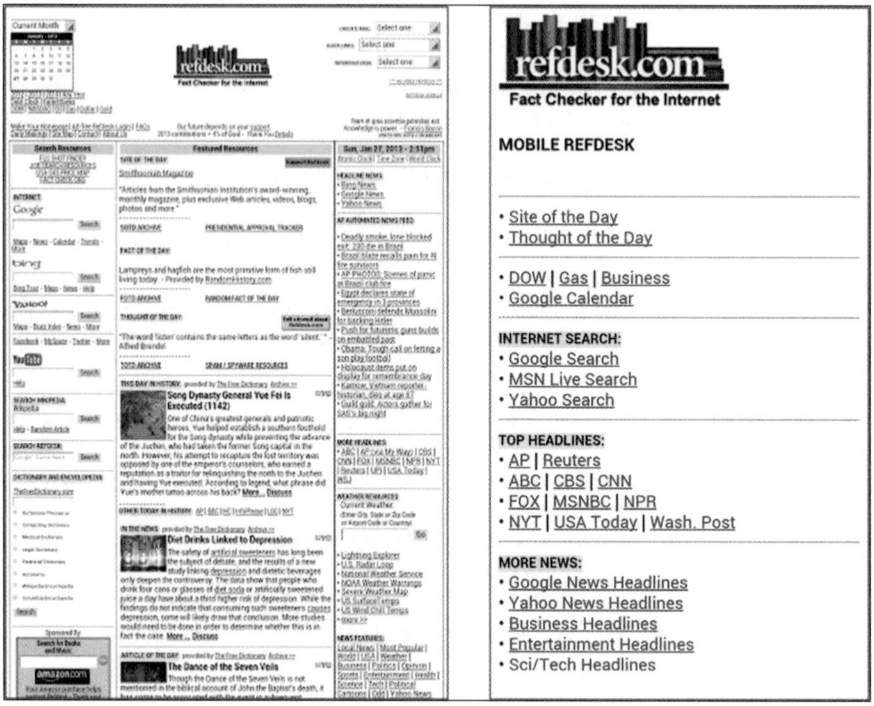

Figure 1-1: A website and the app version of the main site.

Wireless e-mail

On your Galaxy S6 smartphone, you can access your business and personal e-mail accounts, reading and sending e-mail messages on the go. Depending on your e-mail system, you might be able to sync so that when you delete an e-mail on your phone, the e-mail is deleted on your computer at the same time so you don't have to read the same messages on your phone and your computer.

Chapter 5 covers setting up your business and personal e-mail accounts.

Multimedia

Some smartphones allow you to play music and videos on your phone in place of a dedicated MP3 or video player. On the Galaxy S6, you can use the applications that come with the phone, or you can download applications that offer these capabilities from the Play Store.

Chapter 12 covers how to use the multimedia services with your Galaxy S6 phone.

Business applications

Whether your company gives you a Galaxy S6 phone for work or you buy your Galaxy S6 phone yourself, you can use the Galaxy S6 to work with Microsoft Office applications.

Chapter 14 explores how to set up your phone to work with Microsoft Office applications. After you set it up, you'll have unprecedented access to your calendar.

Customizing Your Phone with Games and Applications

Application developers — large and small — are working on the Android platform to offer a variety of applications and games for the Galaxy S6 phone. Compared to most of the other smartphone platforms, Google imposes fewer restrictions on application developers regarding what's allowable. This freedom to develop resonates with many developers — resulting in a bonanza of application development on this platform.

As of this writing, more than one million applications are available from Google's Play Store. For more information about downloading games and applications, turn to Chapter 8.

Downloading games

Chapter 10 of this book is for gamers. Although your phone comes with a few general-interest games, you can find a whole wide world of games for every skill and taste. In Chapter 10, I give you all the information you need to set up different gaming experiences. Whether you prefer standalone games or multi-player games, you can set up your Galaxy S6 phone to get what you need.

Downloading applications

Your phone comes with some very nice applications, but these might not take you as far as you want to go. You might also have some special interests, such as philately or stargazing, that neither Samsung nor your carrier felt would be of sufficient general interest to include on the phone. (Can you imagine?)

Take a deep breath

You don't have to rush to implement every feature of your Galaxy S6 phone the very first day you get it. Instead, pick one capability at a time. Digest it, enjoy it, and then tackle the next one.

I recommend starting with setting up your e-mail and social accounts, but that's just me.

No matter how you tackle the process of setting up your Galaxy S6 phone, it'll take some time. If you try to cram it all in on the first day, you'll turn what should be fun into drudgery.

The good news is that you own the book that takes you through the process. You can do a chapter or two at a time.

Your phone also comes with preloaded *widgets,* which are smaller applications that serve particular purposes, such as retrieving particular stock quotes or telling you how your phone's battery is feeling today. Widgets reside on the extended Home Screen and are instantly available.

Buying applications allows you to get additional capabilities quickly, easily, and inexpensively. Ultimately, these make your phone, which is already a reflection of who you are, even more personal as you add more capabilities.

What's cool about the Android platform

The Samsung Galaxy S6 is the top-of-the-line Android phone. That means you can run any application developed for an Android phone to its full capability. This is significant because one of the founding principles behind the Android platform is to create an environment where application developers can be as creative as possible without an oppressive organization dictating what can and cannot be sold (as long as it's within the law, of course). This creative elbow room has inspired many of the best application developers to go with Android first.

In addition, Android is designed to run multiple applications at once. Other smartphone platforms have added this capability, but Android is designed to let you to jump quickly among the multiple apps that you're running — which makes your smartphone experience that much smoother.

You and Your Shadow: How Your Cellular Carrier Bills You

In the United States, most cellular companies sell phones at a significant discount when you sign up for a service agreement. And most cellular companies offer discounts on phones when you want to upgrade to something newer (as long as you also sign up for another couple of years of service).

So, it's not surprising that most people buy their phones directly from cellular companies or their authorized agents.

If your new Galaxy S6 phone device is an upgrade from an older phone, you might have a service plan that was suitable with your last phone but isn't so great anymore. If this is your first mobile phone (ever, or with this particular carrier), you might start with an entry-level plan, thinking you wouldn't need "that many minutes," only to find that you and your phone are inseparable, and you need a better plan. The good news is that most cellular carriers allow you to change your service plan.

Most cellular service plans have three components of usage:

- ✔ Voice
- ✔ Text
- ✔ Data

I walk you through each of these components and how they affect using your Galaxy S6 in the following sections.

Voice usage

Voice usage is the most common, costly, and complex element of most service plans. Cellular providers typically offer plans with a certain number of anytime minutes and a certain number of night/weekend minutes. Some providers offer plans with reduced rates (or even free calls) to frequently called numbers, to other phones with the same cellular provider, or to other mobile phones in general. If you talk a lot, you might be able to opt for an unlimited voice plan (for domestic calls only).

At its core, a Galaxy S6 phone device is, obviously, a phone. In the early days of smartphones, manufacturers were stung by the criticism that smartphones weren't as easy to use as traditional mobile phones. Indeed, you do have to bring up the phone screen to make a call (more on making and receiving calls in Chapter 3). As an improvement, Samsung has made sure that the screen used to make calls is only one click away from the Home screen.

If keeping track of minutes is important to you and your calling plan, be mindful of all the e-mail and social network updates that prompt you to call someone right away. You might be tempted to make more calls than you did with your old (dumb) mobile phone.

Text usage

A texting "bundle" is an add-on to your voice plan. Some service plans include unlimited texting; others offer a certain number of text messages for a flat rate. For example, maybe you pay an additional $5 per month to get 1,000 free text messages — meaning that you can send and receive a combined *total* of 1,000 messages per month. If you go over that limit, you pay a certain amount per message (usually more for text messages you send than those you receive).

As with voice, the Galaxy S6 phone makes texting very convenient, which in turn makes it more likely that you'll use this service and end up using more texts than you expect. However, nothing obligates you to buy a texting plan.

My advice is to get at least some texting capability, but be ready to decide if you want to pay for more or stay with a minimal plan and budget your texts.

Data usage

Although getting texting may be optional, access to the Internet is essential to get the full experience of your Galaxy S6 phone. The Internet, which is sometimes called "the cloud" (after the way it's symbolized in network diagrams) is where you access the capabilities that make the Galaxy S6 phone so special. Some cellular carriers may let you use the phone on their network without a data plan, but I cannot imagine why you'd want to do that. Although your phone will supplement the coverage you get from your cellular carrier with Wi-Fi, you really need to have a data plan from your cellular carrier to get most of the value out of your investment in your phone. There's just no getting around it.

Most cellular companies price Internet access with usage increments measured in hundreds of megabytes (MB), but more often in gigabytes (GB).

Some cellular carriers make it easy by only offering unlimited data as an option. This is good news: As you customize your phone to keep up with your friends and access your favorite sites, the cost of access won't increase. There are no big surprises in store for people who choose this plan, even if it comes at an initially higher price.

Other carriers just offer very large "buckets" of data. In any case, it can be a challenge to figure out how much data you are going to need without going over the limit and paying a usage penalty. Some carriers try to help you by giving you some tools to estimate your usage by estimating the number of e-mails, web pages, or multimedia files you plan to download.

These plans are a bit iffy. One option is to go with the lowest increment of data, unless you plan to be downloading a large number of videos.

You can use some of the tools I cover later to see how much data you're actually using.

Another school of thought is to go for an increment or two of data larger than what you think you'll need. After you've built up some history, you can call your carrier to scale back your usage if appropriate. An upgrade to the next bucket runs about $10 monthly.

Don't blame me if you don't check your usage! It's easy to check and increase your usage, even mid-billing cycle. While the phone itself has some tools to measure your data usage, most carriers provide tools on the customer-service app they pre-load on your phone to track usage. I suggest you check this amount regularly. It is not an estimate. It is the official answer.

Another consideration: family plans

A popular option is to combine your usage of voice, text, and data with that of your family members. The family unit on the plan gets to share a fixed allotment of voice minutes, texts, and data. This works well, as long as a responsible person checks your usage during the billing period!

Yet one more consideration: international usage

If you travel internationally with your Galaxy S6, you should check with your carrier about your billing options before you travel. Voice and text are usually not too bad when you roam internationally. Data is another story.

Rates for data when you're roaming internationally can be very high. You can end up with a very unpleasant situation if you don't check the rates and plan accordingly.

One final consideration: web subscription fees

Don't forget that some web-based services charge subscription fees. For example, WeatherBug offers a consumer service that gives you weather conditions, but it also offers WeatherBug Plus that provides more information — with a monthly fee to subscribers with no ads. Yup, if you want WeatherBug Plus on your phone, you have to pay the piper. Some of these services can be billed through your cellular carrier (check first), but just make sure you're willing to pony up for the service.

What if I didn't get my phone from a cellular company?

With a few exceptions, such as an "unlocked" GSM phone, each phone is associated with a particular cellular company. (In this context, a *locked* phone can work only on its original carrier.) Maybe you bought a secondhand phone on eBay, or you got a phone from a friend who didn't want his anymore. If you didn't get your phone directly from a cellular provider, you will need to figure out which provider the phone is associated with and get a service plan from that company. Some Galaxy S6 phones sold in the United States all have the cellular company's logo on the phone printed on the front. That makes it easy to know under which carrier a phone will operate.

If there's no logo on the front, you'll have to figure out which cellular carrier it can work with. The quickest way is to take the phone to any cellular store; the folks there know how to figure it out.

To narrow down the possibilities on your own, you need to do some investigation. Take off the back of the phone to find the plate with the model and serial number for the phone. If you see IMEI on the plate, the phone is based on a technology called Global System for Mobile (GSM); it'll work with AT&T, T-Mobile, MetroPCS (or all of them). If you see ESN on the plate, the phone will work with Verizon, Sprint, or U.S. Cellular.

Surviving Unboxing Day

When you turn on your phone the first time, it will ask you a series of ten questions and preferences to configure it. Frankly, they are trying to make this book unnecessary and put me out of business. The nerve!

The good folks at Samsung are well-intentioned, but not every customer who owns a Samsung Galaxy S6 knows, from day one, whether he or she wants a Samsung account, what's a good name for the phone, or what the purpose of a Cloud service, such as Dropbox, and how it would be used.

You can relax. I'll help you answer these questions — or, when appropriate, refer you to the chapter in this book that helps you come up with your answer.

On the other hand, if your phone is already set up, you probably took a guess or skipped some questions. Maybe now you're rethinking some of your choices. No problem. You can go back and change any answer you gave and get your phone to behave the way you want.

The following are the kinds of questions you may be asked. These questions may come in this order, but they may not. They typically include the following:

- ✔ **Language/accessibility:** This option lets you select your language. The default is English for phones sold within the United States. Also, the phone has some special capabilities for individuals with disabilities. If you have a disability and think you might benefit, take a look at these options. They have really tried to make this phone as usable as possible for as many folks as possible.

- ✔ **Wi-Fi:** Your phone automatically starts scanning for a Wi-Fi connection. You can always use the cellular connection when you are in cellular coverage, but if there is a Wi-Fi connection available, your phone will try to use this first. It is probably cheaper and may be faster than the cellular.

  At the same time, you may not want your phone to connect to the Wi-Fi access point with the best signal. It could be that the strongest signal is a fee-based service, whereas the next best signal is free. In any case, this page scans the available options and presents them to you.

- ✔ **Date and time:** This is easy. The default setting is to use the time and date that comes from the cellular network and the date and time format is the US style. Just tap on the next button and move on. This date and time from the cellular network is the most accurate information you'll get, and you don't need to do anything other than be within cellular coverage now and again. If you prefer non-US formatting, such as a 24-hour clock or day/month/year formatting, you can change your phone any way you want.

- ✔ **Sign up for a Samsung account:** Go ahead and sign up for an account. The Samsung account offers you some nice things to help you get your phone back should you lose it. All you need is an account name, such as an e-mail account, and a password.

When you buy a Galaxy S6 smartphone, you are now a customer of multiple companies! These include Samsung for the phone hardware, Google for the phone operating system (Android), and the wireless carrier that provides the cellular service. Plus, if you bought the phone through a phone retailer, such as Best Buy, they are in the mix as well. All of them want to make you happy, which is a good thing for the most part. The only downside is that they want to know who you are so that they can provide you with more services. Don't worry. You control how much they offer you.

- ✔ **Google account sign-up:** "Google account" means an e-mail account where the address ends in @gmail.com. If you already have an account on Gmail, enter your user ID and password here. If you don't have a Gmail account, I suggest waiting until you read Chapter 5. I highly recommend that you create a Gmail account, but there are some considerations on selecting a good name. If you are game, pick a name for your Gmail account now. Otherwise, it can wait until you read Chapter 5.

✔ **Location options:** Your phone knowing your location and providing it to an application can be sensitive issue.

If you're really worried about privacy and security, tap the green check marks on the screen and then tap the button that says Next. Selecting these options prevents applications from knowing where you are. (This choice also prevents you from getting directions and a large number of cool capabilities that are built into applications.) The only folks who'll know your location will be the 911 dispatchers if you dial them.

If you're worried about your security but want to take advantage of some of the cool capabilities built into your phone, tap the right arrow key to move forward. Remember, you can choose on a case-by-case basis whether to share your location. (I cover this issue in Chapter 8.)

✔ **Phone ownership:** This screen asks you to enter your first and last name. Go ahead and put in your real name. If you want to know more, read Chapter 5.

✔ **Cloud services:** The chances are that you will be offered the option to sign up for a cloud service where you can back-up your phone and get access to a gazillion MB of free storage. This can be a tricky decision. You could sign up for every cloud service that comes along. Then you need to remember where you stored that critical file. You could sign up for one, and you may miss a nice capability that is available on another. You could have one cloud service for work and another for personal. Here is what I recommend: Sign up for whatever Cloud service your phone offers during this initial set-up process if you do not already have one. You will learn about all of its bells and whistles later. If you are happy with a Cloud service you already have, such as Dropbox or OneDrive, chances are, they will have all the services you need for you and your phone. You can link your Galaxy S6 to this service by downloading the necessary app (which I cover how to do in Chapter 8).

✔ **Learn about key features:** If you think you don't need this book, go ahead and take this tour of all the new things you can do. If you think you might need this book in any way, shape, or form, tap the Next button. This screen is for setting up the coolest and the most sophisticated capabilities of the phone. I cover many of them in the course of this book. For now, skip this to get to the last screen.

✔ **Device name:** When this screen comes up, you'll see a text box that has the model name. You can keep this name for your phone or you can choose to personalize it a bit. For example, you can change it to "Bill's Galaxy S6" or "Indy at 425-555-1234." The purpose of this name is for connecting to a local data network, as when you're pairing to a Bluetooth device. If this last sentence made no sense to you, don't worry about it. (I go over all of this in Chapter 3.) Tap Finish. In a moment, you see the Home screen, as shown in Figure 1-2.

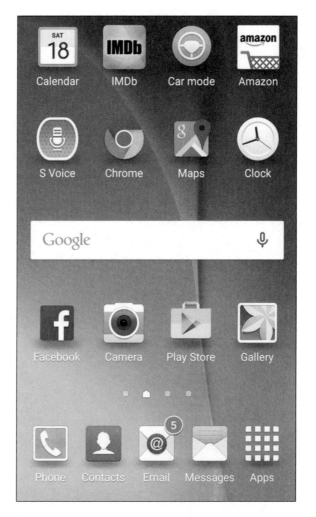

Figure 1-2: The Home screen for the Samsung Galaxy S6.

Beginning at the Beginning

In this chapter, I fill you in on the basics of using your new Samsung Galaxy S6. You start by turning on your phone. (I told you I was covering the basics!) I guide you through charging your phone and getting the most out of your phone's battery. Stick with me for a basic tour of your phone's buttons and other features. Then I end by telling you how to turn off your phone or put it in "sleep" mode.

Unless you're new to mobile phones in general — and smartphones in particular — you might want to skip this chapter. If the term "smartphone" is foreign to you, you probably haven't used one before, and reading this chapter won't hurt. And, just so you know, a *smartphone* is just a mobile phone on which you can download and run applications that are better than what comes preloaded on a phone right out of the box.

First Things First: Turning On Your Phone

When you open the box of your new phone, the packaging will present you with your phone, wrapped in plastic, readily accessible. If you haven't already, take the phone out of the plastic bag and remove any protective covering material on the screen.

First things first. The Power button is on the right side of the phone. You can see where in Figure 2-1. Press the Power button for a second and see whether it vibrates and the screen lights up. Hopefully, your phone arrived with enough electrical charge that you won't have to plug it into an outlet right away. You can enjoy your new phone for the first day without having to charge it.

The phones that you get at the stores of most cellular carriers usually come with the battery installed, partially charged, and registered with the network.

If the screen does light up, don't hold the Power button too long, or the phone might turn off.

If the phone screen doesn't light up (rats!), you need to charge the battery. Here's the rub: It's important to fully charge the battery for 24 hours, or at least overnight, so that it will last as long as possible. That means you have wait to use your beautiful new phone. Sorry.

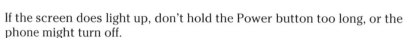

The nitty-gritty of how your phone works

As soon as you turn on your phone, several things happen. As the phone is powering up, it begins transmitting information to (and receiving information from) nearby cellular towers. The first information exchanged includes your phone's electronic serial number. Every mobile phone has its own unique serial number built into the hardware of the phone; the serial number in current-generation mobile phones can't be duplicated or used by any other phone.

This electronic serial number is also called an International Mobile Equipment Identity (IMEI) number. It is 14 or 15 digits long. Cellular equipment is fine with long numbers. We mere mortals have enough trouble remembering ten digit numbers, even with the hack of having only a limited number of area codes. To help us out, you and I get to use the shorter number and the cellular equipment happily keeps track of the ten digit and the 14/15 digit numbers and only shows us what we can handle.

It doesn't matter to the phone or the cellular tower if you're near your home when you turn on your phone — and that's the joy of mobile phones. All cellular networks have agreements that allow you to use cellular networks in other parts of the country and, sometimes, around the world.

That said, a call outside your cellular provider's own network may be expensive. Within the United States, many service plans allow you to pay the same rate if you use your phone anywhere in the United States to call anywhere in the United States. If you travel outside the United States, even to Canada, you might end up paying through the nose. Remember: Before you leave on a trip, check with your cellular carrier about your rates. Even if you travel internationally only a few times yearly, a different service plan may work better for you. Your cellular carrier can fill you in on your options.

Power button

Figure 2-1: The Power button on the Galaxy S6.

Charging Your Phone and Managing Battery Life

Although you probably don't have to plug your phone into an outlet right away, here's a handy rule: The first time you do plug it in, allow it to charge overnight.

You'll hear all kinds of "battery lore" left over from earlier battery technologies. For example, lithium-ion (Li-ion) batteries don't have a "memory" (a bad thing for a battery) as nickel-cadmium (NiCad) batteries did. And the Samsung Galaxy S6 does use Li-ion batteries. That means that you don't have make sure the battery fully discharges before you recharge it.

Your phone comes with a two-piece battery charger (cable and the transformer), as shown in Figure 2-2.

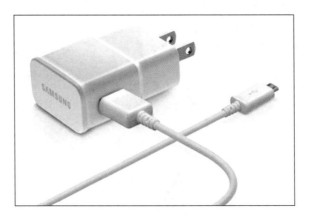

Figure 2-2: The transformer and USB cable for charging your phone.

The cable has two ends: one end that plugs into the phone, and the other that's a standard USB connector. The phone end is a small connector called a *micro USB* that is used on many Samsung devices and is the standard for charging mobile phones and other small electronics — and for connecting them to computers.

To charge the phone, you have two choices:

✔ Plug the transformer into a wall socket and then plug the cable's USB plug into the USB receptacle in the transformer.

✔ Plug the USB on the cable into a USB port on your PC.

Then you plug the small end of the cable into the phone. The port is on the bottom of the phone. You will see that the top is a little smaller than the bottom. It's a trapezoid with rounded edges. Orient the plug with the hole in the phone and make sure you push the little metal plug all the way in.

It doesn't really matter in what order you plug in things. However, if you use the USB port on a PC, the PC needs to be powered on for the phone to charge.

Unplug the transformer when you aren't charging your phone. A charger left plugged in will draw a small but continuous stream of power.

If your phone is off when you're charging the battery, an image of a battery appears onscreen for a moment. The green portion of the battery indicates the amount of charge within the battery. You can get the image to reappear with a quick press of the Power button. This image tells you the status of the battery without your having to turn on the phone.

If your phone is on, you see a small battery icon at the top of the screen showing how much charge is in the phone's battery. When the battery in the phone is fully charged, it vibrates to let you know that it's done charging and that you should unplug the phone and charger.

It takes only a few hours to go from a dead battery to a fully charged battery. Other than the first time you charge the phone, you don't need to wait for the battery to be fully charged. You can partially recharge and run if you want.

In addition to the transformer and USB cable that come with the phone, you have other optional charging tools:

- **Travel USB charger:** If you already have a USB travel charger, you can leave the transformer at home. This accessory will run you about $15. You still need your cable, although any USB-to-micro USB cable should work.

- **Car charger:** You can buy a charger with a USB port that plugs into the power socket/cigarette lighter in a car. This is convenient if you spend a lot of time in your car. The list price is $30, but you can get the real Samsung car charger for less at some online stores.

- **Portable external charger:** You can buy a portable external charger with a micro USB port that you can use to recharge your phone without having to plug into the power socket or cigarette lighter in a car. You charge this gizmo before your travel and only connect it when the charge in your phone starts to get low. These usually involve re-chargeable batteries, but some of these products use photovoltaic cells to transform light into power. As long as there is a USB port (the female part of the USB), all you need is your cable. These chargers can cost from $30 to $100 on up.

- **Wireless charger:** This option is slick. You simply put your phone on a charging mat or in a cradle and the phone battery will start charging! Your Galaxy S6 uses the widely adopted Qi standard (pronounced *chee*). This option saves you from having to plug and unplug your phone.

Ideally, use Samsung chargers — or at least chargers from reputable manufacturers. The power specifications for USB ports are standardized. Reputable manufactures comply with these standards, but less reputable manufacturers might not. Cheap USB chargers physically fit the USB end of the cable that goes to your phone. However, Li-ion batteries are sensitive to voltage; make sure your charger's specifications exactly match those of the genuine Samsung article. An off-brand USB charger can hurt the performance of your battery.

Li-ion batteries do not like extreme heat. A warm room is one thing, but if you leave your phone on the dashboard all day in Phoenix during the summer, your battery will die an untimely and permanent death. When your battery dies, your phone dies because the Galaxy S6 does not have a user-replaceable battery. If your phone is with you, and you can stand the heat, your battery will be fine.

Be aware that the conditions that make for a good charge with a photocell also tend to make for high heat. It will do you little good to have a beautifully functioning charger and a dead phone.

Navigating the Galaxy S6

Galaxy S6 phone devices differ from many other mobile phones in design: They have significantly fewer hardware buttons (physical buttons on the phone). They rely much more heavily on software buttons that appear onscreen.

In this section, I guide you through your phone's buttons.

The phone's hardware buttons

Samsung has reduced the number of hardware buttons on the Galaxy S6. There are only four: the Power button, the Volume button, the Camera button, and the Home button. Before you get too far into using your phone, orient yourself to be sure you're looking at the correct side of the phone. When I refer to the *left* or *right* of the phone, I'm assuming a vertical orientation (meaning you're not holding the phone sideways) and that you're looking at the phone's screen.

The Power button

The Power button we saw back in Figure 2-1 is on right side of the phone, toward the top when you hold it in vertical orientation.

In addition to powering up the phone, pressing the Power button puts the device into sleep mode if you press it for a moment while the phone is On.

Sleep mode shuts off the screen and suspends most running applications.

The phone automatically goes into sleep mode after about 30 seconds of inactivity to save power, but you might want to do this manually when you put away your phone. The Super AMOLED (Active-Matrix Organic Light-Emitting Diode) screen on your Samsung Galaxy S6 is cool, but it also uses a lot of power.

Don't confuse sleep mode with powering off. Because the screen is the biggest user of power on your phone, having the screen go blank saves battery life. The phone is still alert to any incoming calls; when someone calls, the screen automatically lights up.

The Volume button(s)

Technically, there are two Volume buttons: one to increase the volume, and the other to lower it. Their locations are shown in Figure 2-3.

The Volume buttons control the volume of all the audio sources on the phone, including:

- The phone ringer for when a call comes in (ringtone)
- The "notifications" that occur only when you're not talking on the phone, such as the optional ping that lets you know you've received a text or e-mail
- The phone headset when you're talking on the phone
- The volume from the digital music and video player (media)

The volume controls are aware of the context; they can tell which volume you're changing. For example, if you're listening to music, adjusting volume raises or lowers the music volume, but leaves the ringer and phone-earpiece volumes unchanged.

The Volume buttons are complementary to software settings you can make within the applications. For example, you can open the music-player software and turn up the volume on the appropriate screen. Then you can use the hardware buttons to turn down the volume, and you'll see the volume setting on the screen go down.

Another option is to go to a settings screen and set the volume levels for each scenario. Here's how to do that:

1. **From the Home screen, press either Volume button.**

   You can press it either up or down. Doing so brings up the screen shown in Figure 2-4.

   If you press the volume up or down, the ring tone gets louder or softer. Let's hold off on this tweak for now, and go to the next step.

Volume buttons

Figure 2-3: The Galaxy S6 Volume buttons on the left.

Figure 2-4: The ringer volume pop-up.

2. From this screen, tap the Settings icon.

The Settings icon looks like a gear. It's to the right of the slider. Tapping it brings up the screen shown in Figure 2-5.

Ringtone

Media

Notifications

System

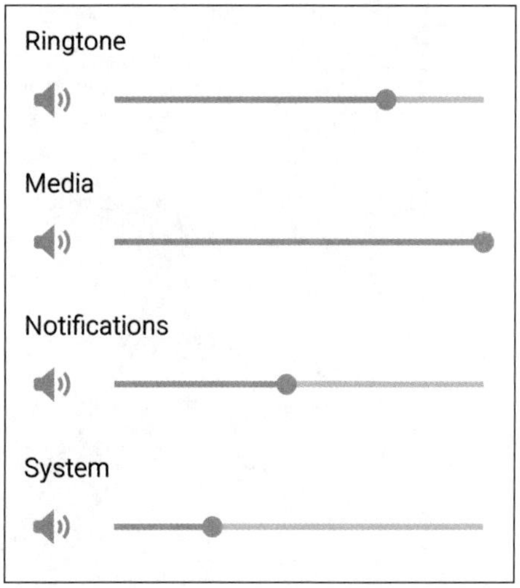

Figure 2-5: The All Volume Settings pop-up.

3. From the screen shown in Figure 2-5, set the volume at the desired setting.

You can adjust the volume of any setting by placing your finger on the dot on the slider image. The dot will get bigger; you can slide it to the left to lower this particular volume setting or to the right to raise it.

The Home button

The biggest button the phone is the Home button (see Figure 2-6). It's on the bottom of the front screen.

Home button

Figure 2-6: The Galaxy S6 Home button on the front.

The Home button brings you back to the home screen from wherever you are in an application. If you're working on applications and feel like you're helplessly lost, don't worry. Press the Home button, close your eyes, tap your heels together three times, and think to yourself, "There's no place like home," and you will be brought back to the Home screen.

You don't really need to do all that other stuff after pressing the Home button. Just pressing the Home button does the trick.

The touchscreen

To cram all the information that you need onto one screen, Samsung takes the modern approach to screen layout. You'll want to become familiar with several finger-navigation motions used to work with your screen.

Before diving in, though, here's a small list of terms you need to know:

- **Icon:** This is a little image. Tapping an icon launches an application or performs some function, such as making a telephone call.

- **Button:** A button on a touchscreen is meant to look like a three-dimensional button that you would push on, say, a telephone. Buttons are typically labeled to tell you what they do when you tap them. For example, you'll see buttons labeled "Save" or "Send."

- **Hyperlink:** Sometimes called a "link" for short, a hyperlink is text that performs some function when you tap it. Usually text is lifeless. If you tap a word and it does nothing, then it's just text. If you tap a word and it launches a website or causes a screen to pop up, it's a hyperlink.

- **Thumbnail:** This is a small, low-resolution version of a larger, high-resolution picture stored somewhere else.

With this background, it's time discuss the motions you'll be using on the touchscreen.

You need to clean the touchscreen glass from time to time. The glass on your phone is Gorilla Glass (made by Corning) — the toughest stuff available to protect against breakage. Use a soft cloth or microfiber to get fingerprints off. You can even wipe the touchscreen on your clothes. However, never use a paper towel! Over time, glass is no match for the fibers in the humble paper towel.

Tap

Often you just tap the screen to make things happen (as when you launch an app) or select options. Think of a *tap* as like a single click of a mouse on a computer screen. A tap is simply a touch on the screen; much like using a touchscreen at a retail kiosk. Figure 2-7 shows what the tap motion should look like.

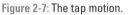

Figure 2-7: The tap motion.

One difference between a mouse click on a computer and a tap on a Galaxy S6 phone is that a single tap launches applications on the phone in the same way that a double-click of the mouse launches an application on a computer.

A tap is different from "press and hold" (see the next section). If you leave your finger on the screen for more than an instant, the phone thinks you want to do something other than launch an application.

Press and hold

Press and hold, as the name implies, involves putting your finger on an icon on the screen and leaving it there for more than a second. What happens when you leave your finger on an icon depends upon the situation.

For example, when you press and hold on an application on the Home screen (the screen that comes up after you turn on the phone), a garbage-can icon appears onscreen. This is to remove that icon from that screen. And when you press and hold an application icon from the list of applications, the phone assumes that you want to copy that application to your Home screen. Don't worry if these distinctions might not make sense yet. The point is that you should be familiar with holding and pressing — and that it's different from tapping.

You don't need to tap or press and hold very hard for the phone to know that you want it to do something. Neither do you need to worry about breaking the glass, even by pressing on it very hard. If you hold the phone in one hand and tap with the other, you'll be fine. I suppose you might break the glass on the phone if you put it on the floor and press up into a one-fingered handstand. I don't recommend that, but if you do try it, please post the video on YouTube.

On average, a person calls 911 about once every year. Usually, you call 911 because of a stressful situation. Like every phone, the Samsung Galaxy S6 has a special stress sensor that causes it to lock up when you need it most. Okay, not really, but it seems that way. When you're stressed, it's easy to think that you're tapping when you're actually pressing and holding. Be aware of this tendency and remember to *tap*.

Moving around the screen or to the next screen

Additional finger motions help you move around the screens and to adjust the scaling for images that you want on the screen. Mastering these motions is important to getting the most from your phone.

The first step is navigating the screen to access what's not visible onscreen. Think of this as navigating a regular computer screen, where you use a horizontal scroll bar to access information to the right or left of what's visible on your monitor, or a vertical scroll bar to move you up and down on a screen.

The same concept works on your phone. To overcome the practical realities of screen size on a phone that will fit into your pocket, the Galaxy S6 phone uses a *panorama* screen layout, meaning that you keep scrolling left or right (or maybe up and down) to access different screens.

In a nutshell, although the full width of a screen is accessible, only the part bounded by the physical screen of the Galaxy S6 phone is visible on the display. Depending upon the circumstances, you have several ways to get to information not visible on the active screen. These actions include drag, flicks, pinch and stretch, and double taps. I cover all these gestures in the following sections.

Drag

The simplest finger motion on the phone is the drag. You place your finger on a point on the screen and then drag the image with your finger. Then you lift your finger. Figure 2-8 shows what the motion looks like.

Figure 2-8: The drag motion for controlled movement.

Dragging allows you to move slowly around the panorama. This motion is like clicking a scroll bar and moving it slowly.

Flick

To move quickly around the panorama, you can flick the screen to move in the direction of your flick (see Figure 2-9).

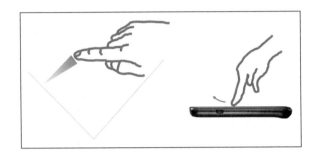

Figure 2-9: Use a flick motion for faster movement.

Better control of this motion comes with practice. In general, the faster the flick, the more the panorama moves. However, some screens (such as the extended Home screen) move only one screen to the right or left, no matter how fast you flick.

Pinch and stretch

Some screens allow you to change the scale of images you view on your screen. When this feature is active, the Zoom options change the magnification of the area on the screen. You can zoom out to see more features at a smaller size, or zoom in to see more detail at a larger size.

To zoom out, you put two fingers (apart) on the screen and pull them together to pinch the image. Make sure you're centered on the spot where you want to see in more detail. The pinch motion is shows in Figure 2-10.

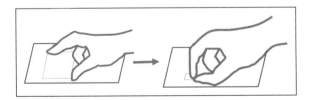

Figure 2-10: Use the pinch motion to zoom out.

The opposite motion is to zoom in. This involves the stretch motion, as shown in Figure 2-11. You place two fingers (close together) and stretch them apart.

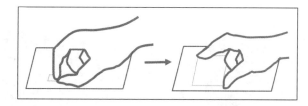

Figure 2-11: Use the stretch motion to zoom in.

Double tap

The double tap (shown in Figure 2-12) just means tapping the same button area on the screen twice in rapid succession. You use the double tap to jump between a zoomed-in and a zoomed-out image to get you back to the previous resolution. This option saves you frustration in getting back to a familiar perspective.

When you double tap, time the taps so that the phone doesn't interpret them as two separate taps. With a little practice, you'll master the timing of the second tap.

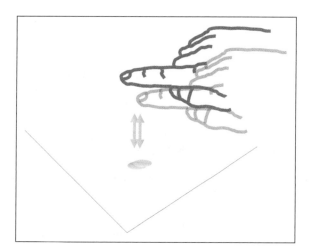

Figure 2-12: The double-tap motion.

The extended Home screen

The Home screen is the first screen you see when the phone is done with setting up. There are additional screens that are off to the right and left. These make up the extended Home screen. They can be seen as a panorama in Figure 2-13.

Home page

Figure 2-13: The Galaxy S6 phone panorama display of the extended Home screen.

At any given moment, you see only one screen at a time. You navigate among the screen by flicking to the right and left. Pressing the home button will always bring you back to one of these screens. Right now, the second screen from the left is designated as the Home screen.

The extended Home screen is where you can organize icons and other functions to best make the phone convenient for you. Out of the box, Samsung and your cellular carrier have worked together to create a starting point for you. Beyond that, though, you have lots of ways you can customize your Home screen for easy access to the things that are most important to you. Much of the book covers all the things that the phone can do, but a recurring theme is how to put your favorite capabilities on your Home screen if you wish.

To start, check out the layout of the Home screen and how it relates to other areas of the phone. Knowing these areas is important for basic navigation.

Figure 2-14 shows a typical Home screen and highlights three important areas on the phone:

- **The notification area:** This part of the screen presents you with small icons that let you know if something important is up, like battery life.
- **The primary shortcuts:** These five icons remain stationary as you move across the home screen. If you notice in Figure 2-14, these have been determined by Samsung and your cellular carrier to be the five most important applications on your phone.
- **The Function keys:** These three keys control essential phone functions, regardless of what else is going on at the moment with the phone.

App shortcuts

Notification area

Recent apps

Back button

Primary shortcuts

Figure 2-14: Important areas on the Galaxy S6 phone and Home screen.

There are a series of dots just above the primary shortcuts on the extended Home screen. You may also notice that one of the dots isn't just a dot — it's a little house. That is the "home" Home screen. The brightest dot indicates where you are among the screens. You can navigate among screens by dragging the screen to the left or right. This moves you one screen at a time. You can also jump multiple screens by tapping on the dot that corresponds to the screen number you want to see, or by dragging the dots to the screen you want to see. Keep reading for more detail on each area.

Adding shortcuts to the Home screen

As seen in Figure 2-14, you have a lot of screen real estate where you can put icons of your favorite applications and widgets. (Widgets are small apps that take care of simple functions, like displaying time or the status of your battery.) You can add shortcuts to the apps and to these widgets to your Home screen by following these steps:

1. **From the extended Home screen page where there is some space for the icon of an app, tap the Apps icon on the primary shortcuts.**

   This brings up a directory of all the Apps you currently have on the phone. The page shown in Figure 2-15 shows just the first page. The number of apps and pages for their icons is practically unlimited. (I cover how to add new apps in Chapter 8.)

2. **Press and hold the icon of the app you want to add.**

   The screen with the app icons will fade and the page with the space for the icon will appear with the icon under your finger.

3. **Move the icon to where you want it to be on the Home screen page and release.**

   Done.

Taking away or moving shortcuts

Say that you put the shortcut on the wrong spot. No problem. Press and hold the icon. The screen will gray out except for your icon. It looks something like Figure 2-16, except the icon you pressed is in full color under your finger.

You then drag the icon to the place on the screen you want it to reside and release. Taking a shortcut off your Home screen is simple: Press and hold the icon on the screen. In a moment, you see the grayed out home page. Drag the doomed shortcut to the garbage can, and off it goes to its maker.

Figure 2-15: An Apps page.

It's gone, but if you made a mistake, you can get it back easily enough. To re-create it, simply go back to the App Menu key and follow the process again.

The notification area and screen

As shown earlier in Figure 2-14, the notification area is located at the top of the phone. Here, you see little status icons. Maybe you received a text or an e-mail, or you'll see an application needs some tending to.

Think of the notification area as a special e-mail inbox where your carrier (or even the phone itself) can give you important information about what's happening with your phone. These little icons at the top tell you the condition of the different radio systems on your phone: The number of bars shown gives you an indication of signal strength, and usually the phone will also tell you what kind of signal you're getting – such as 3G or 4G.

Figure 2-16: The extended Home page in repositioning mode.

You could take the time to learn the meanings of all the little icons that might come up, but that would take you a while. A more convenient option is to touch the notification area and pull it down, as shown in Figure 2-17.

The rest of the screen is written so that you can understand what's going on — and what, if anything, you're expected to do. For example, you could see that you have uploaded a file.

When you're finished reading the notifications, you slide your finger back up to the top. If this screen gets too full, you can clear it by tapping the Clear button. You can also clear notifications one at a time by touching each one and swiping it to the side.

If you want a shortcut to control some key phone capabilities, you can tap one of the five, dark-blue circles. For example, if you want to turn off Wi-Fi, you could just tap the Wi-Fi icon. This would save you from having to get in to Settings to do the same thing.

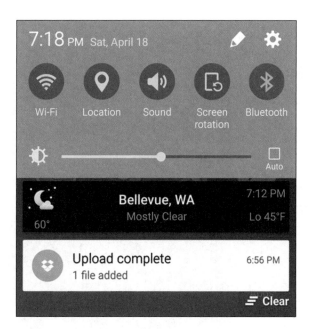

Figure 2-17: Notification area pull down.

If you want to add more of these, simply tap the silhouette of the pencil to see your Quick Settings options. These are seen in Figure 2-18, although you may have slightly different choices on your phone.

For example, many people find the Flashlight capability to be handy. If it is not already there when you pull down the notifications screen, see if it is among the options. If it is, press and hold on the flashlight icon. Then drag it to the top. The other icons scatter and then you release it. You turn on the flashlight by tapping it. Try it and see.

The Device Function keys

At the bottom of the screen, below the rectangular screen display, are three important buttons: the Device Function keys. They're always present for you to navigate your phone even though the backlight might switch off to hide their presence. Whatever else you're doing on the phone, these buttons can take over. You should already know the Home button. The other buttons are equally cool.

Recent Apps button

The button to the left of the Home button is the Recent Apps button. Tapping the button brings up a list of the open apps. This is handy to navigate between running apps. Figure 2-19 shows a typical screen of recent apps.

Figure 2-18: Notification area options.

You can scroll among the open apps by flicking up or down. You can jump to one of these apps by tapping somewhere on the image. You can also shut down one of the apps by tapping the "x" on the upper-right corner. You can shut them all down by tapping the link at the bottom that says Close All.

The Device Function keys are cool because they light up when you're touching them or the screen, but fade away the rest of the time.

The Back button

The Back button on your phone is similar to the Back button in a web browser: It takes you back one screen.

Figure 2-19: Recent Apps screen.

As you start navigating through the screens on your phone, tapping the Back button takes you back to the previous screen. If you keep tapping the Back button, you'll eventually return to the Home screen.

The keyboard

The screen of the Galaxy S6 phone is important, but you'll still probably spend more time on the keyboard entering data on the QWERTY keyboard.

Using the software keyboard

The software keyboard automatically pops up when the application detects a need for user text input. The keyboard, shown in Figure 2-20, appears at the bottom of the screen.

Figure 2-20: Use the software keyboard to enter data.

Using Swype

Some Galaxy S6 phones come with an enhanced data-entering capability called Swype. If it is not on your phone already, you can download it from the Google Play Store. With a little practice, it can dramatically speed your ability to type fast on your phone.

Here's how Swype works: Instead of tapping each discrete key on the keyboard, you leave your finger on the screen and swipe from key to key. The Swype application figures out the words you're wanting to type, including inserting the spaces automatically.

If you like Swype, you can use it anytime you're entering data. If you don't care for it, you can just tap your letters. It's all up to you!

Using voice recognition

The third option for a keyboard is . . . no keyboard at all! Galaxy S6 phones come with voice recognition as an option. It's very easy, and works surprisingly well. In most spots where you have an option to enter text, you see a small version of the microphone icon shown in Figure 2-21.

Just tap this icon and say what you would have typed. You see the phone thinking for a second, and then it shows a screen that looks like the screen shown in Figure 2-22.

When you're done, you can tap the "done" button, or just be quiet and wait. Within a few seconds, you'll see what you said!

Figure 2-21: The voice recognition icon.

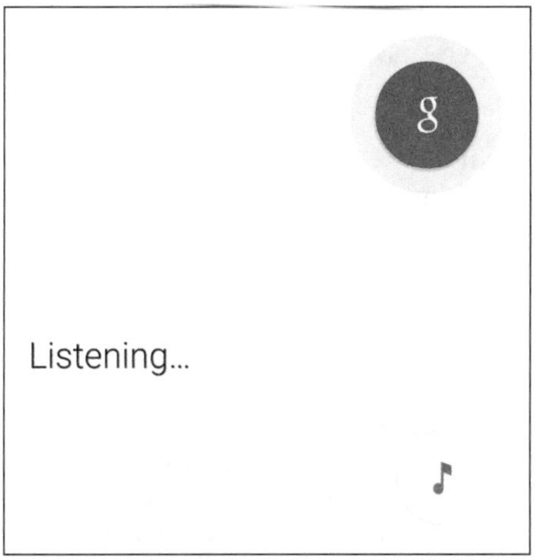

g

Listening...

♪

Figure 2-22: The voice recognition screen.

The orientation of the phone

Earlier in this chapter where I discuss the Power button, I refer to the phone being in vertical orientation (so that the phone is tall and narrow). It can also be used in the *landscape* orientation (sideways, or so that the phone is short and wide). The phone senses in which direction you're holding it, and orients the screen to make it easier for you to view.

The phone makes its orientation known to the application, but not all applications are designed to change their inherent display. That nuance is left to the writers of the application. For example, your phone can play videos. However, the video player application that comes with your phone shows video in landscape mode only.

In addition, the phone can sense when you're holding it to your ear. When it senses that it's held in this position, it shuts off the screen. You need not be concerned that you'll accidentally "chin-dial" a number in Botswana.

Going to Sleep Mode/Turning Off the Phone

You can leave your phone on every minute until you're ready to upgrade to the newest Galaxy S6 phone in a few years, but that would use up your battery in no time. Instead, put your idle phone in sleep mode to save battery power. ***Note:*** Your phone goes into sleep mode automatically after 30 seconds of inactivity on the screen.

You can adjust the sleep time out for a longer duration, which I cover in Chapter 16. Or you can manually put the phone in sleep mode by pressing the Power button for just a moment.

Sometimes it's best to simply shut down the phone if you aren't going to use it for several days or more or the flight attendant tells you it's required. To shut down the phone completely, simply press and hold the Power button for a few seconds. The following options appear:

- ✔ **Silent mode:** Turn off sound, but vibrate if there is an important notification like an incoming call or text.

- ✔ **Airplane mode:** Turns off the radios that communicate to the local Wi-Fi access point and the cellular network so that you can't receive or make voice calls or send or receive texts or data. As the name implies, use this setting when you're flying. If you want to use applications that can operate without a data connection, such as some games, you can. The good news: Because some flights now provide Wi-Fi, the phone *does* allow you to turn Wi-Fi back on when you're in airplane mode if you need it.

- ✔ **Power Off:** Shut down the phone completely.

Good night!

Part II
Communications

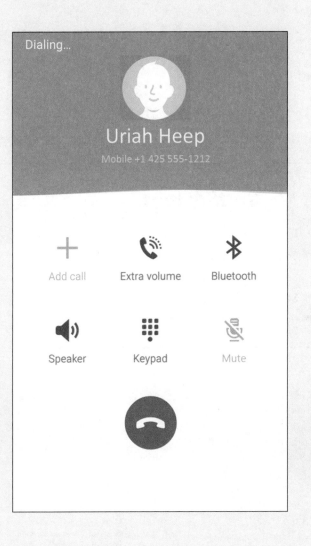

In this part. . .

- ✒ Dial and answer phone calls
- ✒ Connect to a Bluetooth headset
- ✒ Send and receive text messages
- ✒ Set up e-mail accounts on your phone
- ✒ Get all your contacts in one location

Calling People

In This Chapter

▶ Dialing and answering phone calls

▶ Using your call list

▶ Making emergency calls

▶ Connecting to a Bluetooth headset

*A*t its essence, any mobile phone — no matter how fancy or smart — exists to make phone calls. The good news is that making and receiving phone calls on your Galaxy S6 is easy.

In this chapter I show you not only how to make a call, but also how to use your call list to keep track of your calls. And don't skip the section on using your phone for emergencies.

Finally, if you're like many people, you're never doing just one thing at a time, and a Bluetooth headset can make it easier for you to talk on the phone while driving and getting directions, checking e-mail, wrangling kids and dogs, or just plain living life. In this chapter, I show you how to hook up your phone to a Bluetooth headset so you can make and receive phone calls hands-free.

Making Calls

After your phone is on and you're connected to your cellular carrier (see Chapters 1 and 2), you can make a phone call. It all starts from the Home screen. Along the bottom of the screen, above the Device Function keys, are five icons, which are the *primary shortcuts* (see Figure 3-1). The primary shortcuts on your phone may differ slightly, but in this case, from left to right, they are:

T CALL WITH MESSAGE

▸ Phone

▸ Contacts

✔ Chrome (Internet browser)

✔ Messages

✔ Apps

Figure 3-1: The primary shortcuts on the Home screen.

To make a call, follow these steps:

1. From the Home screen, tap the Phone icon.

You will see a screen like the one shown in Figure 3-2. This screen shows any calls you have made or received, such as the one from your carrier to confirm that you phone has been set up correctly.

2. Tap the Dial Pad icon.

This icon is a green circle with little white dots that symbolize the touch pad on a regular landline phone.

3. Tap the telephone number you want to call.

The Keypad screen (see Figure 3-3) appears. This looks like a full-sized version of a touch pad on a regular landline phone. (If you have not made or received any calls at all, tapping the Phone icon takes you right to the Keypad screen.)

Don't be alarmed that you don't hear a dial tone. Smartphones don't connect to a network until after you dial your number and tap Send. At this point, a dial tone would be pointless.

For long distance calls while in the United States, you don't need to dial 1 before the area code — just dial the area code and then the seven-digit phone number. Similarly, you can include the "1" and the area code for local calls. On the other hand, if you're traveling internationally, you need to include the "1" — and be prepared for international roaming charges!

In Chapter 6, you can read about how to make a phone call through your contacts.

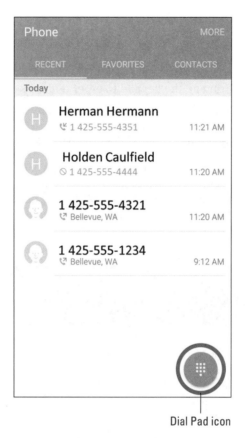

Dial Pad icon

Figure 3-2: The Home screen for the phone.

4. **Tap the green phone button at the bottom of the screen to place the call.**

   The screen changes to the screen seen in Figure 3-4. You have a chance to verify you dialed the person you intended.

   Within a few seconds, you should hear the phone ringing at the other end or a busy signal. From then on, it is like a regular phone call.

5. **When you're done with your call, tap the red phone button at the bottom of the screen.**

   The call is disconnected.

If the other party answers the phone, you have a few options available to you by tapping on the correct icon/hyperlink on the screen, including:

- Put the call on "hold"
- Add another call to have a three-way conversation

- ✔ Increase the volume
- ✔ Switch on a Bluetooth device (more on Bluetooth later in this chapter)
- ✔ Turn on the phone's speaker
- ✔ Bring up the keypad to enter numbers
- ✔ Mute the microphone on the phone

You can do any or all of these, or you can just enjoy talking on the phone.

If the call doesn't go through, either the cellular coverage where you are is insufficient, or your phone got switched to Airplane mode. (It's possible, of course, that your cellular carrier let you out the door without having set you up for service, but that's pretty unlikely!)

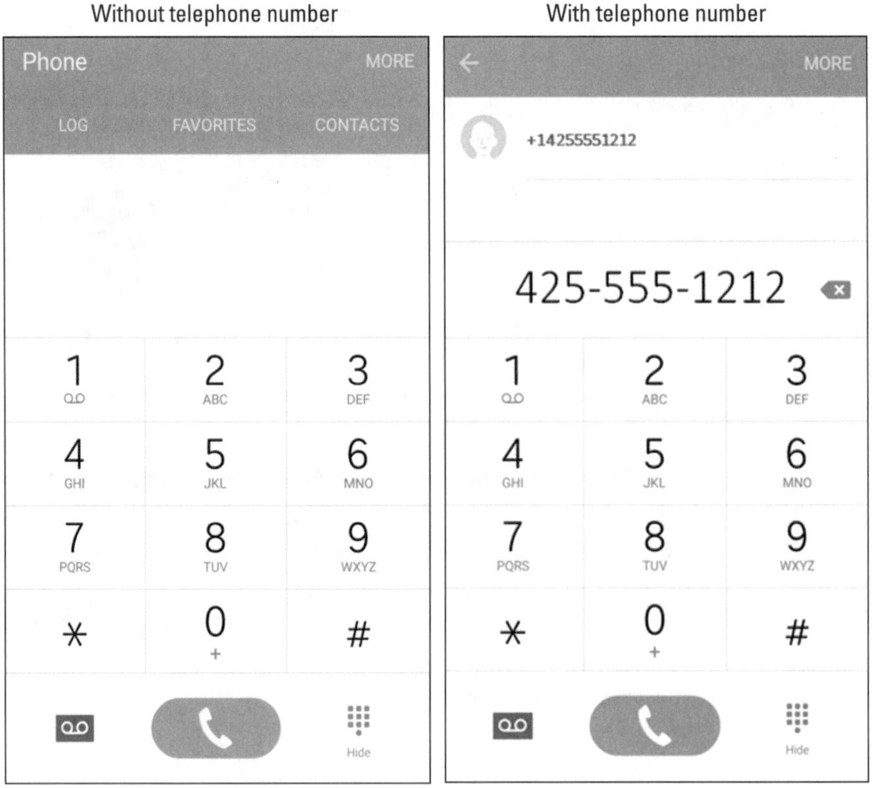

Figure 3-3: Dial the number from the Keypad screen.

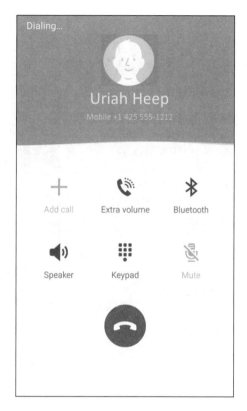

Figure 3-4: Dialing screen.

Check the notification section at the top of the screen. If there are no connection-strength bars, try moving to another location. If you see a small airplane silhouette, bring down the notification screen (see how in Chapter 2) and tap the plane icon to turn off Airplane mode.

If you pull down the notification screen and you don't see the green silhouette of an airplane, scroll the green or gray icons to the left. This icon may be off the page. Alternatively, tap the icon with the boxes in the upper-right corner and you will see all the notification icons.

Answering Calls

Receiving a call is even easier than making a call. When someone calls you, caller ID information appears in a pop-up screen. Figure 3-5 shows some screen options for an incoming call.

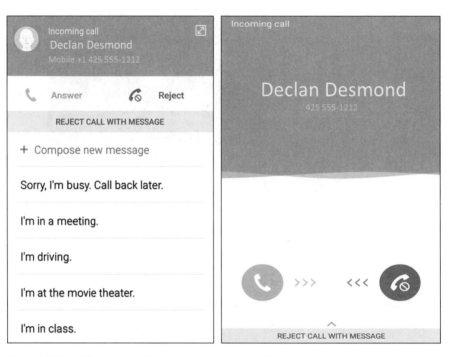

Figure 3-5: Possible screens when you're receiving a call.

To answer the call, tap or slide the green phone button. To not-answer a call, you can simply ignore the ringing, or you can tap or slide the red phone button. The ringing stops immediately and, in either case, the call goes to voicemail.

In Part IV, I fill you in on some exciting options that you can enable (or not) when you get a call. For example, you can specify a unique ringtone for a particular number, or have an image of the caller pop up (if you save your contacts to your phone).

Regardless of what you were doing on the phone at that moment — such as listening to music or playing a game — the answer pop-up screen can appear. Any active application, including music or video, is suspended until the call is over.

For callers to leave you messages, you must set up your voicemail. If you haven't yet set up your voicemail, the caller will hear a recorded message saying that your voicemail account isn't yet set up. Some cellular carriers can set up voicemail for you when you activate the account and get the phone; others require you to set up voicemail on your own. Ask how voicemail works at your carrier store, or look for instructions in the manual included with your phone.

These answer and reject icons are pretty standard on any mobile phone. However, your Galaxy S6 is no standard phone. There is a third option, and what happens depends on your individual phone. In addition to the standard options of answer or reject, you have one more option — to reject *and* send the caller a text message. As your caller is sent to your voicemail, you also can immediately send the caller a text message that acknowledges the call.

Some of the typical "canned" messages that you can send are:

- ✔ Sorry, I'm busy. Call back later.
- ✔ I'm in a meeting.
- ✔ I'm driving.
- ✔ In at the movie theater.
- ✔ I'm in class.

You tap the message that applies. The message is sent as a text right away, which alerts the caller that you're not ignoring him — it's just that you can't talk right now. Nice touch.

You can also create and store your own message, like "Go away and leave me alone," or "Whatever I am doing is more important than talking to you." You could also be polite. To create your own canned message, tap "Compose new message" and type away. It's then stored on your phone for when you need it.

The caller has to be able to receive text messages on the phone used to make the call. This feature doesn't work if your caller is calling from a landline or a mobile phone that can't receive texts.

Keeping Track of Your Calls: The Call List

One of the nice features of mobile phones is that the phone keeps a record of the calls that you've made and received. Sure, you might have caller ID on your landline at home or work, but most landline phones don't keep track of who you called. Mobile phones, on the other hand, keep track of all the numbers you called. This information can be quite convenient, like when you want to return a call and you don't have that number handy. In addition, you can easily add a number to the contact list on your phone.

By tapping the "Log" icon on the phone screen, you get a list of all incoming and outgoing calls. (This hyperlink is located toward the top of the screen shown on the left side in Figure 3-3.) When you tap the log hyperlink, you see a call log like the one shown in Figure 3-6.

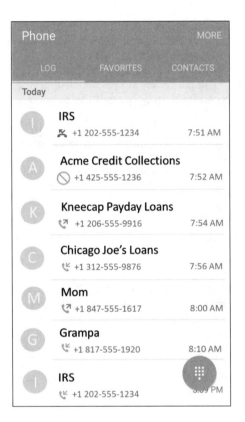

Figure 3-6: A call log.

The tabs along the top include:

- **Outgoing call you made:** An orange arrow points to the number.
- **Incoming call you received:** A green arrow points away from the number.
- **Incoming call you missed:** A red phone silhouette with a broken arrow.
- **Incoming call you ignored:** A blue slash sign is next to the phone number.

The log is a list of all the calls you made or were made to you. This is handy so that you can easily call someone again or call them back. By tapping any number in your call list, you see a screen like the one shown in Figure 3-7. From this screen, you can do several things:

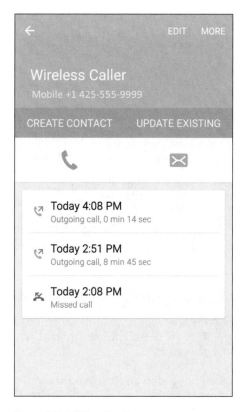

Figure 3-7: Call log detail.

✔ See the date and time the call was logged and all previous calls to and from this number.

✔ Call the number by tapping the green call button. There is an even easier option that I describe in the nearby sidebar, "Samsung Galaxy S6 for Lazybones: Direct Call."

✔ Send a text to that number by tapping the orange envelope icon. (More on this in Chapter 4.)

✔ Mark that number as a favorite by tapping the More hyperlink. Your favorites appears on the Keypad screen (refer to Figure 3-3), which saves you from having to dial the number.

✔ Add the number to your contacts list by tapping the "Create Contact" button if they do not have a contact set up or "Update Existing" if this is someone who has a contact entry, but for whom this is a new number. I cover contacts in more detail in Chapter 6.

Samsung Galaxy S6 for lazybones: direct call

Imagine this scenario. You show up to work, and two co-workers have called in sick. You spend your day hustling to cover for them. You get home and clean the house. It has snowed, so you need to shovel your walk and driveway as well as the walk and driveway of the elderly widow next door. (You are just that kind of person.)

All you want to do is flop down on the sofa and pick up your Samsung Galaxy S6 to call your best friend. You find your friend in the call log, but then pure exhaustion kicks in, and you just don't have it in you to tap that green Phone button to start the dialing process.

No need to worry! Your Samsung Galaxy S6 has taken care of you. Simply put the phone to your ear! After a moment, the phone gives a quick shake and the phone automatically dials that number for you!

Samsung calls this capability *direct call*. Using this feature requires an exceptional level of laziness, which is why I am so fond of it!

Making an Emergency Call: The 411 on 911

Mobile phones are wonderful tools for calling for help in an emergency. The Samsung Galaxy S6, like all phones in the United States and Canada, can make emergency calls to 911.

Just tap the Phone icon on the Home screen, tap **911**, and then tap Send. You'll be routed to the 911 call center nearest to your location. This works wherever you're at within the United States. So, say you live in Chicago but have a car accident in Charlotte; just tap 911 to be connected to the 911 call center in Charlotte, not Chicago.

Even if your phone isn't registered on a network, you don't have a problem as long as you have a charge in the battery. Your phone lets you know that the only number you can dial is a 911 call center, even if the Home screen is locked.

When you call 911 from a landline, the address you're calling from is usually displayed for the operator. When you're calling from a mobile phone, though, the operator doesn't have that specific information. So, when you call 911, the operator might say, "911. *Where* is your emergency?" Don't let this question throw you; after all, you're probably focused on *what* is happening and not on *where*. Take a moment and come up with a good description of where you are — the street you're on, the nearest cross street (if you know it), any businesses or other landmarks nearby. An operator who knows where you are is in a better position to help you with your emergency. Your phone does have a GPS receiver in it that 911 centers can access. However, it's not always accurate; it may not be receiving location information at that moment, as is the case when you're indoors.

When you accidentally dial 911

If you accidentally dial 911 from your phone, don't hang up. Just tell the operator that it was an accidental call. She might ask some questions to verify that you are indeed safe and not being forced to say that your call was an accident.

If you panic and hang up after accidentally dialing 911, you'll get a call from the nearest 911 call center. Always answer the call, even if you feel foolish. If you don't answer the call, the 911 call centers will assume that you're in trouble and can't respond. They'll track you down from the GPS in your phone to verify that you're safe. If you thought you'd feel foolish explaining your mistake to a 911 operator, imagine how foolish you'd feel explaining it to the police officer who tracks you down and is upset with you for wasting the department's time.

When traveling outside the United States or Canada, 911 might not be the number you call in an emergency. Mexico uses 066, 060, or 080, but most tourist areas also accept 911. And most — but not all — of Europe uses 112. Knowing the local emergency number is as important as knowing enough of the language to say you need help.

Syncing a Bluetooth Headset

With a Bluetooth headset device, you can talk on your phone without having to hold the phone to your ear — and without any cords running from the phone to your earpiece. You've probably come across plenty of people talking on Bluetooth headsets. You might even have wondered whether they were a little crazy talking to themselves. Well, call yourself crazy now, because when you start using a Bluetooth headset, you might never want to go back.

Not surprisingly, Galaxy S6 phones can connect to Bluetooth devices. The first step to using a Bluetooth headset with your phone is to sync the two devices. Here's how:

1. **From the Home screen on your phone, tap the Apps icon.**

   This gets you to the list of all the applications on your phone.

2. **Flick or pan to the Settings icon and tap it.**

   The Settings icon is shown here. This screen holds most of the settings that you can adjust on your phone. If you prefer, you can also bring down the notification screen and tap the gear icon or tap the menu button on the Home screen. All these actions will get you to the same place.

   Tapping on the Settings icon brings up the screen shown in Figure 3-8.

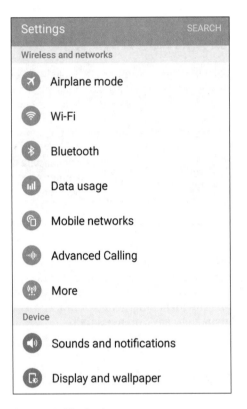

Figure 3-8: The Settings screen.

3. **Tap the Bluetooth icon.**

   This will bring up one of the two screens shown in Figure 3-9. If Bluetooth is off, it will look like the screen to the left. If it is on, it will look like the screen on the right.

4. **Put the phone in to "Pairing mode" by turning "on" Bluetooth or by turning Bluetooth off and on again.**

   This step enables your phone to be visible to other Bluetooth devices. This state will last for about 120 seconds — enough time for you to get your Bluetooth device into pairing mode so both devices can negotiate the proper security settings and pair up every time they "see" each other from now on. For example, the phone in the right image in Figure 3-9 recognizes its old friend, the Bose Color SoundLink. This device and the phone are seen in this image trying to re-establish a connection. The SoundLink and this phone had a connection at one time. That connection was broken. Now they want to pair up again. This is automatic once you exchange the correct security code.

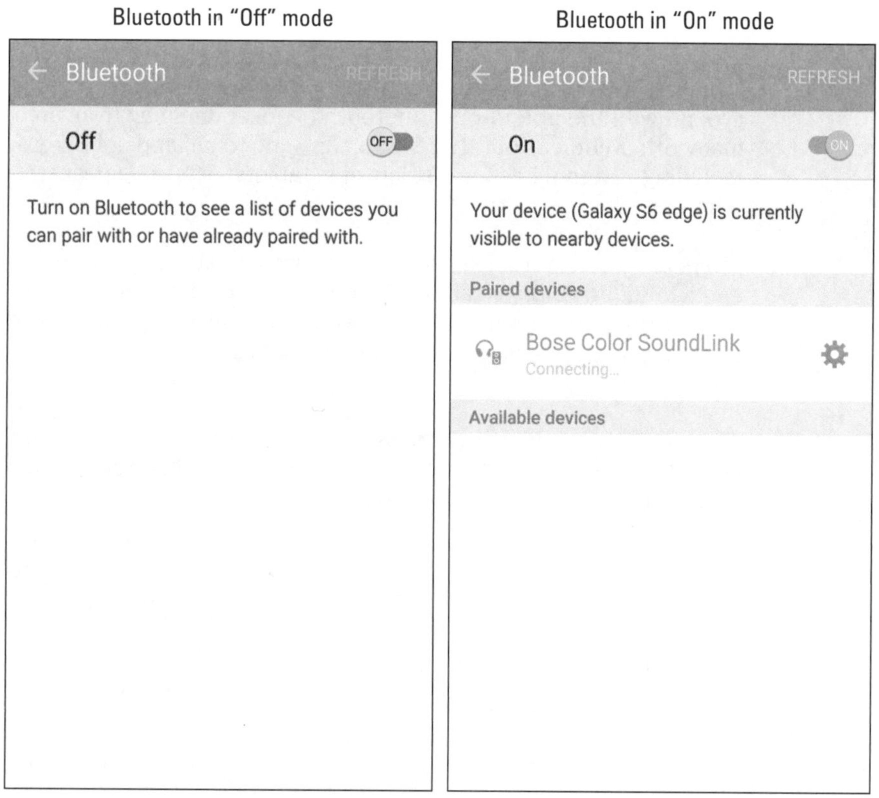

Bluetooth in "Off" mode

Bluetooth in "On" mode

← Bluetooth	REFRESH
Off	OFF

Turn on Bluetooth to see a list of devices you can pair with or have already paired with.

← Bluetooth	REFRESH
On	ON

Your device (Galaxy S6 edge) is currently visible to nearby devices.

Paired devices

🎧 Bose Color SoundLink ⚙
   Connecting...

Available devices

Figure 3-9: The Bluetooth Settings screens.

5. **Next, put your headset into sync mode.**

   Follow the instructions that came with your headset.

   After a moment, the phone "sees" the headset. When it does, you're prompted to enter the security code, and the software keyboard pops up.

6. **Enter the security code for your headset and then tap the Enter button.**

   The security code on most headsets is 0000, but check the instructions that came with your headset if that number doesn't work.

   Your phone might see other devices in the immediate area. If so, it asks you which device you want to pair with. Tap the name of your headset.

   Your headset is now synced to your phone. If you turn one on when the other is already on, they recognize each other and automatically pair up.

Options Other than Headsets

Headsets are not the only option anymore. Although many people walk around with the ubiquitous Bluetooth headset dangling from an ear, there are many other choices out there. You can sync to all kinds of Bluetooth devices, including external keyboards, laptops, tablets, external speakers, and even your car.

There are also external sensors for measuring blood pressure, heart rate, and a lot of other physical information. Some of these are built into wearable devices, like a fitness bracelet. Manufacturers are now embedding computers into home appliances that also connect to your smartphone through Bluetooth!

The good news is that regardless of the technology, you can connect all these devices to your phone simply by using the steps described here. We talk more about these possibilities in later chapters.

Discovering the Joy of Text

In This Chapter

▶ Sending a text message

▶ Sending a text message with an attachment

▶ Receiving a text message

Sure, mobile phones are made for talking. But these days, many people use their phones even more for texting. *Text messages* (which are short messages, usually 160 characters or less, sent by mobile phone) are particularly convenient when you can't talk at the moment (maybe you're in a meeting or class) or when you just have a small bit of information to share ("Running late — see you soon!").

Many mobile phone users — particularly younger ones — prefer sending texts to making a phone call. They find texting a faster and more convenient way to communicate, and they often use texting shorthand to fit more "content" in that character limit.

Even the most basic phones support texting these days, but your Galaxy S6 phone makes sending and receiving text messages more convenient, no matter whether you're an occasional or pathological texter. In this chapter, I fill you in on how to send a text message (with or without an attachment), how to receive a text message, and how to read your old text messages.

> R U there
> Text message 8:16 AM

> How may I serve?
> Text message 8:17 AM

> Your humble servant..
> Text message 8:17 AM

To use text messaging, you must have texting capability as part of your service plan. See Chapter 1 for more information.

This chapter uses images from the Android Messaging application. It is possible that your phone may have as its default the Verizon Messages app or another texting application. If so, you can easily switch to the Messaging app. You can also use the default app, but the images will be somewhat different. Your choice.

Sending the First Text Message

There are two scenarios for texting. The first is when you send someone a text for the first time. The second is when you have a text conversation with a person.

When you first get your phone and are ready to brag about your new Galaxy S6 and want to send a text to your best friend, here's how easy it is:

1. **On the Home screen, tap the Messages icon.**

   The Messages icon looks like an envelope. When you tap it, you will get a mostly blank Home screen for texting. This is shown in Figure 4-1.

   When you have some conversations going, it begins to fill up. More on that soon.

Figure 4-1: The initial Messaging Home screen.

2. Tap the New Message icon (the pencil hovering over a blank page).

Tapping the New Message icon brings up the screen seen in Figure 4-2.

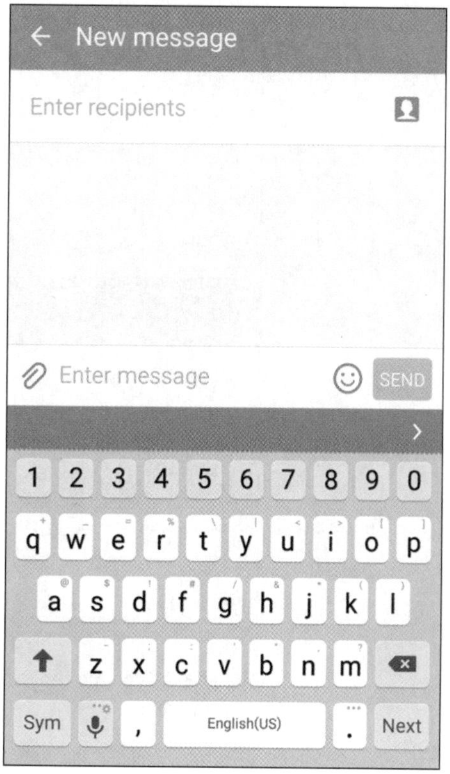

Figure 4-2: A blank texting screen.

3. Tap to enter the recipient's ten-digit mobile telephone number.

A text box appears at the top of the screen with the familiar To field at the top. The keyboard appears at the bottom of the screen.

As shown in Figure 4-3, the top field is where you type in the telephone number. The numerals are along the top of the keyboard.

Be sure to include the area code, even if the person you're texting is local. There's no need to include a "1" before the number.

If this is your first text, you haven't had a chance to build up a history of texts. After you've been using your messaging application for a while, you will have entered contact information, and your phone will start trying to anticipate your intended recipient.

Figure 4-3: Type the recipient's number in the upper text box.

4. **To type your text message, tap the text box that says Enter Message. Figure 4-4 shows you where to enter your text.**

   Your message will appear in the text box to the right of the paper clip icon.

   In the Android Messaging app, your text message can be up to 160 characters, including spaces and punctuation. The application counts down the number of characters you have left.

5. **Send the text by tapping the Send button to the right of your message.**

   The Send button is grayed out before you start typing. After you type something, it turns full-on orange. Once you tap the button, the phone takes it from here. Within a few seconds, the message is sent to your friend's mobile phone.

Figure 4-4: Type your text.

After you build your contact list (read about this in Chapter 6), you can tap a name from the contact list or start typing a name in the recipient text box. If there's only one number for that contact, your phone assumes that's the receiving phone you want to send a text to. If that contact has multiple numbers, it asks you which phone number you want to send your text to.

In most cases, the default for your texting app is for your phone to automatically correct what it thinks is a misspelled word. You can see it guess on the darker gray area under the text message. This capability is called "autocorrect." You may find it very handy, or you may find it annoying. If you like it, you should still verify that it corrected the word in the right way. If you want evidence as to why this is a good idea, search "funny autocorrect examples" in your favorite search engine (although some can be very "racy").

You've probably heard a thousand times about how it's a very bad idea to text while you're driving. Here comes one-thousand-and-one. It's a *very bad idea* to text while you're driving — and illegal in some places. There are Dummies who read this book, who are actually very smart, and then there are DUMMIES who text and drive. I want you to be the former and not the latter.

Carrying on a Conversation via Texting

In the bad ol' pre-Galaxy S days, most mobile phones would keep a log of your texts. The phone kept the texts that you sent or received in sequential order, regardless of who sent or received them.

Texts stored sequentially are old-school. Your Galaxy S6 keeps track of the contact with whom you've been texting and stores each set of back-and-forth messages as a *conversation*.

In Figure 4-5, you can see that the first page for messaging holds *conversations.* After you start texting someone, those texts are stored in one conversation.

As Figure 4-5 shows, each text message is presented in sequence, with the author of the text indicated by the direction of the text balloon.

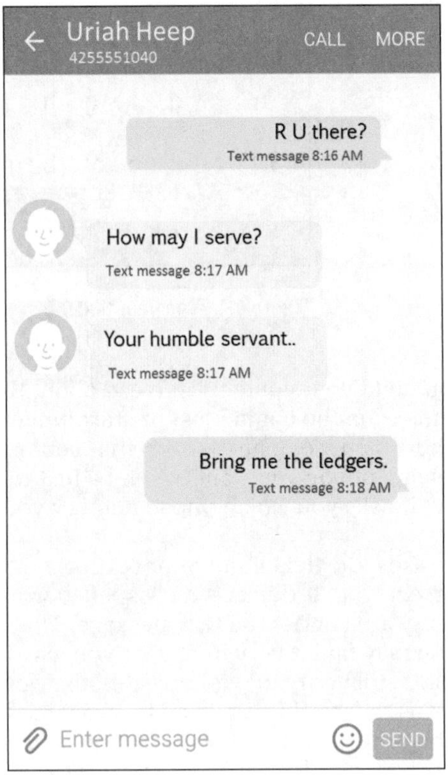

| ← | Uriah Heep | | CALL | MORE |
| | 4255551040 | | | |

R U there?
Text message 8:16 AM

How may I serve?
Text message 8:17 AM

Your humble servant..
Text message 8:17 AM

Bring me the ledgers.
Text message 8:18 AM

✏ Enter message   ☺ SEND

Figure 4-5: A messaging conversation.

Note the Enter Message text box at the bottom of the screen. With this convenient feature, you can send whatever you type to the person with whom you're having a conversation.

In the bad old days, it was sometimes hard to keep straight the different texting conversations you were having. When you start a texting conversation with someone else, there is a second conversation.

Before too long, you'll have multiple conversations going on. Don't worry. They aren't the kind of conversations you need to keep going constantly. No one thinks twice if you don't text for a while. The image in Figure 4-6 shows how the Messaging Home screen from Figure 4-1 can look before too long.

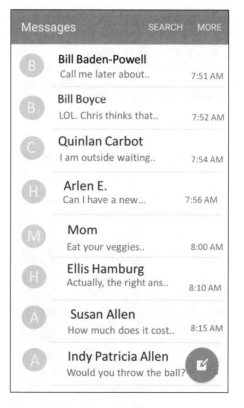

Figure 4-6: The Messaging Home screen showing multiple conversations.

It is easy to change the font size of conversations. To make the fonts larger and easier to read, use the stretch motion. Use the pinch motion to make the fonts smaller so you can see more of the conversation.

Sending an Attachment with a Text

What if you want to send something in addition to or instead of text? Say you want to send a picture, some music, or a Word document along with your text. Easy as pie, as long as the phone on the receiving end can recognize the attachment. Here is the recipe:

1. **From the Home screen, tap the Messages icon.**

2. **Either tap the New Message icon and enter the number of the intended recipient, or pick up on an existing conversion.**

   You'll see the text creation page from Figure 4-2. Enter the information you want like a normal text.

3. **To add an attachment, tap the icon that looks like a paper clip to the left of where you enter text.**

   The paper-clip icon brings up the screen you see in Figure 4-7, which asks what kind of file you want to attach. Your choices include pictures, videos, audio files, and some others I describe later. For now, it's just good that you know you have options.

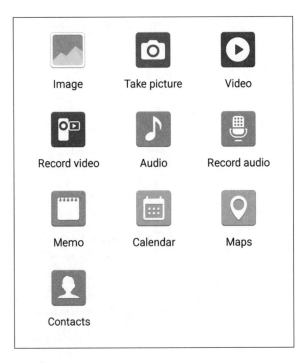

Figure 4-7: File types you can attach to a text.

4. **Tap your choice of file type, and your phone presents you with the options that fall into that category.**

   After you select the file, it becomes an attachment to your text message.

5. **Continue typing your text message, if needed.**

6. **When you're done with the text portion of the message, tap the Send button, and off it all goes.**

A simple text message is an SMS (short message service) message. When you add an attachment, you're sending an MMS (multimedia messaging service) message. Back in the day, MMS messages cost more to send and receive than SMS messages did. These days, that isn't the case in the United States.

Receiving Text Messages

Receiving a text is even easier than sending one.

When you're having a text conversation and you get a new text from the person you're texting with, your phone beeps and/or vibrates. Also, the notification area of the screen (the very top) shows a very small version of the Messages icon.

You can either pull down the notification area from the very top of the screen or start the messaging application. Your choice.

If an attachment comes along, it's included in the conversation screen.

To access the text, you need to unlock the screen. The Messages icon (an envelope) also displays the number of new texts that you have. Tap that icon to open the conversations.

Managing Your Text History

The Messaging Conversations screen stores and organizes all your texts until you delete them. You should clean up this screen every now and then.

The simplest option for managing your messages is to tap the Menu icon and then tap Delete Threads. You can then select and unselect all the conversations that you want deleted. Tap the Delete link at the bottom of the screen, and they disappear.

Another deletion option is to open the conversation. You can delete each text by pressing and holding on the balloon. After a moment, a menu appears from which you can delete that message. This method is a lot slower if you have lots of texts, though.

I recommend that you be vicious in deleting the older texts and conversations. Trust me; deleting all your old messages can be cathartic!

Sending and Receiving E-Mail

. . . .

In This Chapter

▶ Setting up e-mail accounts on your phone

▶ Reading e-mail on your phone

▶ Managing your e-mail folder

▶ Sending e-mail from your phone

. . . .

*I*f you've had e-mail on your phone for a while, you know how convenient it is. If your Galaxy S6 phone is your first mobile phone with the capability to send and receive e-mail, prepare to be hooked.

I start this chapter by showing you how to set up your e-mail, regardless of whether your e-mail program is supported (more on that in a bit). Then I show you how to read and manage your e-mail. Finally, I tell you how to write and send e-mail.

Your phone mainly interacts with your inbox on your e-mail account. It isn't really set up to work like the full-featured e-mail application on your computer, though. For example, many e-mail packages integrate with a sophisticated word processor, have sophisticated filing systems for your saved messages, and offer lots of fonts. As long as you don't mind working without these advanced capabilities, you might never need to get on your computer to access your e-mail again, and you could store e-mail in folders on your phone. In practice, however, phone access to e-mail is best used in working with e-mail that is in your inbox.

SEARCh

al E-Mail Account

read 0   Last synced

Nigerian Banker
Thanks for your money transfer!
We have received your funds, and will...

UK Lotto Headquarters
Congratulations!
You have been approved to collect the sum.

nner Swift
hopping Opportunity
are earning over $1

Using e-mail on your phone requires a data connection. Some cellular carriers solve this problem by obliging you to have a data plan with your phone. If your cellular carrier does not, you won't be able to use e-mail unless you're connected to a Wi-Fi hotspot. I strongly recommend that you get that data plan and enjoy the benefits of wireless e-mail.

Setting Up Your E-Mail

These days, many of us have multiple personal e-mail address for many reasons. Your phone's E-mail app can manage up to ten e-mail accounts. With a Galaxy S6 phone, you may need to create a separate e-mail account through Google's Gmail just for your phone. If you do not get a Gmail account, you'll miss out on so many exciting capabilities. I highly recommend setting up a new Gmail account if you don't have one already (more on that later).

The E-mail app on your phone routinely polls all the e-mail systems for which you identify an e-mail account and password. It then presents you with copies of your e-mail.

Setup is so easy, and having access to all of your e-mail makes you so productive, that I advise you to consider adding all your e-mail accounts to your phone.

Getting ready

In general, connecting to a personal e-mail account simply involves entering the name of your e-mail account(s) and its password(s) in your phone. Have these handy when you're ready to set up your phone.

As mentioned, you can have up to ten e-mail accounts on your phone; however, you do need to pick one account as your favorite. You can send an e-mail using any of the accounts, but your phone wants to know the e-mail account that you want it to use as a default.

Next, you may want to have access to your work account. This is relatively common these days, but some companies see this as a security problem. You should consult with your IT department for some extra information. Technologically, it's not hard to make this kind of thing happen as long as your business e-mail is reasonably modern.

Finally, if you don't already have a Gmail account, I strongly encourage you to get one. Read the nearby sidebar, "The advantages of getting a Gmail account" to find out why.

Setting up your existing Gmail account

If you already have a Gmail account, setting it up on your phone is easy as can be. Follow these steps from the Apps menu:

1. **Find the Gmail icon in the Apps list.**

   Here is a confusing part. The icon on the left in Figure 5-1 is the Gmail app. The icon on the right is for the general e-mail app. The general e-mail app is for your combined e-mail accounts. The general e-mail account is the app that you will use to access any and all of your e-mail accounts.

The advantages of getting a Gmail account

You might already have work and personal e-mail accounts. You might even have an old e-mail account that you check only once in a while because some friends, for whatever reason, haven't updated their profile for you and continue to use an old address.

The thought of getting yet another e-mail address, even one that's free, might (understandably) be unappealing. After all, it's another address and password to remember. However, some important functions on your phone require a Gmail account:

- ✓ The ability to buy applications from the Google Play Store. (This is huge!) I go over the Play Store in Chapter 8.

- ✓ The ability to use the Google Drive for storage. (This is pretty important and almost huge!)

- ✓ Free access to the photo site Picasa (although other sites have many of the same features).

- ✓ Access to the Music and Video Hub. These slick services are explained in Chapter 12.

- ✓ Automatic backup of your contacts and calendar. That's explained in more detail in Chapters 6 and 13.

To make a long story short, it's worth the trouble to get a Gmail account, even if you already have a personal e-mail account.

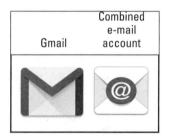

Figure 5-1: The E-mail and Gmail icons.

2. **Tap the Gmail icon.**

   Because your phone does not know if you have a Gmail account yet, it offers you the option of entering your Gmail account or creating a new account. This page is shown in Figure 5-2.

3. **Enter your Gmail account e-mail address.**

   Be sure to include the "@gmail.com" suffix. Tapping Next brings up the screen shown in Figure 5-3.

4. **Enter your existing Gmail password.**

   Go ahead and type your password. When you're ready, tap Next on the keyboard.

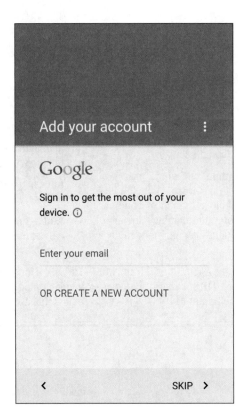

Figure 5-2: Add your account page.

You may get a pop-up re-confirming that you agree with the terms of use and all that legal stuff. Tap OK. You'll see lots of flashing lights and whirling circles while your phone and your Gmail account get to know each other.

If everything is correct, your phone and your account get acquainted and become best friends. After a few minutes, they are ready to serve your needs. There are even a few screens that tell you all the things that your Gmail account will do for you.

If you have a problem, you probably mistyped something. Try retyping your information. From this point on, any e-mail you get in your Gmail account will also appear on your phone!

Setting up a new Gmail account

If you need to set up a new Gmail account, you have a few more steps to follow. Before you get into the steps, think up a good user ID and password.

Figure 5-3: Enter your password on this screen.

Gmail has been around for a while. That means all the good, simple e-mail addresses are taken. Unless you plan to start using this e-mail account as your main e-mail, which you could do if you wanted, you're probably best off if you pick some unusual combination of letters and numbers that you can remember for now to get through this process.

When you have all of this ready, follow Steps 1 and 2 in the previous section, but tap the "Or Create a New Account" hyperlink when you get to the screen shown in Figure 5-2. From there, follow these steps:

1. **Enter your first and last names on the screen and tap Next.**

   Google asks for your name in the screen that appears. This is how they personalize any communications they have with you.

   You may be tempted to use a fake name or some other clever two-word combination in place of a name. Don't do it. You will still be getting e-mail to "Rita Book" or "Warren Peace" long after the humor has worn off.

2. **Enter the username you want to use with Gmail and tap Done.**

   On the screen shown in Figure 5-4, enter the username you want. Hopefully you get this name approved on the first shot.

   Choose your username

   You'll use this username to sign in to your Google Account.

   Username

   somethingobvious2u   @gmail.com

   This username is not available   ⚠

   Suggested usernames:

   notsoobvious6482xg5

   lessobvious49272fde

   veryobscure3030xz28

   ‹   NEXT ›

   Figure 5-4: The Username screen.

   If your first choice isn't available, try again. There is no easy way to check before you go through these steps. Eventually, you hit on an unused ID or you will use one of the suggestions in blue font. When you're successful, it will congratulate you.

3. **Accept the terms and conditions of the account.**

   You may want a lawyer to review these terms and conditions. Or not. Basically, the terms are that you should be nice and not try to cheat anyone. Don't abuse the privilege of having the account.

4. **Prepare a security question and an alternate e-mail address.**

   If you forget your password, Google wants to verify that you're really you and not someone pretending to be you. Google does this check by sending a confirmation e-mail to another account or sending a text to your phone. You can do this now or tap Skip to do it later.

After you tap Done, light flashes and you see the screen working away. This process usually takes less than two minutes. While you wait, you'll see all kinds of messages that it's getting ready to sync things. Don't worry. I'll explain these messages in good time. For now, you can add any other e-mail accounts you want by following the steps in the next section.

Working with non-Gmail e-mail accounts

Your phone is set up to work with up to ten e-mail accounts. If you have more than ten accounts, I'm thinking that you might have too much going on in your life. No phone, not even the Galaxy S6, can help you there!

We will now cover the steps to adding your e-mail accounts. Once you tell your phone all your e-mail accounts, the E-mail screen will let you see the inbox of each account or combine all your e-mail in a single inbox. You can choose which option works best for you.

To get started, have your e-mail addresses and passwords ready. When you have this, go to your phone's Home screen. Look for the Mail icon; it is an envelope with an "@" on it (see Figure 5-1). This is probably on your Home screen as one of the five primary shortcuts just above the device Function keys or in your application list.

Adding your first e-mail account

1. **Tap the Menu icon from the E-mail screen.**

   This brings up a menu like the one shown in Figure 5-5.

2. **Tap the Others icon.**

   This is a generic way to enter lots of kinds of e-mail accounts. If you have an e-mail account on Yahoo!, AOL, Outlook.com, or another e-mail service that is on your screen, you can tap that icon. However, the process and the result will be the same. Tapping one of these icons brings up a screen that looks like the image shown in Figure 5-6.

3. **Carefully enter your full e-mail account name, and then enter your password in the second field.**

   Your e-mail address should include the full shebang, including the @ sign and everything that follows it. Make sure to enter your password correctly, being careful with capitalization if your e-mail server is case-sensitive (most are). If in doubt, select the option that lets you see your password.

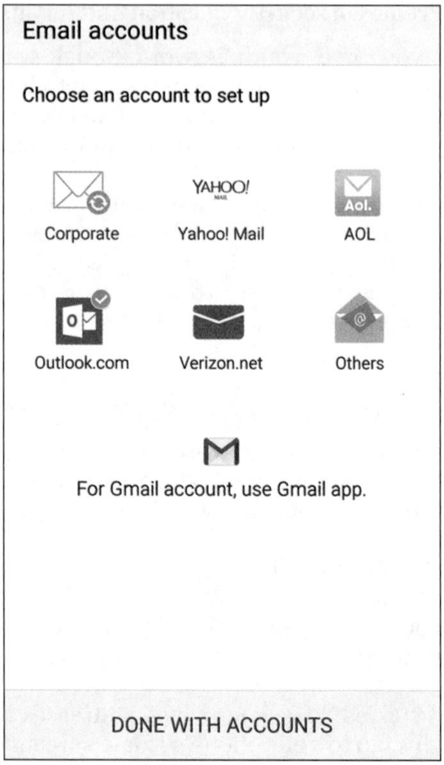

Figure 5-5: The menu for the E-mail app.

4. **Tap Next.**

   You see all kinds of options you can select. Just go with the default settings for now. This will bring up the screen seen in Figure 5-7.

5. **Select your desired Sync Settings.**

   You can select how often you want your phone and the e-mail service to synchronize. There has been a lot of thought and consideration put into the default settings. If you just want to get started, tap Next. If you want to fine-tune things later, it is not hard to go back and adjust these settings. These settings are intended to be gentle on your data usage. If you want images in e-mail to download immediately, store older e-mail messages on your phone, check to see if you have new e-mail all the time, you can change these settings on this page for this e-mail account. If you know what you want that is different from the default settings, make the changes and then tap Next.

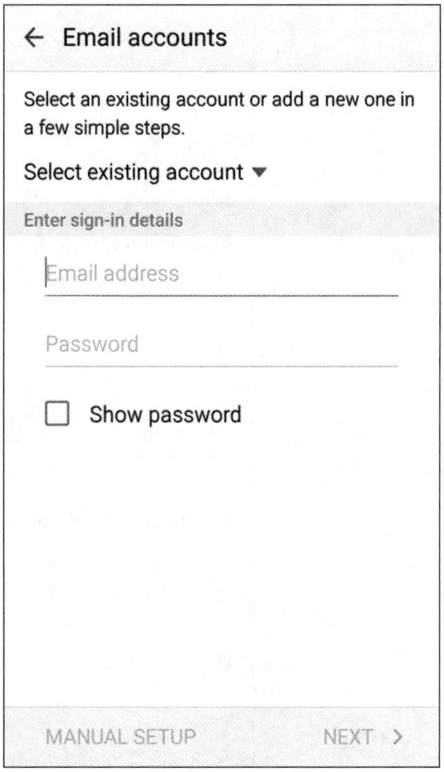

Figure 5-6: The Add Account screen.

6. **Enter a name for the new e-mail account.**

   The next screen is seen in Figure 5-8. This gives you the option to call your e-mail account something other than its address. You can always use the e-mail address for the name, but I recommend choosing something shorter, like Joe's MSN or My Hotmail.

7. **Tap Done.**

   Using Figure 5-9 as an example, you can see that my account is now registered on my phone. It worked!

Adding additional e-mail accounts

Once you have entered your first e-mail account, there are a few different steps to add additional accounts.

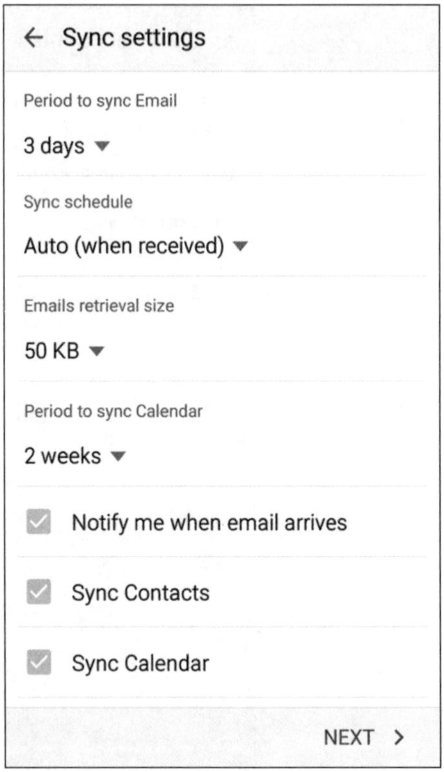

Figure 5-7: The Sync Settings screen.

1. **Tap the More hyperlink at the top right part of the screen.**

   This tap of the More hyperlink brings up the pop-up screen seen in Figure 5-10.

2. **Tap Settings.**

   Tapping Settings brings up the screen seen in Figure 5-11.

3. **Tap Add Account next to the green plus sign.**

   This brings you back to the Set-up e-mail screen seen back in Figure 5-5.

At this point you can add up to nine more accounts, and remember, you will be asked which e-mail account you want to be your primary account. It is entirely up to you. You can send and receive e-mail from all your accounts by selecting it, but only one can be the primary account used if you send an e-mail from another application, such as the Contacts app.

Figure 5-8: Naming your e-mail account.

Setting up a corporate e-mail account

In addition to personal e-mail accounts, you can add your work e-mail account to your phone — if it's based upon a Microsoft Exchange server, that is, and if it's okay with your company's IT department.

Before you get started, you need some information from the IT department of your company:

- The domain name of the office e-mail server
- Your work e-mail password
- The name of your exchange server

If the folks in IT are okay with you using your phone to access its e-mail service, your IT department will have no trouble supplying you with this information.

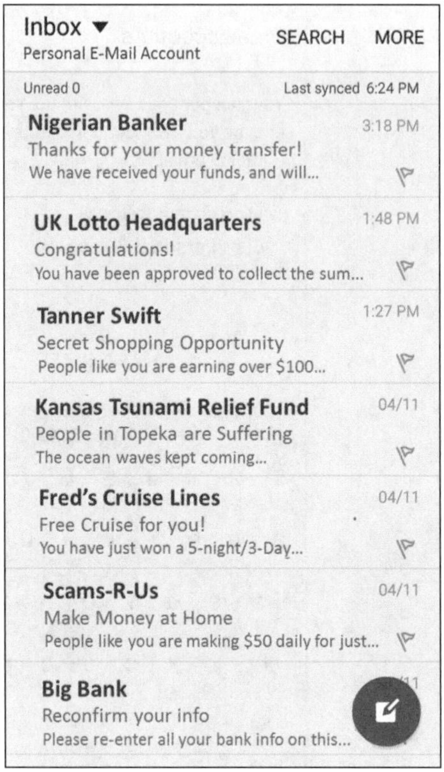

Figure 5-9: The E-mail Home screen.

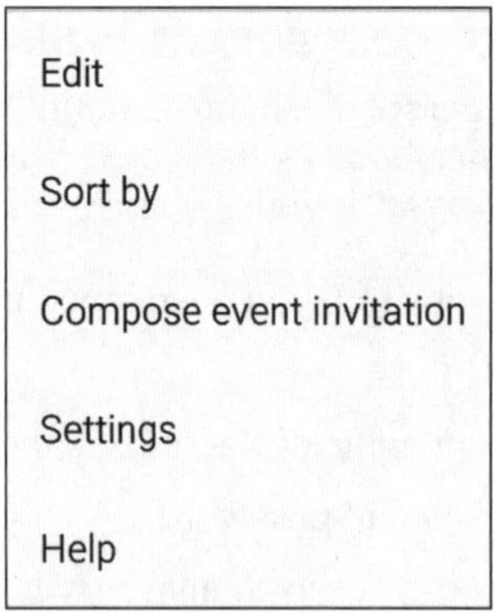

Figure 5-10: The More pop-up.

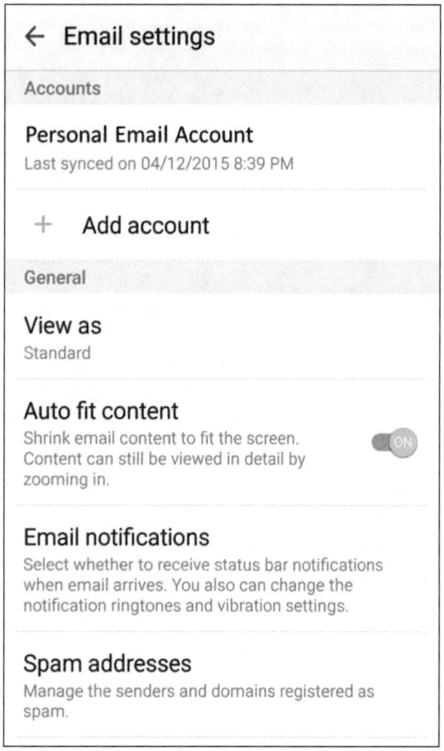

← **Email settings**

Accounts

Personal Email Account
Last synced on 04/12/2015 8:39 PM

+ **Add account**

General

View as
Standard

Auto fit content
Shrink email content to fit the screen.
Content can still be viewed in detail by
zooming in.   ON

Email notifications
Select whether to receive status bar notifications
when email arrives. You also can change the
notification ringtones and vibration settings.

Spam addresses
Manage the senders and domains registered as
spam.

Figure 5-11: The E-mail Settings screen.

Before you set up your work e-mail on your phone, make sure that you have permission. If you do this without the green light from your company, and you end up violating your company's rules, you could be in hot water. Increasing your productivity won't be much help if you're standing out in the parking lot holding all the contents of your office in a cardboard box.

Assuming that your company wants you to be more productive with no extra cost to the company, the process for adding your work e-mail starts at your E-mail Home screen seen in Figure 5-5.

1. **From the E-mail Home screen, tap the Corporate icon.**

2. **Enter your e-mail address and password.**

    The Corporate screen is seen in Figure 5-12. It is similar to the screen shown in Figure 5-6, but this time, in Figure 5-12, I have closed the keypad and can see the full screen.

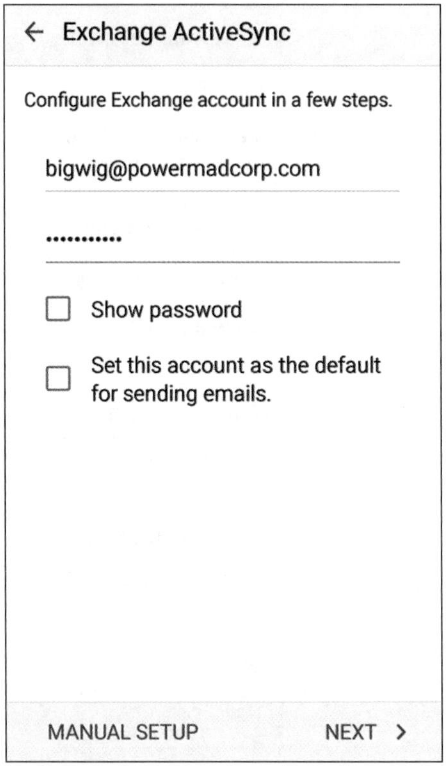

Figure 5-12: The Corporate set up e-mail screen.

3. **Tap Manual Setup.**

   This brings up the screen seen in Figure 5-13.

   The chances are that you haven't got the foggiest notion what any of this means or what you are to do now.

4. **Verify that your IT department is good with you having e-mail on your own device and have them give you the necessary settings.**

   It is increasingly common that a firm will give you access on your phone. At the same time, they do not generally circulate documents with how to make this happen. This would be a big security problem if anyone could get access. Save yourself the time and get help from IT.

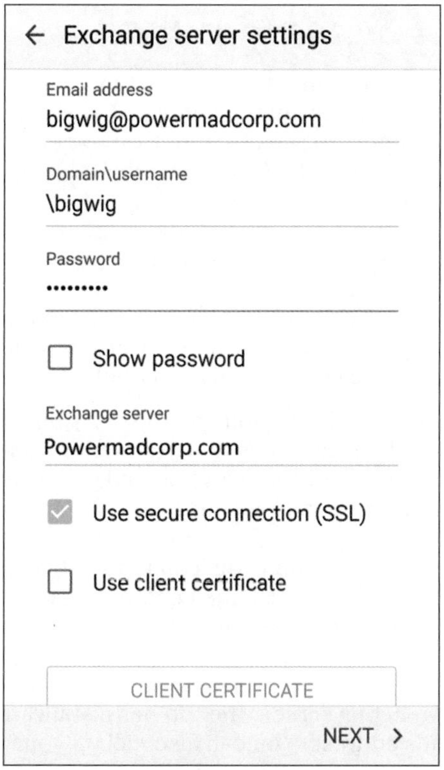

Figure 5-13: The Manual Setup screen for adding corporate e-mail accounts.

Reading E-Mail on Your Phone

In Figure 5-9, you can see how the e-mail screen looks for what I have called Personal E-mail Account. You can also set it up so that this screen combines all your e-mail into one inbox. At any given time, you might want to look at the accounts individually or all together.

To look at all your e-mail in one large inbox, tap the downward pointing arrow next to the word Inbox and select Combined Inbox. This lists all your e-mail in chronological order. To open any e-mail message, just tap it.

If, on the other hand, you want to see just e-mail from one account, tap the box at the top that says Combined Inbox. When you tap this icon, your phone will display all the individual e-mail accounts. Tap on the account you want to focus on at the moment, and your phone will bring up your e-mail in chronological order for just that e-mail address.

Writing and Sending E-mail

After you set up the receiving part of e-mail, the other important side is composing and sending e-mail. At any time when you're in an e-mail screen, simply tap the Menu button to get a pop-up screen. From the pop-up menu, tap the Compose icon (shown here) to open the e-mail composition screen.

Here's the logic that determines which e-mail account will send this e-mail:

✔ If you're in the inbox of an e-mail account and you tap the Compose icon after tapping Menu, your phone sends the e-mail to the intended recipient(s) through that account.

✔ If you're in the combined inbox or some other part of the e-mail app, your phone assumes that you want to send the e-mail from the default e-mail account that you selected when you registered your second (or additional) e-mail account.

When you tap the Compose icon in the Menu pop-up menu, it tells you which account it will use. The E-mail composition screen shown in Figure 5-14 says this e-mail will be coming from this account: `galaxysfordummies @gmail.com`.

As shown in this screen, the top has a stalwart To field, where you type the recipient's address. You can also call up your contacts, a group, or your most recent e-mail addresses. (Read all about contacts in Chapter 6.) Tap the address or contact you want, and it populates the To field.

Below that, in the Subject field, is where you enter the e-mail's topic. And below that is the body of the message, with the default signature, `Sent from my Samsung Galaxy S6`, although your cellular carrier might have customized this signature.

At the top of the screen are three hyperlinks:

✔ **Attach:** Tap this hyperlink to attach a file of any variety to your e-mail.

✔ **Send:** Tap this link to send the e-mail to the intended recipient(s).

✔ **More:** Tap this option and you get the pop-up seen in Figure 5-15. This gives you the following options:

• *Save in Drafts:* This allows you to complete the e-mail later without losing your work.

• *Send e-mail to myself:* This is an alternative to saving the e-mail in your Sent mail folder.

• *Priority:* This option signifies that this is more important than the average e-mail to your recipients.

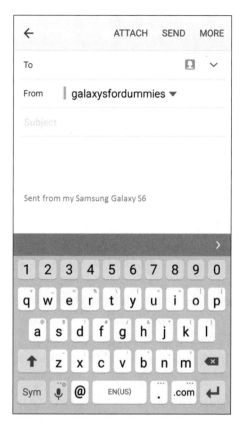

Figure 5-14: The E-mail composition screen.

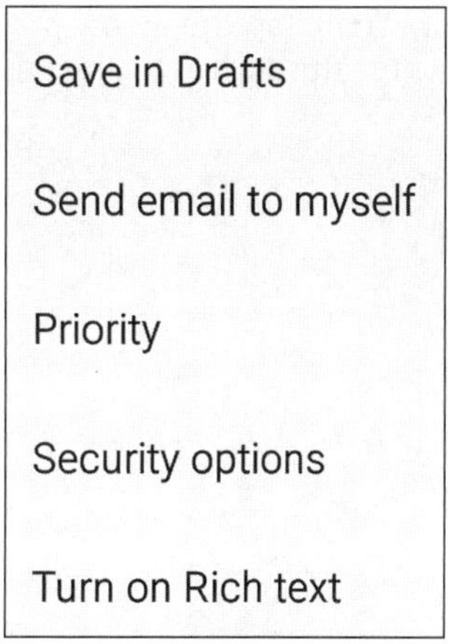

> Save in Drafts
>
> Send email to myself
>
> Priority
>
> Security options
>
> Turn on Rich text

Figure 5-15: Composition e-mail options.

- *Security options:* You have some fancy, 007 options here. You can sign the document or encrypt it.

- *Turn on Rich Text:* To save data usage, e-mail is sent in a default font. If you want to burn a little more data, you can get creative and add more elaborate fonts.

If you change your mind about sending an e-mail message, you can just tap the Back key. If you're partially done with the message, you're asked whether you want to save it in your Drafts folder.

The Drafts folder works like the Drafts folder in your computer's e-mail program. When you want to continue working on a saved e-mail, you open the Drafts folder, tap on it, and continue working.

Replying To and Forwarding E-mail

Replying to or forwarding the e-mail that you get is a common activity. You can do this from your E-mail app. Figure 5-16 shows a typical open e-mail message.

You can Reply by tapping the icon with the return arrow at the bottom of the screen. If other people were copied on the e-mail, you could tap the double return arrow to Reply All.

When you tap either of these options, the Reply screen comes back with the To line populated by the sender's e-mail address (or addresses) and a blank space where you can leave your comments. (In the case of Figure 5-16, you could ask that your Dad not send you any more jokes like these.)

To forward the e-mail, tap the arrow pointing to the right above the word Forward, and enter the addressee just as you do when sending a new e-mail.

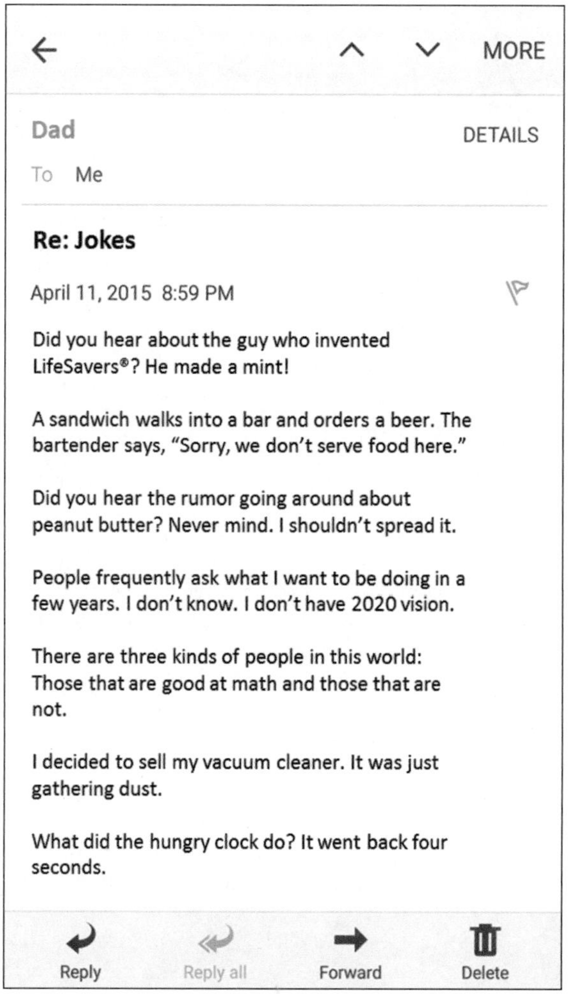

← ∧ ∨ MORE

Dad   DETAILS

To Me

Re: Jokes

April 11, 2015 8:59 PM

Did you hear about the guy who invented LifeSavers®? He made a mint!

A sandwich walks into a bar and orders a beer. The bartender says, "Sorry, we don't serve food here."

Did you hear the rumor going around about peanut butter? Never mind. I shouldn't spread it.

People frequently ask what I want to be doing in a few years. I don't know. I don't have 2020 vision.

There are three kinds of people in this world: Those that are good at math and those that are not.

I decided to sell my vacuum cleaner. It was just gathering dust.

What did the hungry clock do? It went back four seconds.

↩   ↩↩   →   🗑
Reply   Reply all   Forward   Delete

Figure 5-16: An opened e-mail.

Managing Your Contacts

* *

In This Chapter

▶ Putting all your callers, texters, and e-mailers on your phone

▶ Getting all your contacts in one location

▶ Keeping up to date with just a few taps

* *

*Y*ou're probably familiar with using contact databases. Many mobile phones automatically create one, or at least prompt you to create one. You also probably have a file of contacts on your work computer, made up of work e-mail addresses and telephone numbers. And if you have a personal e-mail account, you probably have a contact database of e-mail accounts of friends and family members. If you're kickin' it old school, you might even keep a paper address book with names, addresses, and telephone numbers.

The problem with having all these contact databases is that it's rarely ever as neat and tidy as I've just outlined. A friend might e-mail you at work, so you have her in both your contact databases. Then her e-mail address might change, and you update that information in your personal address book but not in your work one. Before long, you have duplicate and out-of-date contacts, and it's hard to tell which is correct. How you include Facebook or LinkedIn messaging in your contact profile is unclear.

Abraham Lincoln

Mobile
425-555-1111

ɔnnected via

In addition to problems keeping all your contact databases current, it can be a hassle to migrate the database from your old phone. Some cellular carriers or firms have offered a service that converts your existing files to your new phone, but it's rarely a truly satisfying experience. You end up spending a lot of time correcting the assumptions it makes.

You now face that dilemma again with your Galaxy S6: deciding how to manage your contacts. This chapter gives you the advantages of each approach so that you can decide which one will work best for you. That way, you won't have the frustration of wishing you had done it another way before you put 500 of your best friends in the wrong filing system.

Using the Galaxy S6 Contact Database

Your phone wants you to be able to communicate with everyone you would ever want to in any way you know how to talk to them. This is a tall order, and your Galaxy S6 makes it as easy as possible. In fact, I wouldn't be surprised if the technology implemented in the Contacts app becomes one of your favorite capabilities of the phone. After all, your phone is there to simplify communication with friends, family, and co-workers, and the Contacts app on your phone makes it as easy as technology allows.

At the same time, this information is only as good as your contact database discipline. The focus of this section is to help you to help your phone to help you.

Learning the Contact Database on your phone

The fact of the matter is, if you introduced your phone to your e-mail accounts back in Chapter 5, the Contacts list on your phone has all the contacts from each of your contact lists.

Take a look at it and see. From your Home screen, tap the Contacts icon.

If you haven't created a Gmail account, synced your personal e-mail, or created a contact when you sent a text or made a call, your Contacts list will be empty. Otherwise you see a bunch of your contacts now residing on your phone, sorted alphabetically (as shown in Figure 6-1).

Along with the Contacts application that manages the data, this database does more than just store names, phone numbers, and e-mail addresses. You can have the contact include any or all of the following information:

- All telephone numbers, including
  - Mobile
  - Home
  - Work
  - Work fax
  - Pager
  - Other

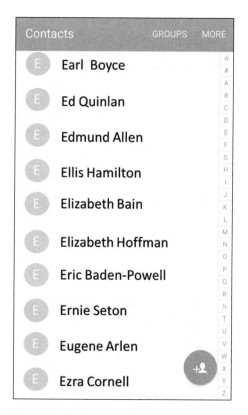

Figure 6-1: The Contacts list.

✔ E-mail addresses
   • Home
   • Work
   • Mobile
✔ Instant Messaging addresses
✔ Company/organization
✔ Job title
✔ Nickname
✔ Mailing address for
   • Home
   • Work
   • Another location

  ✔ Any notes about this person

 • Web address

 • Birthday (or other significant event)

 • A phonetic spelling of the name

As if all this weren't enough, you can assign a specific ringtone to play when a particular person contacts you. I cover the steps to assign a music file to an individual caller in Chapter 12.

Finally, you can assign a picture for the contact. It can be one out of your Gallery; you can take a new picture; or (as I discuss in Chapter 8) you can connect to a social network like Facebook, and use that person's profile picture.

Fortunately, the only essential information is a name. Every other field is optional, and is only displayed if the field contains information to be displayed. Figure 6-2 shows a lightly populated contact.

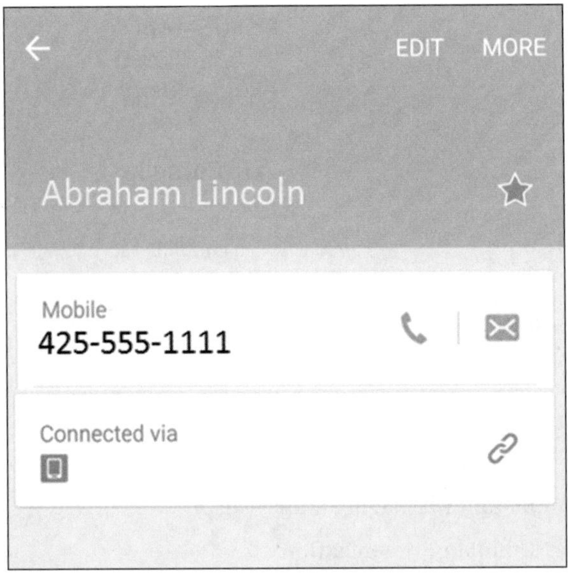

Figure 6-2: A lightly populated contact.

Deciding where to store your contacts

Before we get too far, it is important for you to decide the default option where you want to store your contacts. Deciding this now with the information this section provides you will make your life much easier as you go forward. It is possible to combine contact databases, but even the best tools are imperfect.

The first time you try to save a new contact, the Contacts app will offer you a pop-up screen as seen in Figure 6-3. This lists the options you have and will take your first entry as the option you want as a default.

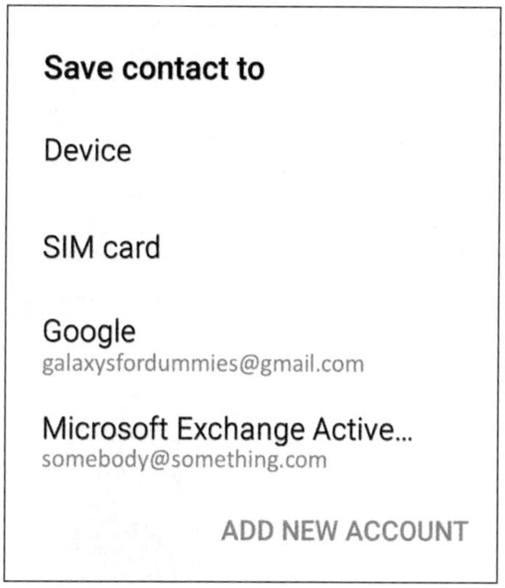

Save contact to

Device

SIM card

Google
galaxysfordummies@gmail.com

Microsoft Exchange Active...
somebody@something.com

ADD NEW ACCOUNT

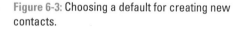

Figure 6-3: Choosing a default for creating new contacts.

Whenever you save a new entry you can manually switch to another of these databases. Save yourself some time and aggravation and decide now what you want to do. Here are your options on where to save new contacts:

✔ Within the memory of your phone

✔ On the SIM card inserted in your phone

✔ Within your Gmail account

✔ As a contact in one of you other accounts

Each of these four options has advantages and disadvantages. If you simply want my advice, I suggest using your Gmail account to store new contacts. If this satisfies you, skip to the next section on linking contacts from other sources. Read on if you need some context.

Here is the deal: If everything is working properly, all options work equally well. However, if you switch phones regularly, ever lose you phone, need to make significant updates to your contacts, or are frequently out of wireless coverage, such as on an airplane, you should consider the options.

The first option mentioned involves storing your contacts within your phone. This is a great option, as long as you have your phone. However, there will come a day when Samsung (or HTC, or LG, etc.) has something faster and better and you will want to upgrade. At that point, perhaps next year or in ten years, you will need to move your contacts to another location if you want to keep them. Plus, if you lose your phone, I sure hope that you have recently used one of the back-up options we explore in Chapter 17.

The second option is to store your new contacts on your SIM card. The SIM card is familiar technology if your previous phone worked with AT&T or T-Mobile. Figure 6-4 shows a profile of a typical SIM card, next to a dime for scale, although yours probably has the logo of your cellular carrier nicely printed on the card. To the right of the SIM card is the newer micro SIM card. This is the same idea, but in a smaller package.

Figure 6-4: A SIM card and a micro SIM card.

If your cellular carrier is Verizon, Sprint, or U.S. Cellular, you may be confused. Your Galaxy S6 has a SIM card. What's the story? These carriers use CDMA technology for voice and for some data features. Up to 3G, the phones using CDMA technology and data services didn't use a SIM card. Today, *all* carriers in the United States are implementing a super high-speed data technology called LTE, also called 4G. Because your phone is capable of LTE, you now have a SIM card.

The cool aspect of using your SIM card is that you can pluck it out of your existing phone and pop it in another phone and all your contacts come with you. It works this easily if you stay with an Android smartphone of recent vintage. It almost works this easily if you, say, switch back to a feature phone (as in the kind of phone that merely makes calls and texts). Another advantage is that your SIM card does not rely on having a wireless connection to update changes.

The next option is to store new contacts on your Gmail account. What this means is that your new contacts are automatically copied from your phone to the Gmail account of Google servers. This keeps the records on your phone, but Google maintains a copy of this record in your Gmail account. You can make changes to a contact on your phone or on your PC.

The two reasons I recommend using your Gmail account are: 1) you can maintain these records with your full-sized keyboard, rather than the smaller keyboard on your phone; and 2) it is easy to get back all these contacts on a new Android phone simply by telling the new phone your Gmail account. Because you will probably enter your Gmail account right away when you get a new phone, your contacts reappear quicker than the fourth option.

The fourth option is to store the contacts in one of your existing e-mail accounts. This may be the best option if you already consider your e-mail, either your personal or work account, to be the primary location where you store contacts. If you already have good database discipline with one of your e-mail accounts, by all means, use this e-mail account as the default place to store new contacts.

If this particular account you currently use for keeping your contacts is not set up yet on your phone, you can tap the "Add New Account" hyperlink shown in Figure 6-3 to go through the process described in Chapter 5 to set up a new e-mail account.

Linking Contacts on your phone

This Contacts list is smart. Allow me to explain some of the things that are going on.

Say your best friend is Bill Boyce. You sent Bill a text earlier to let him know about your new phone. You followed the instructions on how to send a text in Chapter 4 and entered his telephone number. You took it to the next step and tapped Add Contact. When you were prompted to add his name, you did. Now your phone has a contact, "Bill Boyce."

Then you linked your e-mail. Of course your buddy Bill is in your e-mail Contacts list. So while you were reading this chapter, several things happened. First, your phone and your Gmail account synced. Your phone thinks about it, and figures this must be the same person. It automatically combines all the information in one entry on your phone!

Then your phone automatically updates your Gmail account. On the left side of Figure 6-5, you see the Google logo just beneath Bill's e-mail address. This contact is synced with your Gmail account. You didn't have to do anything to make this happen.

Your phone noticed that Bill's work number was in your e-mail contact information, but the mobile phone number you used to text him was not. No problem! Now the contact on your phone includes both the information you had in your e-mail contact as well as his mobile phone.

Now, as slick as this system is, it isn't perfect. In this scenario, both contacts have the same first and last name. However, if the same person also goes by a different name, you have to link these contacts. For example, if you created a contact for Bill Boyce, but your e-mail refers to him as William D. Boyce, your phone will assume that these are two different people.

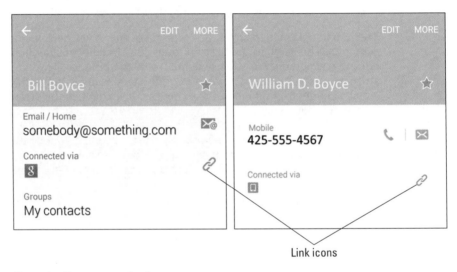

Link icons

Figure 6-5: Two contacts for the same person.

No problem, though. Do you see the chain links icon in Figure 6-5 in the box that says Connected via? Here are the steps to link the two contacts for the same person:

1. **From a contact, tap on the chain icon.**

   This brings up the pop-up shown in Figure 6-6.

   Choose the contact whose name you want to be the primary name. For example, I tapped the link on the Bill Boyce contact, which is saved in Gmail. This will be the name used on the combined contact going forward.

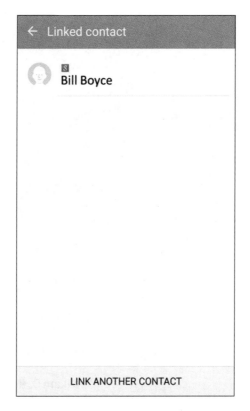

Figure 6-6: The Linking Page for Bill Boyce.

2. Tap the Link Another Contact hyperlink at the bottom of the screen.

Your phone will try to help you with some suggestions, as shown in Figure 6-7. If it gets it all wrong, you can just find the other contact by searching alphabetically.

3. Tap the Contact you want joined.

In this case, the last guess, William D. Boyce, is the one you want. Tap the selection box to the left of his name. The result is shown in Figure 6-8.

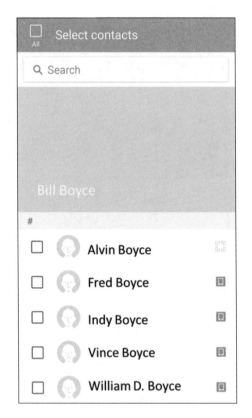

Figure 6-7: Some linking suggestions.

Now tap the hyperlink that says Link in the upper right-hand corner of the screen. This combined link will now have all the information on this one person.

Let no man put this link asunder (unless you made a mistake and want to change it. Then go tap the chain icon to break the link.)

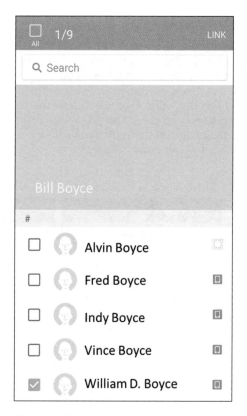

Figure 6-8: The Linked contacts.

Creating Contacts Within Your Database

Your phone is out there trying to make itself the ultimate contact database with as little effort on your part as possible. The interesting thing is that the salesperson in the cellular store probably didn't explain this to you in detail. It's a subtle-but-important capability that's hard to communicate on the sales floor. Here's what happens.

Whenever you make or receive a call, send or receive an e-mail, or send or receive a text, your phone looks up the telephone number or e-mail address from which the message originated to check whether it has seen that address before. If it has, it has all the other information on that person ready. If it doesn't recognize the originating telephone number or e-mail, it asks whether you want to make it a new contact or update an existing one. What could be easier?

Adding contacts as you dial

When you get a call, a text, or an e-mail from someone who isn't in your Contacts list, you're given the option to create a profile for that person. The same is true when you initiate contact with someone who isn't in your Contacts list. Back in Chapter 3, you saw the empty and full dialing screens. The image on the left in Figure 6-9 show the phone trying its best to anticipate the person you are in the process of calling and, if it is not saved already, the image on the right shows how it offers you the option to add this number to your contact list.

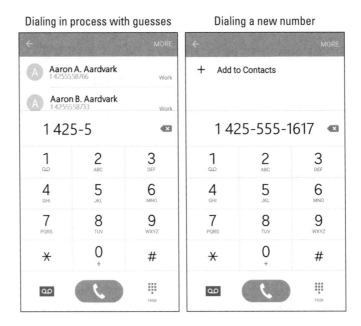

Figure 6-9: The dialing screens in process and when there is a new number.

When you tap Add to Contacts, you're immediately given the option to create a contact or update an existing contact. Your phone doesn't know whether this is a new number for an existing contact or a totally new person. Rather than make an assumption (as lesser phones on the market would do), your phone asks you whether you need to create a new profile or add this contact information to an existing profile.

Keep in mind that if you are calling an existing contact, and your phone guesses the right person, you can save yourself time and tap the phone to dial.

Let's say that you want to enter this number as a new contact. You follow these steps:

1. **Tap the Add a Contact hyperlink.**

   It will first check to see if you want to create a new contact or if you want to add this number to an existing contact. The pop-up as seen in Figure 6-10 gives you these options. If this is a new number for an existing contact, this pop-up saves you from having to link contacts.

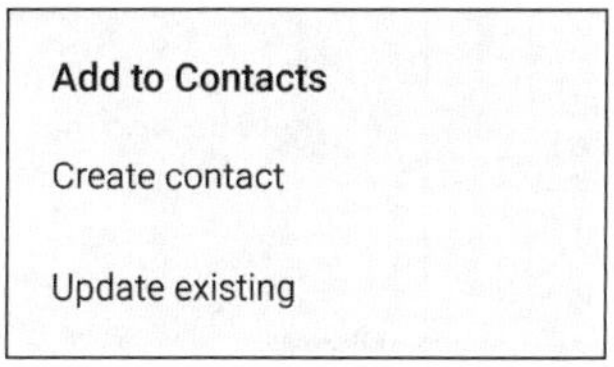

   Add to Contacts

   Create contact

   Update existing

   Figure 6-10: The Add to Contacts pop-up.

2. **Tap the Create Contact hyperlink.**

   Tapping this hyperlink brings up a new contact page. An example is seen in Figure 6-11.

   The number is already populated. You just need to fill in the correct name plus any other information that you wish to have associated with this person.

3. **When done typing in the information for this contact, tap Save at the top of the Contact.**

   Figure 16-11 shows the save button at the top of the screen.

Adding contacts manually

Adding contacts manually involves taking an existing contact database and adding its entries to your phone, one profile at a time. (This option, a last resort, was the only option for phones back in the day.)

1. **Tap the Contacts icon.**

   Doing so brings up the list of existing contact as we saw back in Figure 6-1.

2. **Tap the Add Contacts icon (the + [plus] sign next to a silhouette).**

   This icon is seen in figure 6-12. Tapping it will bring up a blank contact page with nothing populated.

3. **Fill in the information you want to include.**

4. **When you're done entering data, tap Save at the top of the screen.**

   The profile is now saved. Repeat the process for as many profiles as you want to create.

The Save option

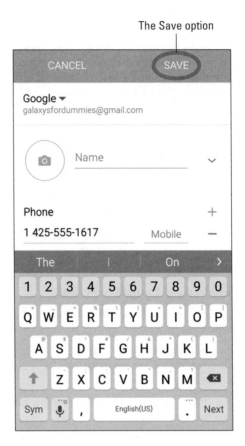

Figure 6-11: A partially populated contact.

Figure 6-12: The Add Contacts icon.

How Contacts Make Life Easy

Phew. Heavy lifting over. After you populate the profiles of dozens or hundreds of contacts, you're rewarded with a great deal of convenience.

Start by tapping a contact. You see that person's profile, as shown in Figure 6-13.

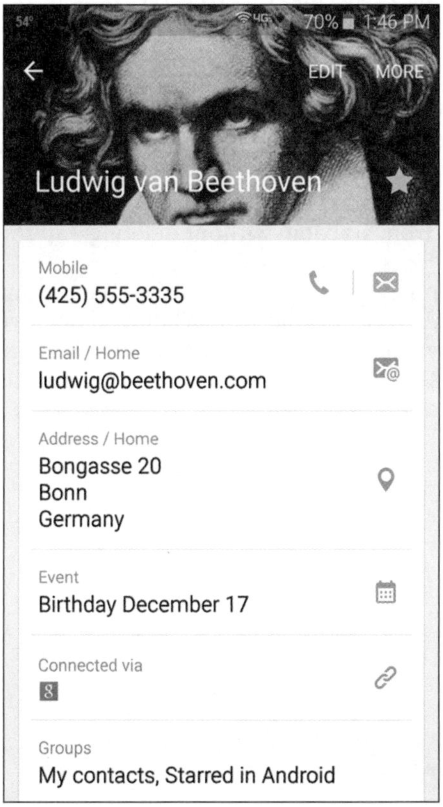

Figure 6-13: A typical Contacts profile.

All the options you have for contacting this contact are but a simple tap away:

✔ Tap the green telephone next to the number to dial that number.

✔ Tap the amber message icon to send a text.

✔ Tap the e-mail icon to create an e-mail.

About the only thing that tapping on a data field won't do is print an envelope for you if you tap the mailing address!

Playing Favorites

Over the course of time, you probably find yourself calling some people more than others. It would be nice to not have to scroll through your entire contacts database to find those certain people. Contacts allow you to place some of your contacts into a Favorites list for easy access.

From within the Contacts app, open the profile and notice the star next to that person's name (refer to Figure 6-13). To the right of the contact name is a star. If that star is gold, that Contact is a Favorite. If not, then not.

To make a contact into a star, tap the blank outline of the star. To demote a contact from stardom without deleting, tap the gold star.

You won't immediately see a difference in your Contacts other than the appearance of the gold star. When you open your phone, however, this contact now appears under your Favorites tab. This is like a mini-contact database. It looks similar in structure to you regular contact database, but it only includes your favorites.

Part III

Live on the Internet: Going Mobile

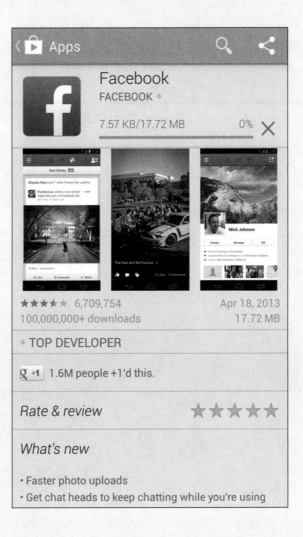

Visit www.dummies.com/extras/samsunggalaxys6 for great Dummies content online.

In this part. . .

- ✔ Surf the Internet from your phone and visit websites
- ✔ Get to know Google's Play Store and add exciting new apps to your phone
- ✔ Set the Browsing settings to get to your favorite websites quickly

7

You've Got the Whole (Web) World in Your Hands

In This Chapter

▶ Surfing the Internet from your phone

▶ Changing the browsing settings

▶ Visiting websites

▶ Adding and deleting bookmarks

*I*f you're like most people, one of the reasons you got a smartphone is because you want Internet access on the go. You don't want to have to wait until you get back to your laptop or desktop to find the information you need online. You want to be able to access the Internet even when you're away from a Wi-Fi hotspot — and that's exactly what you can do with your Galaxy S6 phone. In this chapter, I show you how.

The browser that comes standard with your Galaxy S6 works almost identically to the browser that's currently on your PC. You see many familiar toolbars, including the Favorites bar and search engine. And the mobile version of the browser includes tabs that allow you to open multiple Internet sessions simultaneously.

This chapter goes into much more detail on using the Internet browser on your Galaxy S6, as well as the websites you can access from your phone, and discusses some of the trade-offs you can make when viewing a web page.

oogle

☰   Web   Images   0 +

Google

ference, Facts, News - Free and Family

Starting the Browser

You have three options for getting access to information from the Internet via your Galaxy S6 phone. Which one you use is a personal choice. The choices are:

- **Use the regular web page:** This option involves accessing a web page via its regular address (URL) and having the page come up on your screen. The resulting text may be small.

- **Use the mobile web page:** Many websites offer a "mobile" version of their regular web page. This is an abbreviated version of the full website that can be more easily read on a mobile device.

- **Find whether there's a mobile app associated with the web page:** Many websites have found that it is most expedient to write a mobile application to access the information on its website. The app reformats the web page to fit better on a mobile screen — a convenient option if you plan to access this website regularly. I cover the trade-offs about this option later in this chapter and explore how to find and install such apps in Chapter 8.

With this background, let's head to the Internet. On your Galaxy S6 phone, you may have a few choices on how to get there. Figure 7-1 shows four possible icons that can get you there. Tap any of these and you can start surfing.

Figure 7-1: Possible paths to the Internet on your Galaxy S6.

If you want a little more understanding as to why there are multiple options, read the next section on Internet terminology. If not, skip ahead.

For our purposes, tap either the Chrome icon or the Google icon to get started. These icons will typically be on the Home screen. Alternatively, tap the Application icon and find the Chrome or Google icon.

If you love Bing, you are not out of luck. Bing is either on your phone or you can get it installed (I cover how to install things like Bing in Chapter 8). For now, let's stay with Chrome and Google. Things on other browsers and search engines are mostly similar and choosing the Chrome/Google pair simplifies things.

Basic Internet terminology for dummies

The term *Internet access* can mean a few different things. In some circumstances, the word "Internet" can mean a "web browser." This is an app that will display pages on the Internet. In other circumstances, the word "Internet" may refer to a "search engine." You use a search engine to find either information you are seeking or to bring you to a website. Then you use a web browser to look at the information.

Chances are the web browser on your phone that you will use is an app from Google called "Chrome," but it may be the search engine from Microsoft called "Bing." The goal with your phone is to get you where you want with minimal fuss. It is easier for the people that are bringing you this phone and service (Samsung, Google, and your wireless carrier) to give you three icons that essentially point to the same thing than to explain the terminology. Tapping the Internet icon, the Chrome icon, or the Google icon, will most likely bring up the Chrome web browser.

As long as you're connected to the Internet (that is, you are either near a Wi-Fi hotspot or in an area where you have cellular service), your home page appears. If you tap the Google icon, it will be Google. If you tap Chrome, your default home page could be blank or the Google home page, but many cellular carriers set their phones' home pages to their own websites.

If you're out of coverage range, or you turned off the cellular and Wi-Fi radios because you turned on Airplane mode, you get a pop-up screen letting you know that there is no Internet connection. (Read about Airplane mode in Chapter 2.)

If you should be in coverage but are not connected, or when you get off the airplane, you can reestablish your connections by pulling down the Notification screen and either tapping the Wi-Fi icon at the top or turning off Airplane mode.

Accessing Mobile (or Not) Websites

The browser on your phone is designed to work like the browser on your PC. At any time, you can enter a web address (URL) by tapping the text box at the top of the screen. You can try this by typing in the address of your favorite website and seeing what happens.

For example, the page seen in Figure 7-2 is the regular version of the website Refdesk.com.

Figure 7-2: The regular version of the website Refdesk.com.

As you can see, the website is all there. Also as you can see, the text is very small. This particular website is designed to take you to a lot of useful links throughout the Internet. So this is an extreme example of a regular website.

You can stretch and pinch to find the information you need. (*Stretching* and *pinching* are hand movements you can use to enlarge/shrink what you see onscreen, as covered in Chapter 2.) With a little bit of practice you can navigate your familiar websites with ease.

The other option is to find the mobile version of a website. As a comparison, Figure 7-3 shows the mobile version of Refdesk.com. It has fewer pictures, the text is larger, and the mobile version loads faster — but it's less flashy.

In the case of RefDesk, you can get to the mobile version by entering **m.refdesk.com** into the text block at the top from the software keyboard. Refdesk.com is far from the only website to offer a mobile version. Many sites — from Facebook to Flickr, Gmail to Wikipedia — offer mobile versions.

Figure 7-3: The mobile version of Refdesk.com.

So how do you get to the mobile websites? If a website has a mobile version, your phone browser will usually bring it up. Samsung has gone out of its way to work to make the web experience on the Galaxy S6 phone as familiar as possible to what you experience on your PC.

The most common difference between the address of a mobilized website and a regular one is `.com/mobile` at the end of the address. For example, the mobile version of Amazon.com is `www.amazon.com/mobile`.

If your phone doesn't automatically bring up the mobile version of a site, the simplest way to find it is to search for the desired site along with the term *mobile*. For example, the first option you get from searching for *IMDB mobile* on your phone is the mobilized website for the Internet Movie Database.

Getting Around in the Browser

If you tapped one of the icons seen in Figure 7-1, you have opened up the browser. Now would be a good time to try some of your favorite websites. Go ahead and tap in a few website addresses and see how they look!

One of the early goals for browsers that work on smartphones was to replicate the experience of using the Internet on a PC. For the most part, the browsers on your phone achieve that goal, even if you probably need to practice your zooming and panning.

One popular capability of PC browsers is the ability to open multiple tabs. This allows you to quickly jump between sessions of, say, Google, Facebook, LinkedIn, and Wikipedia by clicking on a tab. If you only had one tab, your browser would need to wait as the website's home page was re-loaded.

If you want to have multiple tabs open simultaneously, you will need to take a couple of steps to change the settings. If you can only handle one browsing session at time, feel free to skip to the next section on bookmarks.

1. **From the browser screen, tap the Menu icon.**

   Tapping the Menu icon, the three vertical dots to the right of the website address, brings up the menu options seen in Figure 7-4.

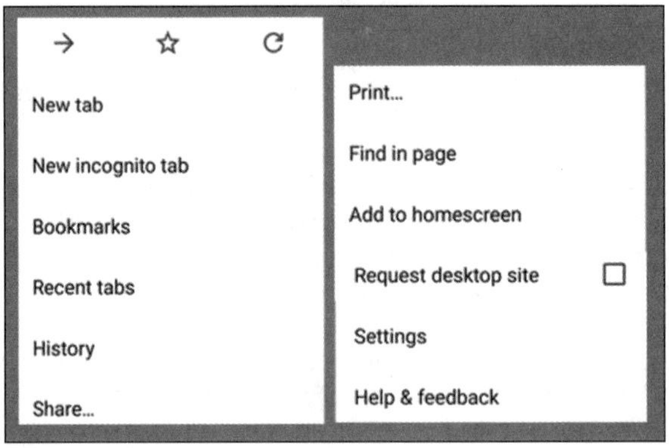

Figure 7-4: The Chrome Menu options.

2. **Tap Settings.**

   Tapping the Settings brings up the screen shown in Figure 7-5.

3. **Tap the Merge Tabs and Apps setting.**

   Tapping this setting brings up the screen shown in Figure 7-6.

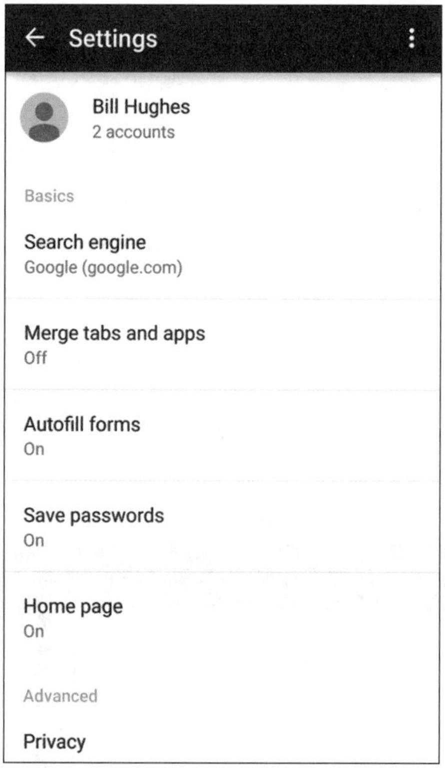

Figure 7-5: The Chrome Settings screen.

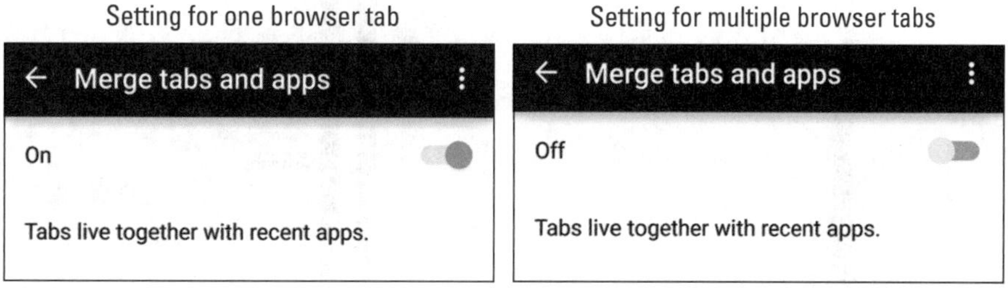

Setting for one browser tab

Setting for multiple browser tabs

Figure 7-6: The Merge tabs and apps selection.

4. Tap the toggle switch to the off position to get multiple tabs.

Tapping the toggle switch turns off this option. Turning off the option is necessary to see multiple tabs. Figure 7-7 shows the options.

The tab count tells you how many tabs are open. Because we just enabled the capability to have multiple tabs, there is only one. To add other tabs, tap the tab count box. This brings up a screen like the one shown on the left in Figure 7-8.

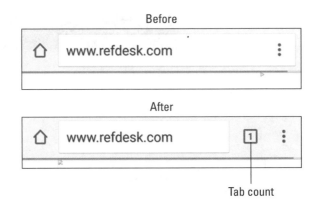

Before

After

Tab count

Figure 7-7: The browser screen before and after allowing multiple tabs.

One tab

Two tabs

Figure 7-8: The tab manager with one tab and with two tabs.

If you just want a new window for a second browser tab, tap the + (plus) sign in the upper left corner of the screen. You get a second browser screen. The right screen shows RefDesk in the second tab. You navigate among the multiple tabs by swiping up or down. If you just want to close an open tab, tap the "x" in that tab's upper right-hand corner. It will disappear.

Using Bookmarks

As convenient as it is to type URLs or search terms with the keyboard, you'll find it's usually faster to bookmark a web address that you visit frequently. Making bookmarks is a handy way to create a list of favorite sites that you want to access over and over again.

A *bookmark* is roughly the equivalent of a Favorite on a Microsoft Internet Explorer browser.

Adding bookmarks

When you want to add a website to your bookmark list, simply visit the site. From there, follow these steps:

1. **Tap the Menu options icon.**

   This brings up the screen we saw back in Figure 7-4.

2. **Tap the outline of a star.**

   This brings up the screen seen in figure 7-9.

   The first textbox is the name you want to give to your bookmark. In this case, the default is "Conditions & Forecast - WeatherBug.com." You can choose to shorten it to just WeatherBug, or anything you want to call it. When ready, tap Next on the keyboard.

   The second textbox is the web address (URL). You probably want to leave this one alone.

3. **Tap the Save button at the bottom right corner of the screen.**

   This puts a thumbnail of the website in your Bookmark file. This is shown in Figure 7-10.

You access this screen through the Menu options shown in Figure 7-4. The next time you come to Bookmarks, you can tap this thumbnail, and this page will refresh and come up in its own window.

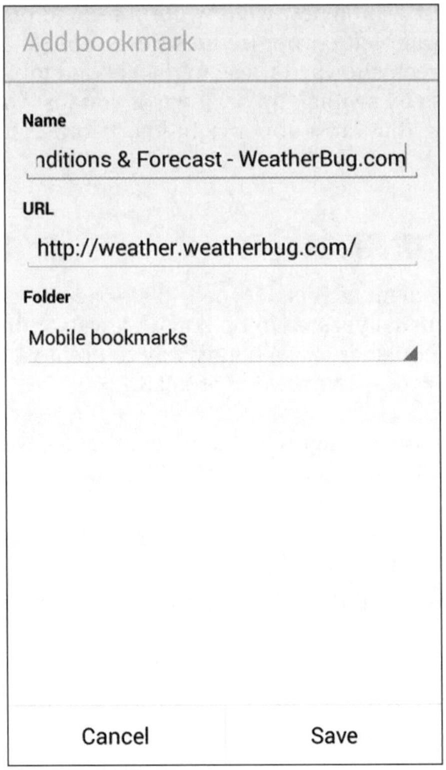

Figure 7-9: The Bookmark screen for your new addition.

Bookmark housekeeping

Bookmarks are cool and convenient, but you don't always want to save them forever. When a bookmark has served its purpose, rather than have it take up prime real estate on your Bookmarks screen, you can delete it. Press and hold the thumbnail of the website you want to delete. Doing so brings up a pop-up like the one shown in Figure 7-11.

To delete a bookmark, tap Delete Bookmark. Your phone confirms that this is indeed what you want to do. Tap Yes and the bookmark is gone.

On the other hand, say you really like this site. You can make it your home page. Tap Set as Homepage. Boom. Done. It's now your home page.

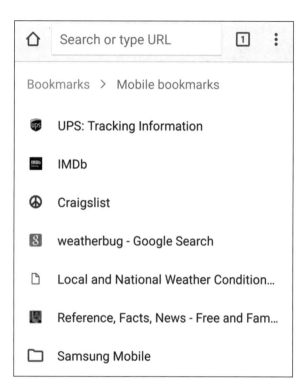

Figure 7-10: The Bookmark screen with your new addition.

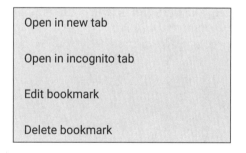

Figure 7-11: Bookmark housekeeping options.

Deciding Between Mobile Browsing and Mobile Apps

When you open the browser, you can use any search engine you want (for example, Bing or Yahoo!). This is a very familiar approach from your experience with PCs. However, you may get very tired of all the pinching and stretching of the screen.

Many companies are aware of this. What they have done is to develop a mobile app that provides you the same information as is available on their website that is formatted for a smartphone screen. Companies in particular will put the information from their website in a mobile app and then add some important mobile features.

For example, it is very convenient to order a custom-made pizza from the website of a national pizza chain. You can order your desired variety of crusts and toppings. The website version also offers directions to the nearest store. The mobile app can take this one step further and give you turn by turn directions as you drive to pick up your pizza.

This capability of providing turn by turn directions makes no sense for a desktop PC. This capability could make sense for a laptop, but few laptops have GPS receivers built-in. It is also too cumbersome and probably unsafe to rely on turn by turn directions from a laptop. It is much easier to get turn by turn directions over a smartphone.

This is just one example where downloading a mobile app offers a superior experience. The best part is, you get to choose what works for you on your Galaxy S6.

Playing in Google's Play Store

In This Chapter

▶ Getting to know Play Store

▶ Finding Play Store on your phone

▶ Seeing what Play Store has to offer

▶ Downloading and installing Android apps

▶ Rating and uninstalling apps

*O*ne of the things that makes smartphones (such as the phones based on the Google Android platform) different from regular mobile phones is that you can download better apps than what comes standard on the phone. Most traditional mobile phones come with a few simple games and basic apps. Smartphones usually come with better games and apps. For example, on your Galaxy S6 phone, you get a more sophisticated contact manager, an app that can play digital music (MP3s), basic maps, and texting tools.

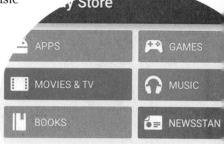

To boot, you can download even better apps and games for phones based on the Google Android platform. Many apps are available for your Galaxy S6 phone, and that number will only grow over time.

So where do you get all these wonderful apps? The main place to get Android apps is the Google Play Store. You might be happy with the apps that came with your phone, but look into the Play Store and you'll find apps you never knew you needed and suddenly won't be able to live without.

In this chapter, I introduce you to the Google Play Store and give you a taste of what you find there. For information on how to buy and download apps, keep reading.

Exploring the Play Store: The Mall for Your Phone

The Play Store is set up and run by Google, mainly for people with Android phones. Adding an app to your phone is similar to adding software to your PC. In both cases, a new app (or software) makes you more productive, adds to your convenience, and/or entertains you for hours on end — sometimes for free. Not a bad deal.

There are some important differences, however, between installing software on a PC and getting an app on a mobile phone:

- **Smartphone apps need to be more stable than computer software because of their greater potential for harm.** If you buy an app for your PC and find that it's unstable (for example, it causes your PC to crash), sure, you'll be upset. If you were to buy an unstable app for your phone, though, you could run up a huge phone bill or even take down the regional cellular network. Can you hear me now?

- **There are multiple smartphone platforms.** These days, it's pretty safe to assume that computer software will run on a PC or a Mac or both. On the other hand, because of the various smartphone platforms out there, different versions within a given platform aren't always compatible. The Play Store ensures that the app you're buying will work with your version of phone.

Getting to the Store

You can access the Play Store through your Galaxy S6 phone's Play Store app or through the Internet. The easiest way to access the Play Store is through the Play Store app on your Galaxy S6 phone. The icon is shown in Figure 8-1.

If the Play Store app isn't already on your Home screen, you can find it in your Apps list. To open it, simply tap the icon.

Figure 8-1: The Play Store icon.

When you tap the Play Store icon, you're greeted by the screen shown in Figure 8-2.

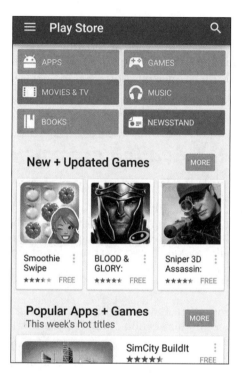

Figure 8-2: The Play Store Home screen.

As new apps become available, the highlighted apps will change, and the Home screen will change from one day to the next, but the categories tend to be consistent over time. These categories are:

✔ **Apps:** This showcase highlights valuable apps or games that you might not otherwise come across. Apps is the first Play Store category you see (the leftmost screen on the panorama).

✔ **Games:** These apps are for fun and enjoyment. As it happens, games are the most-downloaded type of app. The popularity of any given game is a good initial indication that it is worth considering.

Throughout this book, I use the blanket term *apps* to refer to games and other kinds of apps. Some purists make a distinction between apps and games. The thing is, from the perspective of a phone user, they're the same: You download an app and use it, whether for fun or to be more productive.

✔ **Movies and TV:** As with music, you can download multimedia files and view your favorite movies and TV shows. You can watch these on your Galaxy S6's screen. More on this in Chapter 12.

✔ **Music:** You can buy your digital music at the Play Store. I talk more about buying music in Chapter 12.

✔ **Books:** Have you been thinking about getting an e-reader, such as a Nook or a Kindle? Before you spend your hard-earned cash, take a look at the book library here and see whether you like reading on your phone! If you like the way the Nook or the Kindle work, both are available as apps you can download and use to access your accounts on the Barnes & Noble website or Amazon.com.

✔ **Newsstand:** Same idea as with books, only this category is for periodicals.

Seeing What's Available: Shopping for Android Apps

When you head to the local mall with a credit card but without a plan, you're asking for trouble. Anything and everything that tickles your fancy is fair game. Similarly, before you head to the Play Store, it helps to have a sense of what you're looking for so you don't spend more than you intended.

The apps for your Galaxy S6 phone fall into the following subcategories:

✔ **Games:** Your Galaxy S6 phone takes interactive gaming to a new level. Games in this section of the Play Store fall into the following categories:

- *Arcade and Action:* Think of games that are based on what you find in arcades: shooting games, racing games, and other games of skill and/or strategy.

- *Brain and Puzzle:* Think crossword puzzles, Sudoku, and other word or number games.

- *Cards and Casino:* Find an electronic version of virtually every card or casino game. (If you know of any game that's missing, let us know so we can write the app and sell it to the three people who play it.)

- *Casual:* This crossover category includes simpler games, some of which are also arcade, action, or cards, but are distinguished by the ease with which you can pick them up, play them, and then put them down. Solitaire may be the most widespread example of a casual game.

✔ **Apps:** The "non-games" fall into many subcategories:

- *Comics:* These are apps that are meant to be funny. Hopefully, you find something that tickles your funnybone.

- *Communication:* Yes, the Galaxy S6 phone comes with many communications apps, but these Play Store apps enhance what comes with the phone: for example, tools that automatically send a message if you're running late to a meeting, or text you if your kids leave a defined area.

- *Demo:* These small, sometimes frivolous apps don't quite fit any-where else.

- *Entertainment:* Not games per se, but these apps are still fun: trivia, horoscopes, and frivolous noisemaking apps. (These also include Chuck Norris "facts." Did you know that Chuck Norris can divide by 0?)

- *Finance:* This is the place to find mobile banking apps and tools to make managing your personal finances easier.

- *Health:* This is a category for all apps related to mobile medical apps, including calorie counters, fitness tracking, and tools to help manage chronic conditions, such as diabetes.

- *Lifestyle:* This category is a catch-all for apps that involve recre-ation or special interests, like philately or bird-watching.

- *Maps & Search:* Many apps tell you where you are and how to get to where you want to go. Some are updated with current conditions, and others are based on static maps that use typical travel times.

- *Multimedia:* The Galaxy S6 phone comes with the music and video services, but nothing says you have to like them. You might prefer offerings that are set up differently or have a selection of music that isn't available elsewhere.

- *News & Weather:* You find a variety of apps that allow you to drill down till you get just the news or weather that's more relevant to you than what's available on your extended Home screen.

- *Productivity:* These apps are for money management (such as a tip calculator), voice recording (such as a standalone voice recorder), and time management (for example, an electronic to-do list).

- *Reference:* These apps include a range of reference books, such as dictionaries and translation guides. Think of this section as similar to the reference section of your local library and bookstore.

- *Shopping:* These apps help you with rapid access to mobile shop-ping sites or do automated comparison shopping.

- *Social:* These are the social networking sites. If you think you know them all, check here just to be sure. Of course, you'll find Facebook, LinkedIn, Twitter, and Pinterest, but you'll also find dozens of other sites that are more narrowly focused and offer apps for the convenience of their users.

- *Software Libraries:* Computers of all sizes come with software libraries to take care of special functions, such as tools to manage ringtones, track app performance, and protect against malware.

- *Sports:* Sports sites to tell you the latest scores and analysis can be found in this part of the Play Store.

- *Themes:* Your phone comes with color schemes or "themes." This part of the Play Store offers a broader selection.

- *Tools:* Some of these are widgets that help you with some fun capabilities. Others are more complicated and help you get more functionality from your phone.

- *Travel:* These apps are useful for traveling, including handy items such as currency translations and travel guides.

 Many of your favorite websites are now offering apps that are purpose-built for your phone. The previous chapter talks about how you can access websites on your phone. You can use the full site with your high-resolution screen or use the mobile version. A third alternative can be an app that makes the information you want from your phone even easier to access.

Each app category comes with the apps divided into the following categories:

- **Top Free:** All apps in the "top free" category are available at no charge.

- **Top New Free:** This option gets you out in front of the curve to find the best new free apps before the unwashed masses find them.

- **Top Paid:** All apps in this category charge a fee.

- **Top Grossing:** These are the apps that are both popular and cost money. This is often a good indication that the app is really good, or at least that it has a crack marketing team. (If the app is not good, the customer comments will show that right away.)

- **Top New Paid:** All apps in this category charge a fee and are also new.

- **Trending:** Our friends at Google show the apps that are catching on. It's worth considering the apps that reside in this category.

- **Featured:** These apps are relatively new and might or might not charge you to download and use them.

In general, you'll probably want to see what you get with a free app before you spend money on the commercial equivalent. Many software companies know this, and offer a lower-feature version for free and an enhanced version for a charge. Enjoy the free-market mechanisms on this site and never feel regret for enjoying a free app.

 Free apps are great. But don't be afraid of buying any apps that you're going to use frequently. Apps usually cost very little and the extra features may be worth it. Some people (including me) have an irrational resistance to paying $1.99 monthly for something I use all the time. Frankly, this is a little silly. Let's all be rational and be willing to pay a little bit for the services we use.

Installing and Managing an Android App

To make the process of finding and downloading an app less abstract, I'll show you how to download and install one in particular as an example: the Facebook for Android app.

Downloading the Facebook app

Follow these steps to download the Facebook app from the Google Play Store:

1. **Tap the Play Store icon.**

2. **In the Query box, type** Facebook.

   Doing so brings up a search results screen like the one shown in Figure 8-3.

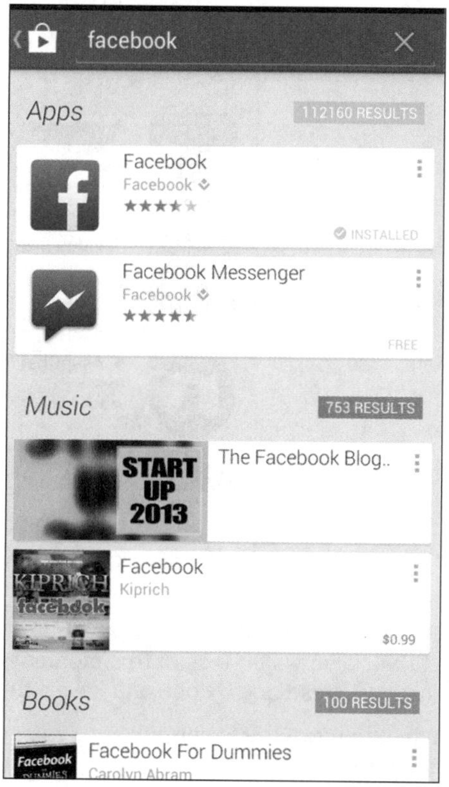

Figure 8-3: The Facebook search results.

You want to get the Facebook *app*, so you can tap the line with the Facebook icon. (Let's ignore that it is right there at the top of the list. Many of the apps you really want will not be at the top.)

3. **Tap the More icon to the right of the app's title.**

   When you tap the More icon, it brings up only apps that include the Facebook name. This screen is shown in Figure 8-4.

   As you can see in the search results, several options include the word *Facebook*. The other lines in the Apps section are for apps that include

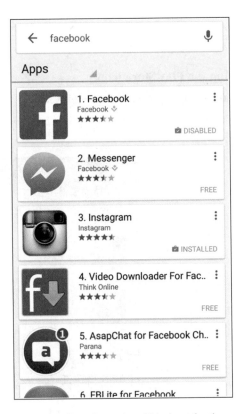

Figure 8-4: Search results within Apps for the term Facebook.

the word *Facebook*. These are typically for apps that "enhance" Facebook in their own ways — as of this moment, 112,160 of them. Rather than go through these one by one, stick with the one with the Facebook icon.

When you tap the Facebook app, you get a lot of information, as shown in Figure 8-5.

Before continuing to the next step, I want to point out some important elements on this page:

- **Title line:** The top section has the formal name of the app just above the green Install button. After you click this to download and install the app, you'll see some other options. I give some examples later in this chapter.

- **Description:** This tells you what the app does.

- **What's New:** This information is important if you have a previous version of this app. Skip this section for now.

- **Screen captures:** These representative screens are a little too small to read, but they do add some nice color to the page.

Figure 8-5: The Facebook app screen in panorama.

- **Feedback statistics:** This particular app has about 4.0 stars out of five. That's not bad at all. The other numbers tell you how many folks have voted, how many have downloaded this app, the date it was released, and the size of the app in MB.

- **All Reviews:** This section gets into more details about what people thought of the app beyond the star ranking.

- **More by Facebook:** The app developer in this case is Facebook. If you like the style of a particular developer, this section tells you what other apps that developer offers.

- **Similar apps:** Just in case you are not sure about this, the good folks at Google offer some alternatives.

- **Users also installed:** Play Store tells you the names of other apps downloaded by that the customers who downloaded this app. It's a good indicator of what else you may like.

- **Developer:** This section gives you contact information for the developer of this app.

- **Flag as inappropriate:** This is how you tell the Play Store whether this app is naughty or nice.

4. **Tap the dark green button that says Install.**

   Before the download process begins, the Google Play Store tells you what this app plans to do on your phone. The App permissions screen is shown in Figure 8-6.

App permissions

Facebook needs access to:

Storage
Modify or delete the contents of your USB storage

Other Application UI
Draw over other apps

System tools
Read battery statistics

Microphone
Record audio

Your location
Approximate location (network-based), precise location (GPS and network-based)

Camera
Take pictures and videos

Your applications information
Retrieve running apps

~~Your accounts~~

ACCEPT

Figure 8-6: The Facebook permissions screen.

This information lists all the permissions you will be granting the app when you download it.

This is similar to the license agreements you sign when installing software on your PC. Hopefully you read them all in detail and understand all the implications. In practice, you hope that it's not a problem if lots of other people have accepted these conditions. In the case of a well-known app like Facebook, you're probably safe, but you should be careful with less-popular apps.

Back in Chapter 1, you were presented with the option to prevent an app from having access to your location information. I mentioned that you could allow apps to know where you are on a case-by-case basis. Here is where that issue comes up. Each app asks you for permission to access information, such as your location. If you don't want the app to use that information or share it somehow, here's where you find out whether the app uses this information. You may be able to limit the amount of location information. If you're not comfortable with that, you should decline the app in its entirety.

5. **Tap the green Accept button.**

Before the download process starts, your app may want to know two things:

- *Do you want your phone to automatically update when Facebook (or the app provider) releases a newer version?* In general, this is the most convenient option. It's rare, but not unheard of, for an update to make things worse.

- *Do you want to wait for the update to take place only when you have a Wi-Fi connection?* This prevents your phone from downloading a huge app update over the cellular network. In most cases, using a Wi-Fi connection is a better option. Facebook asks you this question in the pop-up shown in Figure 8-7.

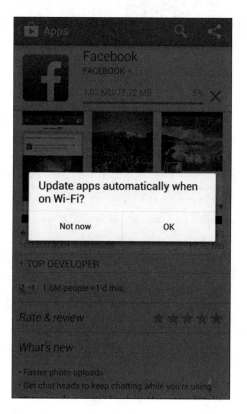

Figure 8-7: The automatic update pop-up screen.

6. **Tap OK.**

This process is like downloading apps to your PC over the Internet. The screens shown in Figure 8-8 illustrate the progress of downloading and installing the app.

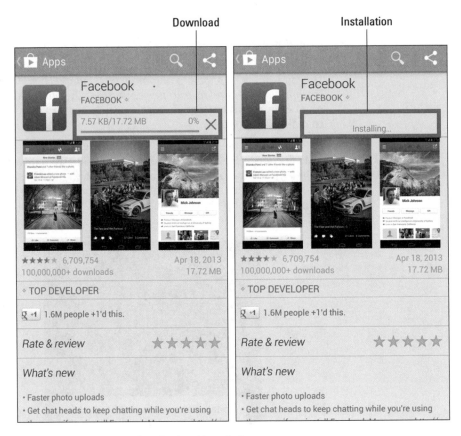

Figure 8-8: The Facebook download and installation screens.

This may happen so fast that you look away for a second and when you look back, it's done. Sometimes the Play Store lets you keep on shopping while the app downloads in the background (as shown in Figure 8-9). If you like, you can watch the process in the notification portion of your screen.

When the installation process is complete, the Facebook icon appears on your Apps screen along with some other recently added apps, such as Angry Birds and Pandora (as shown in Figure 8-10).

If you want this app to be on your Home screen, press and hold the icon.

Creating a Facebook account

You can get started with the Facebook app immediately by tapping on Open from the Facebook App screen. You could also tap the Facebook icon from the Apps screen. If you added this app to your Home screen, you can tap its icon there. In any case, opening the app for the first time brings up the screen shown in Figure 8-11.

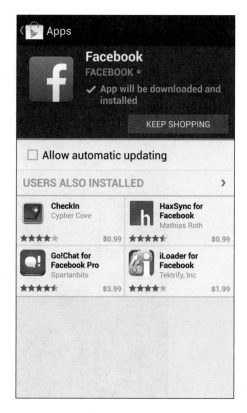

Figure 8-9: The Facebook app screen.

If you don't already have a Facebook account, you can create an account here. Toward the bottom of the screen is the option to sign up for Facebook.

If you already have a Facebook account, all you need to do is enter your e-mail address and Facebook password in the screen shown in Figure 8-11. Hopefully you can recall your Facebook password. It could be the same as your e-mail password, even though using the same password for multiple accounts is bad security discipline. Obviously, you'll need to get back to your PC to figure out your password if you cannot remember it.

To sign up for Facebook, use an e-mail account or your mobile number as well as a password. The first step is to enter your information onscreen, shown in Figure 8-12.

After you enter this information, Facebook sends a verification message. If you provide an e-mail address, the app sends you an e-mail. If you use your mobile phone number, it sends you a text.

Figure 8-10: The Facebook icon on the Apps screen.

The e-mail or text contains a code. Enter this code, and your Facebook account is validated. To get the most out of Facebook, I recommend checking out *Facebook For Dummies, 5th Edition* (Wiley) by Carolyn Abram.

It will ask you questions about your preferences for syncing Contacts. You can choose to put all of your Facebook friends into your phone's Contacts database. This goes so far as to use your Facebook image as your Contacts image. The options for syncing are shown in Figure 8-13 and outlined here:

- **Sync all:** This option syncs with your existing contacts and makes new contacts for Facebook friends who don't already have an entry in your phone's Contacts database.

- **Sync with existing contacts:** Same idea as Sync All, but if they don't already have an entry, it doesn't create a new contact.

- **Don't sync:** As the name implies, this keeps Contacts as Contacts and Facebook friends as Facebook friends, and doesn't mix the two.

Figure 8-11: The Facebook login screen.

When you've made your selection, tap the word Sync in the upper-right corner, and you're done. It's really amazing, all the ways that this information integrates into your phone. Pictures of your contacts start appearing in your Contacts database. You also see (for example) the option to post pictures from your Gallery to your Facebook page — for openers.

Within the Facebook app itself, you see the latest posts from your friends in an instant. You get your daily serving of cute kitten images, stories from proud parents about their children, and messages from old flames wondering about what might have been.

Accessing Facebook Settings

You can get to Facebook Settings by tapping the Menu button and then tapping Settings. I especially urge you to consider how many notifications you want to receive. Even the most hard-core Facebook fan may need a break from all the notifications.

Figure 8-12: The Sign Up for Facebook screen.

Figure 8-14 shows you the Facebook Settings options. You can just go along with the defaults.

Or, if you prefer, you can also adjust the settings to your liking. A few of the options are:

- **Facebook chat:** You can choose to chat or not when you're running this app.

- **Refresh interval:** You get to decide how often the Facebook app polls the Internet to see whether there are new posts. The default is every hour. Polling more often keeps you better informed, but it can drive up costs. Your choices are shown in Figure 8-15.

  If you choose Never, it looks for status updates only when you first open the app.

- **Messenger location services:** If you change your mind about having Facebook know where you are, here is how you would change the setting.

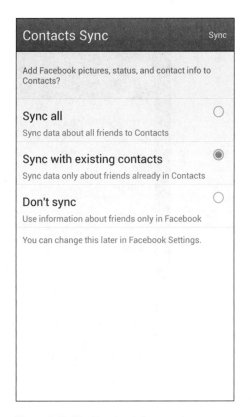

Figure 8-13: The Facebook Sync options.

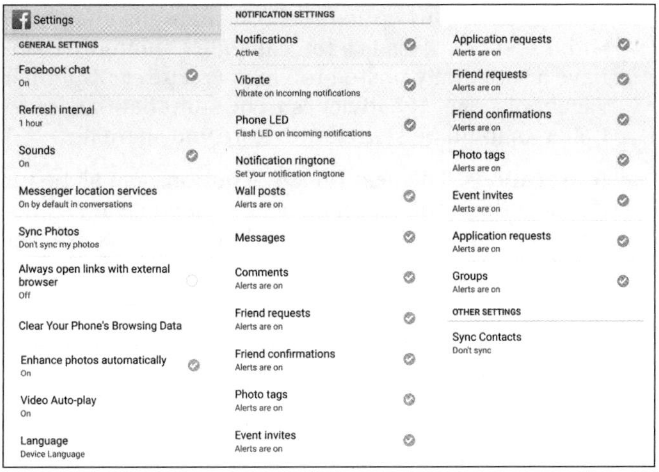

Figure 8-14: The Facebook Settings options.

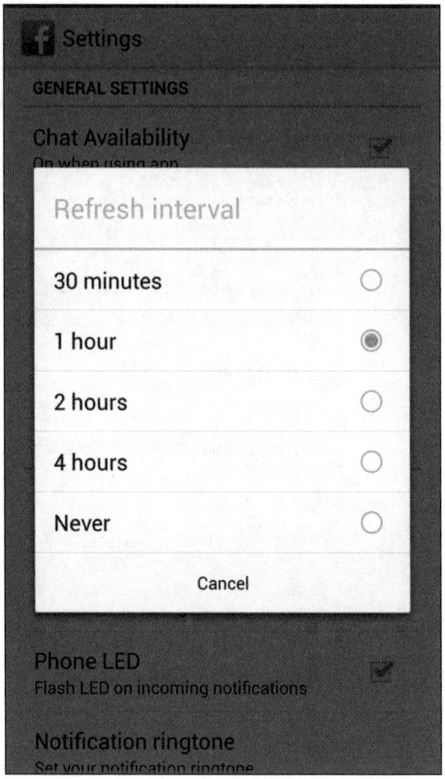

Figure 8-15: The Facebook Refresh Interval.

✔ **Sync photos:** This option lets you share the images in your Gallery app with Facebook. This is a fun capability, but more than a few people have accidentally posted too many pictures from their phone to their Facebook page. My advice is to be sure that the photo you select in Gallery should be shared — before you share it.

✔ **Notifications:** The next bunch of options can all be turned off if you deselect the Notification check box. If you want some but not all of these notifications, leave the Notification check box selected, and deselect the notifications you don't want.

The next selections offer you various ways you can be notified of a change occurring on your Facebook account:

  • *Vibrate:* Every time something happens on Facebook, your phone vibrates.

  • *Phone LED:* Every time something happens on Facebook, an LED lights up.

- *Notification ringtone:* Every time something happens on Facebook, your phone makes a noise. Tap this choice and you see all the options.

These selections let you select which Facebook events trigger a notification alert, including:

- *Wall posts*

- *Messages*

- *Comments*

- *Friend requests*

- *Friend confirmations*

- *Photo tags*

- *Event invites*

- *App requests*

- *Groups*

✔ **Sync Contacts:** This option brings back the screen shown in Figure 8-13 in case you want to change your Sync status.

There are lots of combinations and permutations for Facebook. Choose wisely.

Rating and Uninstalling Your Apps

Providing feedback to an app is an important part of maintaining the strength of the Android community. It's your responsibility to rate apps honestly. (Or you can blow it off and just take advantage of the work others have put into the rating system. It's your choice.)

If you want to make your voice heard about an app, here are the steps:

1. **Open the Play Store.**

   See Figure 8-2.

2. **Tap the Menu button.**

   Doing so brings up a drop-down menu like the one shown in Figure 8-16.

3. **Tap the Line that says My Apps.**

   This tap brings up the screen shown in Figure 8-17, which lists all the apps on your phone. Keep on scrolling down. You'll eventually see them all.

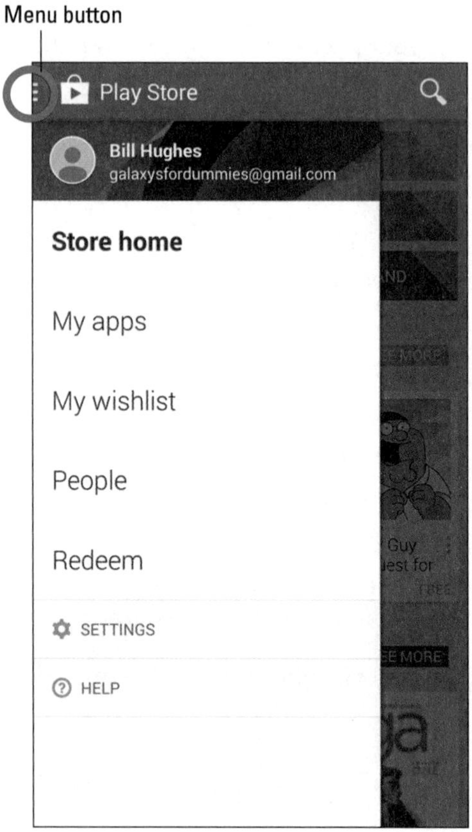

Menu button

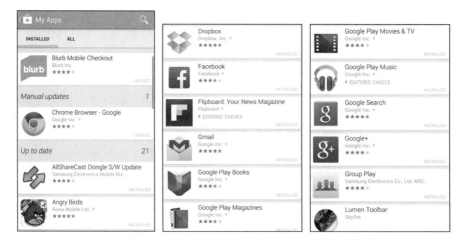

Figure 8-16: The menu from the Play Store.

Figure 8-17: The My Apps screen in panorama.

Tapping on one of these apps is how you rate them or uninstall them, as shown in Figure 8-18.

Uninstall option

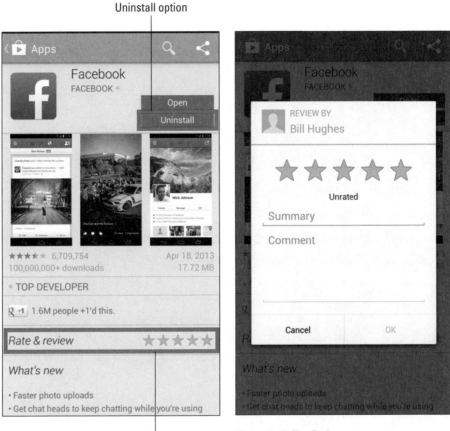

Rate and review

Figure 8-18: The My Apps page for Facebook.

Figure 8-19: The Rating pop-up.

If you love the app, rate it highly. You get a pop-up, as shown in Figure 8-19, where you can rank the app and tell the world what you think. If you hate the app, give it one star and blast away. Then you can remove it from your phone by tapping the Uninstall button.

Part IV
Entertainment Applications

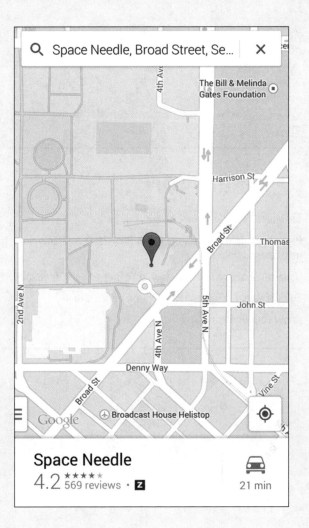

Visit www.dummies.com/extras/samsunggalaxys6 for great Dummies content online.

In this part. . .

- ✐ Take pictures and video on your Galaxy S6
- ✐ Peruse the games available in the Play Store and download the best ones to your phone
- ✐ Use your phone to find a location on a map and get directions
- ✐ Enjoy a single song, podcasts, or an entire album
- ✐ Know your licensing options

Sharing Pictures

In This Chapter

▶ Taking pictures and video with your phone

▶ Organizing your pictures and video

▶ Sharing pictures and video with friends and family

*A*s I stated in Chapter 1, the Samsung Galaxy S6 should really be called a smartcamera with a phone. If you're like many mobile phone users, you love that you can shoot photographs and video with your phone.

You probably carry your phone with you practically everywhere you go, so you never again have to miss a great photograph because you left your camera at home.

And don't think that Samsung skimped on the camera on your Galaxy S6. Boasting 16MP of muscle, this camera is complemented with lots of shooting options. Then, you can view your shots on that wicked Super AMOLED screen. Samsung also includes a Gallery app for organizing and sharing. Plus, the camera can shoot stills *and* video.

It's truly amazing to consider the number of options that you have for your photographs and your videos. Samsung keeps on adding new options, filters, and ways to share these files. It would not be surprising if your phone now has more capabilities than your digital camera.

These capabilities actually cause a problem. There are so many options that it can be overwhelming. Research has shown that people fall into one of three categories: The first group tends to use the default settings. If they want to alter the image, they'd prefer to do it on their own PCs. The second group likes to explore some of the capabilities on the phone and will have some fun looking at the scenarios, but keep things within reason. The third group goes nuts with all the capabilities of the phone.

To accommodate everyone, this chapter starts with the basics. I cover how to use the camera on your phone, view your pictures, and share them online. This works for everybody.

I then focus on the most popular settings for the second. There are some important capabilities.

For the third group, the best that can be done is to lead you in the right direction. As much as I would like to, it would be impossible to cover all the options and combinations. In my count there are 2.43 billion possible combinations of filters, lighting, and modes. If you were to start now and take a picture every 10 seconds, you would not run out of combinations for over 700 years. This would not even include all the options for sharing these images.

A super-fast primer on Super AMOLED

All Samsung Galaxy S6 phones have a Super AMOLED screen. Allow me to take a moment to explain what makes this so good — and what makes you so smart for having bought the Samsung Galaxy S6.

To start, think about a typical LCD screen, like what your TV or PC might have. LCDs are great, but they work best indoors where it's not too bright. LCDs need a backlight (fluorescent, most commonly), and the backlight draws a fair amount of power, although much less power than a CRT. When used on a phone, an LCD screen is the largest single user of battery life, using more power than the radios or the processor. Also, because of the backlight on an LCD screen, these screens display black as kinda washed-out, not a true black.

The next step has been to use light-emitting diodes (LEDs), which convert energy to light more efficiently. Monochrome LEDs have been used for decades. They are also used in mongo-screens (Jumbotrons) in sports arenas. Until recently, getting the colors right was a struggle. (Blue was a big problem.) That problem was solved by using organic materials (*organic* as in carbon-based, as opposed to being grown with no pesticides) for LEDs.

The first organic LEDs (OLEDs) looked good, drew less power, and offered really dark blacks — but still had two problems. Their imaging really stank in bright light, even worse than did LCD screens. Also, there was a problem with *crosstalk:* individual pixels would get confused, over time, about whether they were on or off. You'd see green or red pixels remaining onscreen, even if the area was clearly supposed to be dark. It was very distracting.

The solution to the pixels' confusion is called Active Matrix, which tells the pixels more frequently whether they are to be on or off. When you have Active Matrix technology, you have an Active Matrix Organic LED, or AMOLED. The image you get with this technology still stinks in bright light, but at least it's some improvement.

Enter the Super AMOLED technology, made by Samsung. When compared with the first AMOLED screens, Super AMOLED screens are 20 percent brighter, use 20 percent less power, and cut sunlight reflection by 80 percent. This is really super!

This screen still uses a significant share of battery life, but less than with earlier technologies. With Super AMOLED, you even save more power if you use darker backgrounds where possible.

Realistically, neither you nor your phone will last that long. To keep things in the realm of reality, I introduce only the most important and valuable options and go from there.

Say Cheese! Taking a Picture with Your Phone

Before you can take a picture, you have to open the Camera app. The traditional way is to simply access the Camera application from the Application list. Just tap the Camera icon to launch the app.

Because the camera is so important, here are a few more ways to get to the Camera app. First, press the Home button twice. Boom. There it is.

Next, unless you have turned off the capability for security purposes, there is a camera icon on your lock screen. If you swipe the icon across the screen, the Camera app bypasses the security setting. You can snap away, but you can't access the photo gallery or any other files.

Here is a suggestion. If you see something suspicious, but are not ready to call 911, go ahead and start taking photos of what concerns you. If you need to, you can go back to the lock screen and slide the phone icon to the right to call 911, again without needing to unlock.

A closely related application on your phone is the Gallery, which is where your phone stores your images. The icons for these two apps are shown in Figure 9-1.

Figure 9-1: The Camera and Gallery icons.

With the Camera app open, you're ready to take a picture within a second or two. The screen becomes your viewfinder. You'll see a screen like the one shown in Figure 9-2.

And how do you snap the picture? Just tap the big Camera icon on the right: the camera within the oval. The image in your viewfinder turns into a digital image.

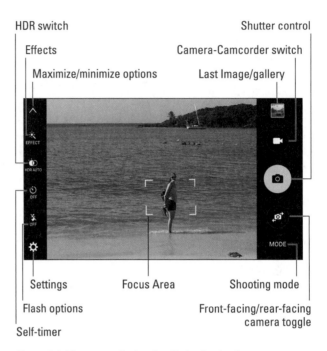

HDR switch

Effects

Maximize/minimize options

Shutter control

Camera-Camcorder switch

Last Image/gallery

Settings   Focus Area   Shooting mode

Flash options   Front-facing/rear-facing
camera toggle

Self-timer

Figure 9-2: The screen is the viewfinder for the Camera app.

A few picture-taking options are right there on the viewfinder. Going clockwise from the upper-right corner, the options include:

- **Gallery:** This is a thumbnail of the most recent image. Tapping the thumbnail opens the Gallery app, which I discuss a bit later in this chapter.

- **Camera/Video camera switch:** This icon takes you from the camera to the video camera.

- **Shutter control:** This icon takes the picture.

- **Rear-facing camera to front-facing camera switch:** This icon takes you from the 16 megapixel (MP) rear-facing camera to the not-too-shabby 5MP front-facing camera. This is a good option for selfies as you can see what the shot will look like before you snap it.

- **Mode:** This icon gives you some fancy options that are not for the faint-of-heart. I cover these in the next section.

- **Settings:** Settings also gives some fancy options that are covered in the next section.

- **Flash options:** Even if you want to keep it simple, you will want to know how to control your flash. Sometimes you need a flash for your photo. Sometimes you need a flash for your photo, but it's not allowed, as when you're taking images of fish in an aquarium, newborns, or some animals. (Remember what happened to King Kong?) Regardless of the situation, your phone gives you control of the flash. Tap the Settings icon at the top of the viewfinder. You have the options of Off, On, or Auto Flash, which lets the light meter within the camera decide whether a flash is necessary. The options are seen in Figure 9-3.

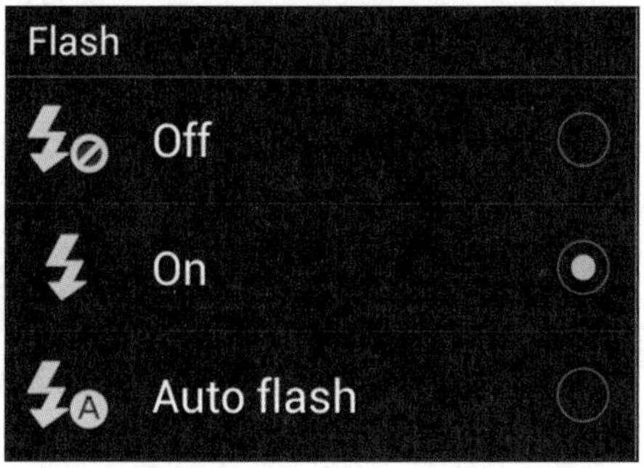

Figure 9-3: Flash options.

✔ **Self-timer:** This lets you set a delay between the instant you tap the shutter and when the camera takes the picture. This is primarily for selfies to avoid having your hand in the way of the camera.

✔ **HDR switch:** Your phone can automatically compensate when the light sources add a blue or red tint. You do this by having the HDR in Auto mode. You can also remove this capability, but why?

✔ **Effects:** More fancy options you can apply to your images, which I discuss later in this chapter.

✔ **Maximize/minimize options:** Tap this arrow to make the options on the left go away.

✔ **The brackets in the center of the screen:** These brackets serve two purposes. First, they show you what the autofocus thinks is most interesting, typically a face if it can find one. You can move the brackets if you want them to focus on something else. Also, they help you with magnification. If you want to control how much background you see in your shot, Samsung has a slick way to zoom in on a shot. When you're in Camera mode, you can zoom in and out by pinching or stretching the screen.

  • Stretch the screen to zoom in.

  • Pinch the screen to zoom out.

The viewfinder tells you how much you have zoomed into the shot, as shown in Figure 9-4.

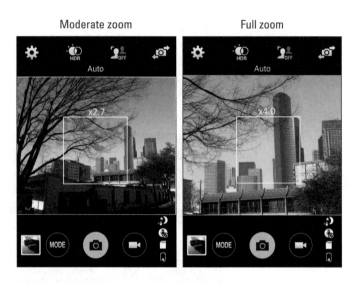

Moderate zoom   Full zoom

Figure 9-4: The Viewfinder when zooming.

For skeptics only

If you've ever used a cameraphone, you might be thinking, "Why make such a big deal about this camera's phone? Cameraphones aren't worth the megapixels they're made of." Granted, in the past, many cameraphones weren't quite as good as a digital camera, but Samsung has addressed these issues with the Galaxy S6:

✔ **Resolution:** The resolution on most cameraphones was lower than what you typically get on a dedicated digital camera. The Galaxy S6, however, sports a 16 mega-pixel (MP) camera — and that's good enough to produce a 8×10 inch print that's indistinguishable from what you could pro-duce with an analog camera, and 4×6's are plenty large for most uses.

✔ **Photo transfer:** With most cameraphones, the photos are hard to move from the camera to a computer. With the Samsung Galaxy S6, however (remember: it uses the Android operating system), you can quickly and easily send an image, or a bunch of images, anywhere you want, easily and wirelessly. (I address how to do this later in this chapter when discussing the Gallery App.)

✔ **Screen resolution:** In practice, many camer-aphone users just end up showing their pic-tures to friends right on their phones. Many cameraphone screens, however, don't have very good resolution, which means your images don't look so hot when you want to show them off to your friends. The good news is that the Samsung Galaxy S6 has a bright, high-resolution screen. Photos look really good on the Super AMOLED screen.

✔ **Organization:** Most cameraphones don't offer much in the way of organizational tools. Your images are all just there on your phone, without any structure. But the Samsung Galaxy S6 has the Gallery application that makes organizing your photos easier. It's also set up to share these photos easily.

You probably know that it's not a good idea to touch the lens of a camera. At the same time, it's practically impossible to avoid touching the lenses on your Galaxy S6. This can create a problem where there can be a build-up of oil and dirt on your high-resolution lens. You should clean the lens of your camera from time to time with a microfiber cloth to get the most out of your camera. Otherwise your high-resolution images might look like you live in a perpetual fog bank.

After you take a picture, you have a choice. The image is automatically stored in another application: the Gallery. This allows you to keep on snapping away and come back to the Gallery when you have time. I cover the Gallery application more in the upcoming section, "Managing Your Photo Images."

However, if you want to send that image right away, here's what you do:

1. **From the viewfinder screen, tap the Last Image icon.**

   The viewfinder shows a thumbnail of the most recent image you took. This image is at the top right corner of the viewfinder. When you tap it, it brings up the Gallery application as shown in Figure 9-5.

Figure 9-5: The Gallery app.

This brings up the current image along with the some other most recent photos.

2. **Tap the thumbnail of the image you want to share.**

   It also brings up some options as seen in Figure 9-6. Right now, you're interested in the Share option.

Figure 9-6: Gallery options for the current image.

3. **Tap the Share button.**

   This brings up the options you can use to forward the image; see Figure 9-7 (although your phone might not support all the options listed here and may have a few others not in this image):

   • **Dropbox:** This is a Cloud storage service. There are many other services that give you storage out on the Internet. There is a special folder specifically for your images.

   • **Messaging:** Attach the image to a text message to someone's phone as an MMS message.

   • **Bluetooth:** Send images to devices, such as a laptop or phone, linked with a Bluetooth connection.

   • **Photos:** Picasa is a website owned by Google, created to help its subscribers organize and share photos. The main advantage for subscribers is that they can send links to friends or family for them to see a thumbnail of images, rather than sending a large number of high-resolution files. Read more on Picasa in the next section.

   • **Email:** Send the image as an attachment with your primary e-mail account.

   • **Facebook:** You can take a picture and post it on your Facebook account with this option.

   • **Gmail:** If your main e-mail is with Gmail, this option and the Email option are the same.

- **Google+:** Google+ is a social networking site that is second in popularity only to Facebook. If you signed up for Google+ when you connected your phone, you can use this service to host images immediately.

- **Wi-Fi Direct:** Talk about slick! This option turns your phone into a Wi-Fi access point so that your Wi-Fi–enabled PC or another smartphone can establish a connection with you.

The point is that there is an overabundance of options. If an app on your device works with images, this is the place you can upload that image. If one of these options doesn't quite suit your need to share your pictures, perhaps you're being too picky!

Figure 9-7: Sharing options for the current image.

Getting a Little Fancier with Your Camera

Using the default Camera settings to snap pics is perfectly fine for those candid, casual, on-the-go shots: say, friends in your well-lit living room. However, your Samsung Galaxy S6 phone camera can support much more sophisticated shots. Your digital SLR camera has a bigger lens than your phone, but I can assure you that your phone has a much bigger brain than your camera. I suggest that even the users who want these default settings get familiar with the camera's Mode settings. These are easy to access and will improve the image quality with minimal effort.

The Mode setting

The Mode setting is where you make some basic settings that describe the situation under which you will be taking your shot. The default is a single picture in Automatic mode. The Mode icon is a round button underneath the button for the shutter release.

Tapping on this icon brings up the options shown in Figure 9-8.

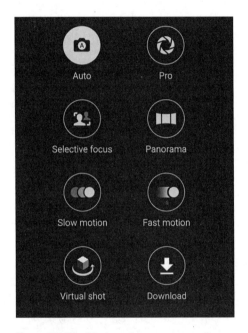

Figure 9-8: The Mode options pop-up on the camera viewfinder.

Tapping the Mode icon brings up a number of choices:

- ✔ **Auto:** Taking a single photo at a time is the default setting, which assumes average light. It's a good place to start.
- ✔ **Pro:** This mode gets you to all kinds of camera settings that someone who knows what he or she is doing would want to control rather than let the camera make the choice.

✔ **Selective focus:** This setting lets you get within 20 inches of an object, which is too close for the normal autofocus.

✔ **Panorama:** This setting lets you take a wider shot than you can with a single shot. Press the Camera button while you rotate through your desired field of view. The application then digitally stitches the individual photos into a single wide angle shot.

✔ **Slow Motion:** This switches you in to video mode to slow down really fast shots.

✔ **Fast Motion:** This also switches you to video and speeds things up.

✔ **Virtual shot:** Put an image in the viewfinder and walk around it. The phone figures out where you are and it creates a virtual tour. If this does not prove to you that your phone is a "smarticle," nothing will.

✔ **Download:** This setting lets you download some additional capabilities. Figure 9-9 shows some of the very cool capabilities you can snag. The good news is that you only download the one you want.

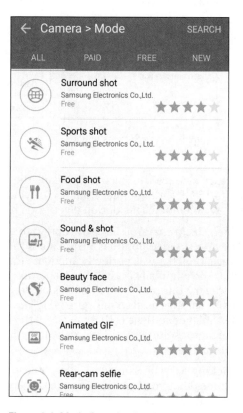

Figure 9-9: Mode Download options.

Choose the option that sounds right and snap away.

These modes help when you're taking the shot. You can also edit an image later. You would probably find it easier to do complicated image editing on your desktop computer instead of your phone. However, you can make some edits on your phone and send your photo off right away. Your choice.

Settings options on the Viewfinder

Tapping the Settings icon on the viewfinder brings up a number of choices, which are shown in Figure 9-10:

← Camera settings		Location tags	OFF
Picture size (rear) 16M (16:9) 5312x2988		**Review pictures** Review the picture as soon as you take it.	OFF
Video size (rear) HD 1280x720		**Quick launch** Open Camera by pressing the Home key twice in quick succession.	ON
Tracking AF Focus on and track a subject selected on the preview screen.	OFF	**Voice control**	ON
Video stabilization	OFF	**Volume keys function** Take pictures	
Grid lines	OFF	**Shutter sound**	ON
		Reset settings	

Figure 9-10: The Settings options.

- ✔ **Picture size (rear):** This really means the camera resolution. You can go up to 16 MP for high image quality, or you can choose a lower resolution to save memory. This option gives you choices.

- ✔ **Video size (rear):** You have the option to get really carried away here. The lowest video option is VGA. This is the resolution of your old, analog television. That was perfectly adequate for us for many decades, but HD is the minimally acceptable resolution for thoroughly modern folks. However, your phone scoffs at this puny resolution, and can take it to four higher settings as seen in Figure 9-11. The only reason to hesitate to use these higher settings is that, just as with still pictures, videos recorded in higher resolutions take more memory. It is good to know these resolutions are there.

- ✔ **Tracking AF:** The Samsung Galaxy S6 can spot a person's face and assumes that you want it to be the place where you focus if you toggle this option to the On position. Otherwise, if you don't use this mode, the camera may assume that you want whatever is in the center of the viewfinder to be in focus.

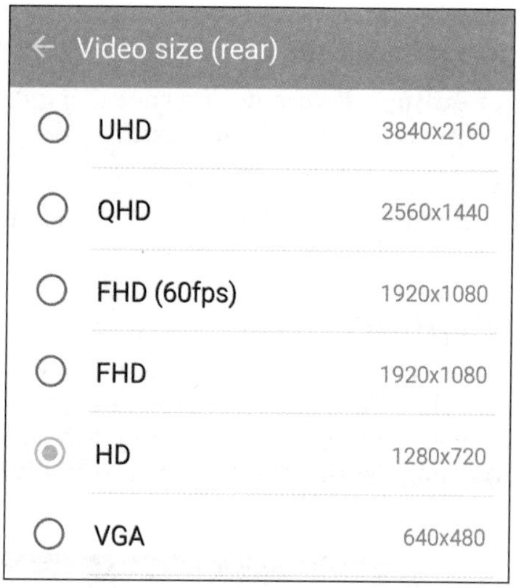

Figure 9-11: Your phone's camcorder resolution options.

✔ **Video stabilization:** If too much caffeine is causing your shots to blur, this capability is your answer.

✔ **Grid lines:** Some people like to have a 3×3 grid on the viewfinder to help frame the shot. If you are one of these people, toggle on this option.

✔ **Location tags:** The Samsung Galaxy S6 uses its GPS to tell the location of where you took the shot. If this is too intrusive, you can leave out this information on the images description.

✔ **Review pictures:** Some people want to see the shot right away. Others want to take a bunch of pictures and look at them at their leisure. If you want to see the image right away to see if you need to take a second picture, turn on this toggle. It will jump you in to the Gallery app right away.

✔ **Quick launch:** I mentioned earlier that you could launch the camera by pressing the Home button twice. If you would rather not, here is where you can disable that setting.

✔ **Voice control:** Your camera is listening to you. If you say, "Smile," "Cheese," "Capture," or "Shoot," the camera will snap a shot. This is simpler than using the self-timer. If you say "record video," the video-recorder will start recording. In either case, you can tell it to zoom by saying "zoom." Or not if you turn off this option.

✔ **Volume keys function:** Your voice can only control the camera, the video-camera, or the zoom function one at a time. You use this option to select which one you want to use.

✔ **Shutter sound:** It can be satisfying to hear the click when you take a picture. If you would rather not, turn that sound off here.

✔ **Reset settings:** If you mess something up, tap Reset Settings and it will take you back to the default settings.

✔ **Help:** If you mess something up, but are too stubborn to reset the settings, the Help option will help you figure it all out.

Effects options

As seen back in Figure 9-2, there is a magic wand icon on the left side of the viewfinder. That's not just for Harry Potter fans. Tapping that icon brings up a number of effects that you can apply to your image. If you tap the arrow, it brings up a long list of choices. Some examples are shown in Figure 9-12.

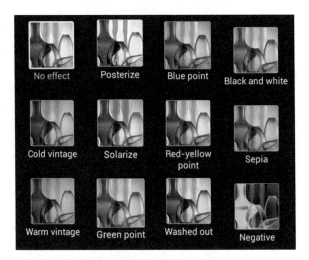

Figure 9-12: Some examples of Effects options.

Select the option that sounds right and snap away.

The Digital Camcorder in Your Pocket

Your Samsung Galaxy S6 Camera application can also function as a digital camcorder.

Starting the camcorder

All you need to do to use your phone as a video recorder is to put your camera into Camcorder mode. From the camera viewfinder, shown in Figure 9-13, you tap the icon with the silhouette of a movie camera in the upper-right corner and you switch from photographer to videographer.

At this point, recording video automatically starts. You get the notification that says "Rec" in red and the timer from when it started.

The recording continues until you either tap the stop button, which is the circle with the dark square in the center on the right side of the viewfinder, or the pause button, which is the button with the parallel slashes in the middle. If you press the stop button, the screen will revert back to the still camera.

Stop button

Camera button

Pause button

Figure 9-13: Your phone's camcorder viewfinder.

If you press the pause button while in camcorder mode, the buttons to the right morph into two additional buttons. You can tap the upper button to switch back to the camera. Your other option is to tap the button with the red dot to begin recording again.

Your phone is not only recording the video; it's also recording the sound. Be careful what you say!

Taking and sharing videos with your camcorder

Just as you share photos you take with the camera, you can immediately share a video, play it, or delete it by tapping the video viewer. Also, the video is immediately saved on your camera. It's stored in the Gallery app (described earlier in this chapter) or is viewable from your Video Player app (covered in Chapter 12).

You can get fancy with some of the settings for your camcorder, but you won't find nearly as many settings as you have for your camera (fortunately!). Two settings, Video Size and Image Stabilization, are available in Settings from the Menu button.

You cannot get to the Settings screen from the camcorder viewfinder. You must go back to camera mode. From there you tap the Settings icon to get to these options.

Use Image Stabilization unless you like the feeling of being seasick. It's turned on by default.

Managing Your Photo Images

After you take some great pictures, you need to figure out what to do with them. Earlier in this chapter, I describe how to send an image immediately to another site or via e-mail. This will likely be the exception, though.

In most cases, it's easier to keep on doing what you were doing and go back to the Gallery application when you have some time to take a look at the images and then decide what to do with them. Your choices include:

- ✔ Store them on your phone within the Gallery app.
- ✔ Transfer them to your PC to your photo album application by sending them with e-mail.
- ✔ Store them on an Internet site, like Picasa or Flickr.
- ✔ Print them from your PC.
- ✔ E-mail or text them to your friends and family.
- ✔ Any combination of the preceding choices.

Unlike many regular phones with a built-in camera, the Galaxy S6 makes it easy to access these choices. You need to determine the approach(es) you want to take to keep your images when you want them to stick around. The rest of this chapter goes through your options.

Even though the Camera application and the Gallery application are closely related, they are two separate apps. Be sure that you keep straight which application you want to use.

The Gallery Home screen (shown back in Figure 9-5) shows how the app first sorts the images on your phone into folders, depending upon when they originated.

All your photos from the Camera app are placed in files sorted by date. The application takes a shot at grouping them when a series of pictures or videos are taken about the same time.

Using Images on Your Phone

In addition to sharing photos from your camera, your Galaxy S6 phone allows you to use a Gallery photo as wallpaper or as a photo for a contact. And if the fancy shooting settings in the Camera application aren't enough, you can wrangle minor edits — as in cropping or rotating — when you have an image in the Gallery application.

The first step is to find the image that you want in Gallery. If you want to do something to this image other than send it, tap the Edit button at the bottom of the screen as we saw back in Figure 9-6. Some of the options include:

- **Slideshow:** This displays each of the images for a few seconds. You can not only set the speed for transition, but also add music and select among several image transitions.

- **Crop:** Cut away unnecessary or distracting parts of the image. The application creates a virtual box around what it considers to be the main object. You can move the box around the image, but you cannot resize it. You then can either save this cropped image or discard.

- **Set As:** Make this image your wallpaper or set it as the image for a contact.

- **Print:** This option allows you to print if you have set up a local printer to communicate with your phone either through Wi-Fi or Bluetooth.

- **Rename:** These options allow you to rotate the image right or left. This is useful if you turned the camera sideways to get more height in your shot and now want to turn the image to landscape (or vice versa).

- **Details:** See the information on the image: its metadata, which is fixed and cannot change.

Deleting Images on Your Phone

Not all the images on your phone are keepers. When you want to get rid of an image, press and hold the image you want to delete. In a second, a checkbox with the image selected will appear. Also, you will have the links appear at the top to either Share or Delete. If you want to delete this image, tap Delete. The camera verifies that this is your intent. After you confirm, the image goes away.

If you want to delete more images, you can tap all the images you want to make go away. It is selected if it has a green checkmark on the image. Tap away, then hit delete. It will confirm with you once. Tap again and these images are gone forever.

When I say that the photos you delete are gone forever, I do mean *for-ev-er*. Most of us have inadvertently deleted the only copy of an image from a PC or a digital camera. That's not a pleasant feeling, so be careful.

Playing Games

In This Chapter

▶ Perusing the games available in the Play Store

▶ Downloading games to your phone

▶ Providing feedback

*G*ames are the most popular kind of download for smartphones of all kinds. In spite of the focus on business productivity, socializing, and making your life simpler, games outpace all other application downloads. The electronic gaming industry has larger revenues than the movie industry — and has for several years!

The fact of the matter is that your Samsung Galaxy S6, with its large Super AMOLED screen, makes Android-based games more fun. And because you already have one, maybe you should take a break and concentrate on having fun!

The Play Store Games Category

The Games category of Google Play Store (shown in Figure 10-1) is huge, and it includes everything from simple puzzles to simulated violence. All games involve various combinations of intellect, skill (either cognitive or motor), and role-playing.

We could have a lively and intellectually stimulating debate on the merits of games versus applications. For the purposes of this book, the differences between games and apps are as follows:

   ✔ Apps and Games are in different sections of the Play Store.

   ✔ If a person likes a game, he or she tends to play it for a while, maybe for a few weeks or even months, and then stops using it. A person who likes an app tends to keep on using it.

✔ People who use their phones for games tend to like to try a wide range of games.

Games

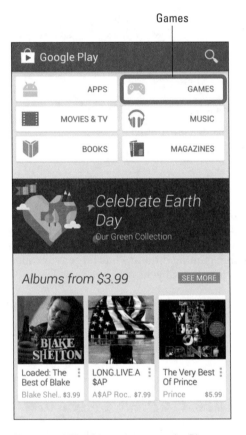

Figure 10-1: The Games button on the Play Store screen.

For these reasons, I will pick up where I left off in Chapter 8 and expand on some elements of the Google Play Store that are relevant for gamers.

The Games Home tab

When you tap on the Games option shown in Figure 10-1, you go to the Home screen for Games. If you scroll down, you see many suggested games. This is shown in panorama in Figure 10-2.

Figure 10-2: The Games Home tab.

If you aren't sure what games you might like to try, don't worry: There are lots of options. The categories shown in Figure 10-2 will probably be different from what you will see. These categories are regularly updated with the latest games.

The Games Categories tab

If you scroll to the left from the tab that says Home, you see a tab for Categories. These are seen in Figure 10-3.

In the Play Store, Games are divided into the following genres:

- **Action:** These involve shooting projectiles that can range from marshmallows, to bullets, to anti-ballistic missiles. They also involve fighting games with every level of gore possible.
- **Adventure:** Games that take you to virtual worlds where you search for treasure and/or fight evil. Zombies and vampires are traditional evildoers.
- **Arcade:** Game room and bar favorites.
- **Board:** Versions of familiar (and some not-so-familiar) board games.
- **Card:** All the standard card games are here.
- **Casino:** Simulations of gambling games; no real money changes hands.
- **Casual:** Games that you can easily pick up and put aside (unless you have an addictive personality).

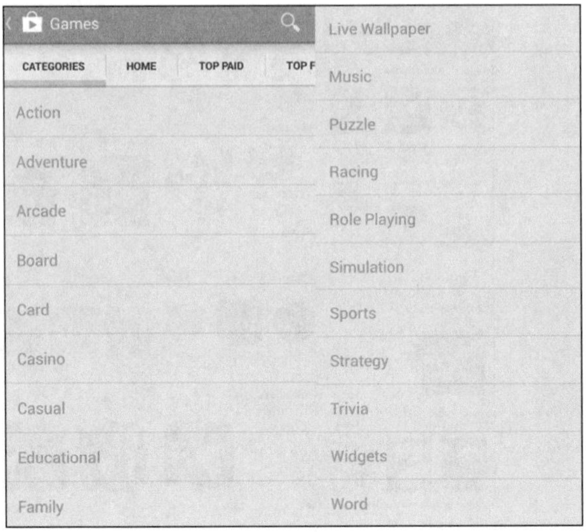

Figure 10-3: The Games Categories tab.

- ✓ **Educational:** Enjoyable games that also offer users enhanced skills or information.

- ✓ **Family:** These are really games for younger children, but using the term "family" makes it sounds like Mom and Dad are somehow involved rather than using this to keep junior occupied while you are stuck in traffic.

- ✓ **Music:** This category includes a wide range of games that involve music in one way or another. These games may include trivia, educational games involving learning music, or sing-a-long songs for kids

- ✓ **Puzzle:** Includes games like Sudoku, word search, and Trivial Pursuit.

- ✓ **Racing:** Cars, go-karts, snowboards, jet skis, biplanes, jets, or spacecraft competing with one another.

- ✓ **Role Playing:** In a virtual world, become a different version of who you are in real life, be it for better or worse.

- ✓ **Simulation:** Rather than live in the virtual world of some game designer, create and manage your own virtual world.

- ✓ **Sports:** Electronic interpretations of real-world activities that incorporate some of the skill or strategy elements of the original game; vary based upon the level of detail.

- ✓ **Strategy:** Emphasize decision-making skills, like chess; a variety of games with varying levels of complexity and agreement with reality.

- ✓ **Trivia:** A variety of games where that reward you if you know things like the name of family dog from the TV show "My Three Sons." Its name was Tramp, but you knew that already.

✔ **Widgets:** Widgets include a range of simple capabilities that range from offering a flashlight, showing the status of your battery, to some entertaining features such as acting as a remote control for your TV.

✔ **Word:** These are the games that are universally popular, such as Sudoku.

Many games appear in more than one category.

Each game has a Description page. It's similar to the Description page for apps, but it emphasizes different attributes. Figure 10-4 is an example Description page.

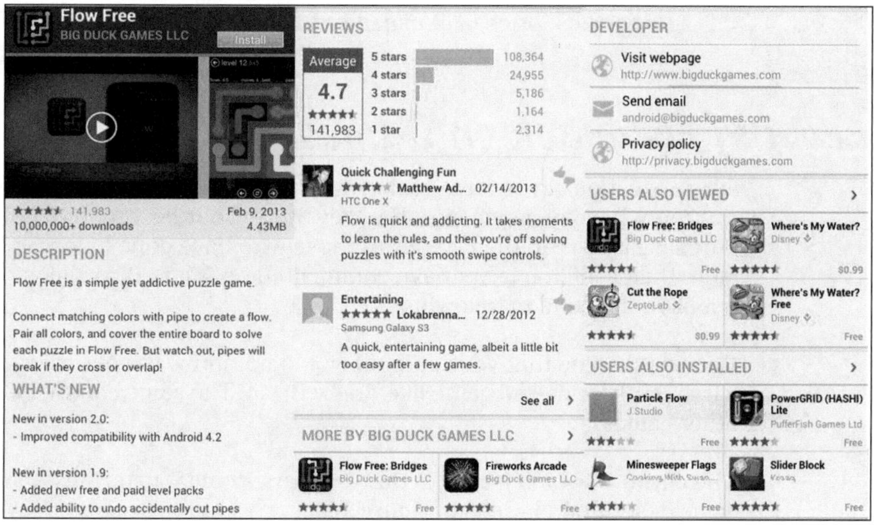

Figure 10-4: A Description page for Flow Free.

When you're in a category that looks promising, look for these road signs to help you check out and narrow your choices among similar titles:

✔ **Ratings/Comments:** Gamers love to exalt good games and bash bad ones. The comments for the game shown in Figure 10-4 are complimentary, and the overall ranking next to the game name at the top suggests that many others are favorable.

✔ **Description:** This tells you the basic idea behind the game.

✔ **What's New:** This section tells what capabilities have been added since the previous release. This is relevant if you have an earlier version of this game.

✔ **Reviews:** Here is where existing users get to vent their spleen if they do not like the game, or brag about how smart they are for buying it ahead of you. The comments are anonymous, include the date the comment was left, and tell you the kind of device the commenter used. There can be applications that lag on some older devices. However, you have the Galaxy S6, which has the best of everything (for now).

✔ **More Games by Developer:** If you have a positive experience with a given game, you may want to check that developer's other games. The More By section makes it easier for you to find these other titles.

✔ **Users Also Viewed/Users Also Installed:** This shows you the other apps that other people who downloaded this app have viewed or downloaded. These are some apps that you may want to check out.

✔ **Price:** As a tie-breaker among similar titles, a slightly higher price is a final indication of a superior game. And because you're only talking a few pennies, price isn't usually a big deal.

Leaving Feedback on Games

For applications in general, and games in particular, the Play Store is a free market. When you come in to the Play Store, your best path to finding a good purchase is to read the reviews of those who have gone before you. Although more than a million users have commented on Angry Birds, most games do not have that kind of following.

One could argue that your opinion would not move the overall rating for a frequently reviewed game like Angry Birds. The same cannot be said for other games.

One of the new paid games is Dungeoneers from Monsterious Games. The game description is seen in Figure 10-5.

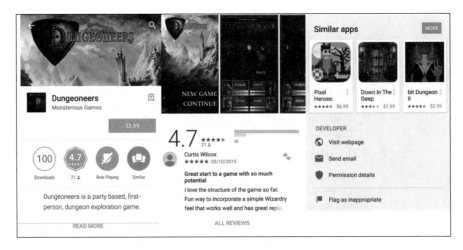

Figure 10-5: A game description for Dungeoneers.

A Description page, before you download it to your phone, will show either the Install button or the price of the game; the feedback areas will be grayed out. The Description page after you download the game to your phone will offer the options to Open or Uninstall, and the feedback areas will be active.

As of this writing, Dungeoneers has been reviewed by 21 gamers, most of whom are pretty darn enthusiastic. Your opinion matters more for this game than for the heavily reviewed games. After you've downloaded and played a game, you can help make the system work by providing your own review. This section reviews the process, starting from the first screen of the Play Store, which was shown in Figure 10-1:

1. **Tap the Menu icon.**

   This brings up a pop-up menu like the one shown in Figure 10-6.

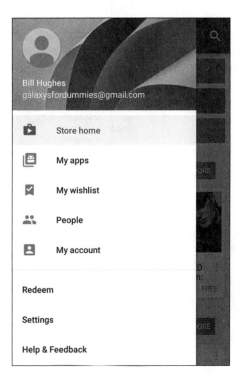

Figure 10-6: The Menu pop-up for the Play Store applications.

2. **Tap My apps.**

   This brings up the applications that you've downloaded, as shown in Figure 10-7. The Play Store does not distinguish between games and apps. They're all in the same list.

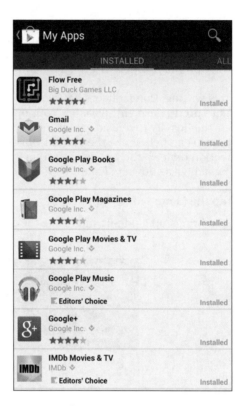

Figure 10-7: Check out your downloads.

3. **Tap the game for which you'd like to leave feedback.**

   Tapping the title of the game normally brings up the game description similar to what is shown in Figures 10-4 and 10-5. After you've downloaded a game, however, a Rate & Review section appears that lets you leave feedback. See Figure 10-8 to see this section for Angry Birds.

4. **Tap the stars on the screen.**

   This brings up a pop-up screen as shown on the left of Figure 10-9.

5. **Tap the number of stars you believe this game deserves.**

   The right image shown in Figure 10-9 illustrates the result for a five-star review.

   You then make a name for your review and enter any comments. You cannot enter comments without first choosing the number of stars for this game.

6. **When you're done, tap Submit.**

   Your comments are sent to the Play Store for everyone to see. For the sake of the system, make sure your comments are accurate!

Review section

Figure 10-8: The Game Description page with space for feedback.

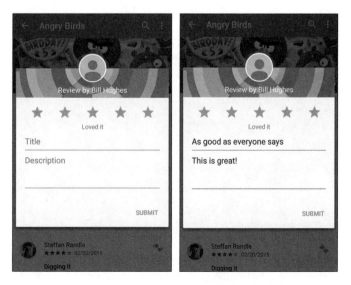

Figure 10-9: The ratings stars pop-up screen before and after entering feedback.

11

Mapping Out Where You Want to Be

In This Chapter

▶ Deciding what you want to use for navigation

▶ Using what's already on your phone

▶ Using maps safely

*H*aving a map on your phone is a very handy tool. At the most basic level, you can ask your phone to show you a map for where you plan to go. This is convenient, but only a small part of what you can do.

With the right applications, your Galaxy S6 phone can do the following:

✔ Automatically find your location on a map

✔ Give directions to where you want to go

  • As you drive, using historical driving times

  • As you drive, using real-time road conditions

  • While you walk

  • As you take public transportation

✔ Give turn-by-turn directions as you travel

  • With two-dimensional representations of the road and intersections

  • With three-dimensional representations of the roads, buildings, and intersections

✔ Tell others where you are

✔ Use the screen on your phone as a viewfinder to identify landmarks as you pan the area (augmented reality)

min (9.3 mi)

Normal traffic via WA-520 W

⚠ This route has tolls.

Start navigation

There are also some mapping applications for the Galaxy S6 for commercial users, such as CoPilot Mobile Live from ALK Technologies, but I don't cover them in this book.

GPS 101: First Things First

You can't talk smartphone mapping without GPS in the background, which creates a few inherent challenges of which you need to be aware. First off (and obviously), there is a GPS receiver in your phone. That means the following:

- **Gimme a sec.** Like all GPS receivers, your location-detection system takes a little time to determine your location when you first turn on your phone.

- **Outdoors is better.** Many common places where you use your phone — primarily, within buildings — have poor GPS coverage.

- **Nothing is perfect.** Even with good GPS coverage, location and mapping aren't perfected yet. *Augmented reality,* the option that identifies local landmarks on the screen, is even less perfect.

- **Turn me on.** Your GPS receiver must be turned on for it to work. Sure, turning it off saves battery life, but doing so precludes mapping applications from working.

- **Keep it on the down-low.** Sharing sensitive location information is of grave concern to privacy advocates. The fear is that a stalker or other villain can access your location information in your phone to track your movements. In practice, there are easier ways to accomplish this goal, but controlling who knows your location is still something you should consider, particularly when you have applications that share your location information.

Good cellular coverage has nothing to do with GPS coverage. The GPS receiver in your phone is looking for satellites; cellular coverage is based upon antennas mounted on towers or tall buildings.

Mapping apps are useful, but they also use more battery life and data than many other applications. Be aware of the impact on your data usage and battery life. Leaving mapping applications active is convenient, but it can also be a drain on your battery and your wallet if you don't pay attention to your usage and have the wrong service plan.

Practically Speaking: Using Maps

The kind of mapping application that's easiest to understand is one that presents a local map when you open the application. Depending on the model of your phone, you may have a mapping applications preloaded, such as Google Maps, TeleNav, or VZ Navigator. You can find them on your Home screen and in your Application list.

It's not a large leap for a smartphone to offer directions from your GPS-derived location to somewhere you want to go in the local area. These are standard capabilities found in each of these applications.

This section describes Google Maps and Google Maps Navigation; these are both free and might come preinstalled on your phone. If not, you can download them from the Google Play Store. Other mapping applications that might come with your phone, such as Bing Maps or TeleNav, have similar capabilities, but the details will be a bit different. Or you might want to use other mapping applications. That's all fine.

In addition to the general-purpose mapping applications that come on your phone, hundreds of mapping applications are available that can help you find a favorite store, navigate waterways, or find your car in a crowded parking lot. For example, Navigon and TCS offer solutions that base their navigation on real-time traffic conditions and give you turn-by-turn directions using three-dimensional images of the neighborhoods in which you are driving. For more, see the section, "Upgrading Your Navigation," at the end of this chapter.

As nice as mapping devices are, they're too slow to tell you to stop looking at them and avoid an oncoming car. If you can't control yourself in the car and need to watch the arrow on the map screen move, do yourself a favor and let someone else drive. If no one else is available to drive, be safe and don't use the navigation service on your phone in the car.

The most basic way to use a map is to bring up the Google Maps application by tapping the Google Maps icon. The first screen that you see when you tap the Google Maps icon is a street map with your location. Figure 11-1 shows an example of a map when the phone user is in the Seattle area.

The location of the user is a blue arrow head at the center of the map. The resolution of the map in the figure starts at about one mile square. You can see other parts of the map by placing a finger on the map and dragging away from the part of the map that you want to see. That brings new sections of the map onto the screen.

Turn the phone to change how the map is displayed. Depending on what you're looking for, a different orientation might be easier.

Map menu   Search box   Voice commands

Local services   Centering icon   Directions

Figure 11-1: You start where you are.

Changing map scale

A resolution of one square mile will work, under some circumstances, to help you get oriented in an unfamiliar place. But sometimes it helps to zoom out to get a broader perspective, or zoom in to help you find familiar landmarks, like a body of water or a major highway.

To get more real estate onto the screen, use the pinch motion as discussed in Chapter 2. This shrinks the size of the map and brings in more of the map around where you're pinching. If you need more real estate on the screen, you can keep pinching until you get more and more map. After you have your bearings, you can return to the original resolution by double-tapping the screen.

On the other hand, a scale of one square mile might not be enough. To see more landmarks, use the stretch motion to zoom in. The stretch motion expands the boundaries of the place where you start the screen. Continue stretching and stretching until you get the detail that you want. Figure 11-2 shows a street map both zoomed in and zoomed out. The map on the left is zoomed in in Satellite view. The map on the right is zoomed out in Terrain view.

The app gives you the choice of Satellite view or Terrain view by tapping the menu button, the three parallel lines, on the top-left corner of the map. This brings up a pop-up similar to the one shown in Figure 11-3.

Bring up the Satellite view by tapping Satellite. You get the Terrain view by tapping Terrain. You can also bring up other views that are useful to you, including transit routes and bicycling paths. I show you some of the other options later in this chapter.

If you're zooming in and can't find where you are on the map, tap the dot-surrounded-by-a-circle icon (refer to Figure 11-1 for the centering icon). It moves the map so that you're in the center.

Zoomed in image   Panned out image

Figure 11-2: A street image zoomed in and zoomed out.

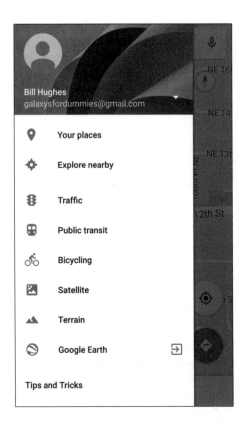

Figure 11-3: The Map Menu pop-up.

Finding nearby services

Most searches for services fall into a relatively few categories. Your Maps application is set up to find what you're most likely to seek. By tapping the Local Services icon at the bottom of the page (refer to Figure 11-1), you're offered a quick way to find the services near you, such as restaurants, coffee shops, bars, hotels, attractions, ATMs, and gas stations, as shown in Figure 11-4.

Not only that, it is aware of the time of day. There are different suggestions during breakfast time than in the evening. Just scroll down and tap one of the topical icons, and your phone performs a search of businesses in your immediate area. The results come back as a regular Google search with names, addresses, and distances from your location. An example is shown in Figure 11-5.

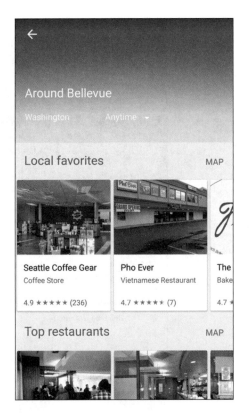

Figure 11-4: Tap to find a service on the map.

In addition to the location and reviews, the search results include icons and other relevant information:

- ✔ **Directions:** Tap the car icon to get turn-by-turn directions from your location to this business.

  You might need to download Google Maps Navigation to your phone to get the turn-by-turn directions. This is a free app from the Play Store. For more on how to download applications, read Chapter 8.

- ✔ **Call:** Tap this to call the business.

- ✔ **Save:** Tap the star to set this place as one of your favorites.

- ✔ **Website:** Tap this to be taken to the website for this business.

- ✔ **Map:** Tap the Google location icon to see a map of where you are in relation to this business, but without directions.

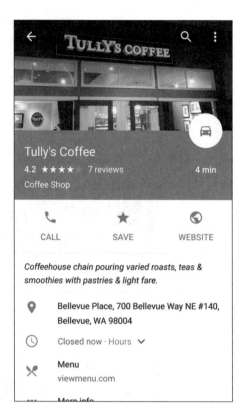

Figure 11-5: The results of a service selection.

✔ More options, which include:

- *Street view:* See the location in Google Street View. As shown at the bottom of Figure 11-6, Street View shows a photo of the street address for the location you entered.

- *Hours:* If this establishment has shared its hours of operation, you can find them here.

- *Menu:* If this establishment has shared its menu, you can find it here.

- *Reviews:* This includes all kinds of information about how people have experienced this location.

- *More:* Run another Google search on this business to get additional information, such as reviews from other parts of the web.

Just how deeply you dive into using this information is up to you. In any case, having this kind of information when you're visiting an unfamiliar location is handy.

Figure 11-6: A street map search result.

Getting and Using Directions

You probably want to get directions from your map application. I know I do. You can get directions in a number of ways, including:

- ✔ Tap the Search text box and enter the name or address of your location, for example, **Seattle Space Needle** or **742 Evergreen Terrace, Springfield, IL.**

- ✔ Tap the Services icons (refer to Figure 11-2), tap the Attractions icon (refer to Figure 11-4), and select your location.

Any of these methods lead you to the map showing your location, as shown in Figure 11-6.

It might seem intuitive to expect that when you search for a specific attraction (such as the Seattle Space Needle), you get only the Seattle Space Needle. Such a result, however, is sometimes too simple. If a given search may have multiple results, such as for chain stores, Google Map gives you several choices and you may need to choose your favorite. Typically, the app will give you the closest option.

To get directions, tap the Directions icon. This brings up the pop-up screen shown in Figure 11-7.

This gives you the options of:

- **Driving:** Turn-by-turn directions as you drive from where you are to the destination.
- **Public transportation:** This option tells you how to get to your destination by taking public transportation using published schedules.
- **Cycling:** This option is for the cyclist among us that includes bike trails in addition to city streets.
- **Walking navigation:** Turn-by-turn directions as you walk to your destination.

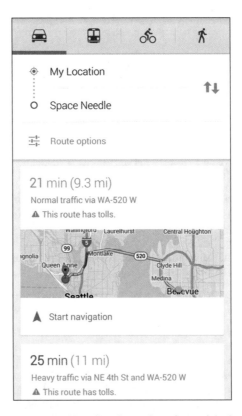

Figure 11-7: Your direction options, from original location to the target.

For each of these options, you can either use the options at the bottom of the screen to:

- ✔ **Get directions:** Sequential directions, as shown in Figure 11-8, but without telling you when to turn.
- ✔ **Navigate:** Rather than show you a map, this option puts you in a navigation app that monitors where you are as you travel and tells you what to do next.

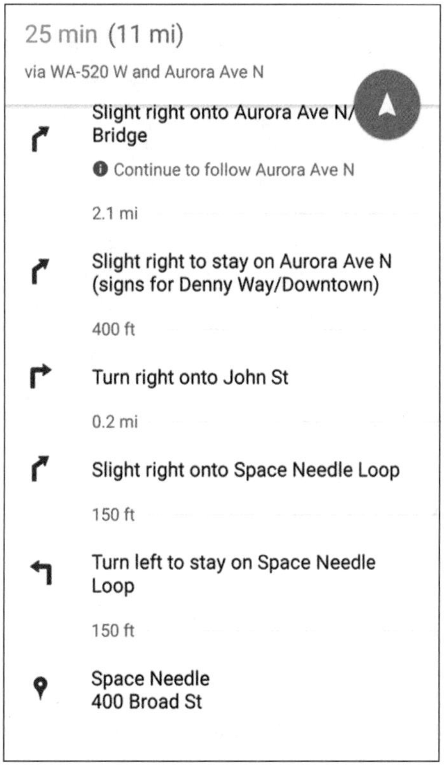

25 min (11 mi)

via WA-520 W and Aurora Ave N

↱ Slight right onto Aurora Ave N/ Bridge

ⓘ Continue to follow Aurora Ave N

2.1 mi

↱ Slight right to stay on Aurora Ave N (signs for Denny Way/Downtown)

400 ft

↳ Turn right onto John St

0.2 mi

↱ Slight right onto Space Needle Loop

150 ft

↰ Turn left to stay on Space Needle Loop

150 ft

📍 Space Needle
400 Broad St

Figure 11-8: Step-by-step directions to the target.

Upgrading Your Navigation

As a rule, free navigation applications like Google Maps Navigation use historical averages to determine travel times. The applications that charge a modest monthly fee (between $5 and $10 monthly), like VZ Navigator, have real-time updates that avoid taking you on congested routes. They also tend to have 3D images that provide better context for landmarks. (See Figure 11-9.)

Figure 11-9: Comparing 2D navigation to 3D navigation.

As you can see in Figure 11-9, the 2D map is perfectly usable and accurate, but the 3D map gives you context and additional information about the build-ings around you, which can give you an extra level of confidence. So if you frequently depend on your mapping app to get where you're going, you may find it worth your while to spend money for a paid app.

Paying an extra $5 to $10 monthly feels like a lot for some of us. Keep in mind, however, that:

✔ This is relatively modest compared to what you're paying monthly for your service.

✔ The price of a dedicated GPS receiver, with almost exactly the same capabilities, is between $125 and $200. The monthly cost of the service is comparable to the one-time fee of the GPS receiver. Plus, you don't have the hassle of lugging an additional device and its wiring.

1. Wannabe (Radio Edit)
Spice Girls - Spice

(Radio Edit)
pice

1. Wannabe (Rac
Spice Girls - Spice

12

Playing Music and Videos

In This Chapter

▶ Enjoying a single song, podcasts, or an entire album
▶ Viewing videos
▶ Knowing your licensing options

*M*ost smartphones have built-in digital music players. Having a single device that you can use as a phone *and* as a source of music is quite convenient because then you need only one device rather than two, and you eliminate extra cords for charging and separate headphones for listening. Your Samsung Galaxy S6 is no exception. You can play digital music files and podcasts all day and all night on your phone.

In addition, by virtue of the Super AMOLED screen on your Galaxy S6 smartphone, your phone makes for an excellent handheld video player. Just listen on the headset and watch on the screen, whether you have a short music video or a full-length movie.

To boot, your Galaxy S6 comes with applications for downloading and listening to music as well as downloading and watching videos. These apps are very straightforward, especially if you've ever used a CD or a DVD player.

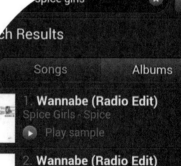

Being Mindful of Carrier Quirks

The only possible pitfall for playing music and videos on your smartphone is that each cellular carrier has its own spin: Some carriers want you to use their proprietary music stores; some give you the freedom to enjoy the flexibility that comes with owning an Android-based phone. You can use the basic multimedia tools that come with the phone, or download the myriad of options that you have via the Play Store. (Read all about the Play Store in Chapter 8.)

To keep things straight, read on to see the options you have regardless of what cellular carrier you use — including the use of the basic multimedia applications that came with your phone. Lots and lots of options for entertainment exist out there. The truth is that there isn't that much difference among them when it comes to playing. The differences lie in price and selection.

Therefore, I cover the basic functions, but I encourage you to find the entertainment that you prefer. Trust me — it's out there somewhere. Find the music you like and subscribe to as many services as it takes to bring you joy. Remember, the whole point is enjoyment. Enjoy yourself!

Getting Ready to be Entertained

Regardless of the model phone you have, the particular app you use for entertainment, and whether you're listening to audio or watching video, here's where I cover some common considerations up front.

The first is the use of headsets. Yeah, you use *headphones* with your MP3 player, but your phone uses a *headset.* The vocabulary is more than just semantics; a headset has headphones plus a microphone so you can make and take phone calls.

Secondly, you need to know about connecting your Galaxy S6 phone to a television and/or stereo. After I talk about that, I cover the issue of licensing multimedia material.

Choosing your headset

You can use wired or wireless (Bluetooth) headsets with your Samsung Galaxy S6 phone. Wired headsets are less expensive than Bluetooth headsets, and of course, wired headsets don't need charging, as do the Bluetooth headsets.

On the other hand, you lose freedom of mobility if you're tangled up in wires. In addition, the battery in Bluetooth headsets lasts much longer than the battery in your phone.

Wired headsets

At the bottom of your Galaxy S6 phone is a headset jack. If you try to use your regular headphone jack in this jack, you'll hear the audio, but the person on the other end of the call may not hear you because the headphones don't come with a microphone. In such a case, your phone tries to use the built-in mic as a speakerphone. Depending upon the ambient noise conditions, it may work fine or sound awful. Of course, you can always ask the person you're talking to whether he or she can hear you.

To address that problem, your phone might come with a wired headset. In that case, just plug it in to use the device. The Galaxy S6 uses ear buds, like those shown in Figure 12-1.

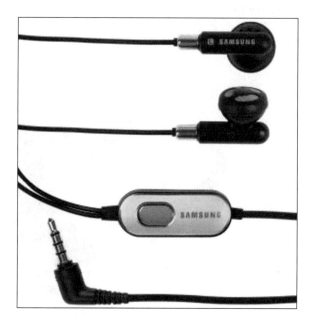

Figure 12-1: A typical wired headset with ear buds and a 3.5mm plug.

Some people dislike ear buds. You can obtain other styles at a number of retail franchises that offer the following options, including:

- ✔ Around-the-ear headphones that place the speakers on the ear and are held in place with a clip.

- ✔ A behind-the-neck band that holds around-the-ear headphones in place.

- ✔ An over-the-head band that places the headphones on the ear.

The laws in some regions prohibit the use of headphones while driving. Correcting the officer and explaining that these are really "headsets" and not "headphones" won't help your case if you're pulled over. Even if not explicitly illegal in an area, it's still a bad idea to play music in both ears at a volume that inhibits your ability to hear warnings while driving.

Ear buds can have a greater chance of causing ear damage if the volume is too loud than other options. The close proximity to your ear drum is the culprit. There are probably warnings on the ear bud instructions, but I wanted to amplify this information (<har har>).

In any case, give yourself some time to get used to any new headset. There is often an adjustment period while you get used to having a foreign object in or around your ear.

Stereo Bluetooth headsets

The other option is to use a stereo Bluetooth headset. Figure 12-2 shows a typical model.

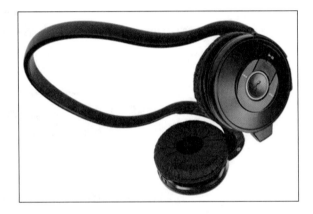

Figure 12-2: A behind-the-neck Bluetooth stereo headset.

A stereo Bluetooth headset is paired the same way as any other Bluetooth headset. (Read how to do this in Chapter 3.) When your Galaxy S6 phone and the headset connect, the phone recognizes that the headset operates in stereo when you're listening to music or videos.

There are also several variations on how to place the headphone part of the headset near your ear with a Bluetooth headset. Be aware that some products on the market are strictly Bluetooth head*phones* and not headsets; they don't have microphones. In this case, you might want to remove your headphones when a call comes in, or move the phone near your mouth. Of course, this effort defeats some of the convenience of having a Bluetooth connection.

Choosing your Bluetooth speaker

In the last few years, developers released a flurry of products known as *Bluetooth speakers*. Among the better-known Bluetooth speakers are products such as the Dre Beats Pill. These speakers include a range of options: some of which are very small and convenient; others are designed to offer excellent audio quality.

Although these speakers (which come in a range of sizes) are not as portable as the Bluetooth headset — they're a little difficult to use as you're walking down the street — they're usually pretty easy to take with you and set up when you're at a desk or in someone's living room. They also do not need a cable to make a connection, and are always ready to go.

Soen Audio's Transit (see Figure 12-3) is an excellent example of a high-quality Bluetooth speaker. Its list price is close to $200.

Figure 12-3: The Soen Audio Transit Bluetooth speaker.

If you like high-quality sound, this is the quality of Bluetooth speaker that you'd want to get. On the other hand, if you're just looking for background enjoyment, you can get a Bluetooth speaker for less than half that price.

Connecting to your stereo

Although being able to listen to your music on the move is convenient, it's also nice to be able to listen to your music collection on your home or car stereo. Your Galaxy S6 phone presents your stereo with a nearly perfect version of what went in. The sound quality that comes out is limited only by the quality of your stereo.

In addition, you can play the music files and playlists stored on your phone, which can be more convenient than playing CDs. If you stereo receiver is older, setting this up involves plugging the 3.5mm jack from the cable shown in Figure 12-4 into the 3.5mm jack available on newer stereos.

When you play the music as you do through a headset, it will play through your stereo. Although each stereo system is unique, the correct setting for the selector knob is AUX.

Figure 12-4: The patch cable with 3.5mm plugs.

Newer stereo receivers recognize that mobile phones are a great place to access music. These receivers support a Bluetooth connection to your phone. If you are in the market for a new receiver, make sure you get one with Bluetooth capability. In either case, you will be entertained. Enjoy yourself.

Licensing your multimedia files

It's really quite simple: You need to pay the artist if you're going to listen to music or watch video with integrity. Many low-cost options are suitable for any budget. Depending upon how much you plan to listen to music, podcasts, or watch videos, you can figure out what's the best deal.

Stealing music or videos is uncool. Although it might be technically possible to play pirated music and videos on your phone, it's stealing. Don't do it. If your financial circumstances do not allow you to afford to pay for your music, I suggest you listen to Internet Radio. With just a little work on your part, you can get free unlimited music.

You can buy or lease music, podcasts, or videos. In most cases, you pay for them with a credit card. And depending upon your cellular carrier, you might be allowed to pay for them on your monthly cellular bill.

Listening up on licensing

Here are the three primary licensing options available for music files and podcasts:

- ✔ **By the track:** Pay for each song individually. Buying a typical song costs about 79 to 99 cents. Podcasts, which are frequently used for speeches or lectures, can vary dramatically in price.

- ✔ **By the album:** Buying an album isn't a holdover from the days before digital music. Music artists and producers create albums with an organization of songs that offer a consistent feeling or mood. Although many music-playing applications allow you to assemble your own playlist, an album is created by professionals. In addition, buying a full album is often less expensive than on a per-song basis. You can get multiple songs for $8 to $12.

✔ **With a monthly pass:** The last option for buying audio files is the monthly pass. For about $15 per month, you can download as much music as you want from the library of the service provider.

If you let your subscription to your monthly pass provider lapse, you won't be able to listen to the music from this library.

In addition to full access to the music library, some music library providers offer special services to introduce you to music that's similar to what you've been playing. These services are a very convenient way to learn about new music. If you have even a small interest in expanding your music repertoire, these services are an easy way to do it.

Whether buying or renting is most economical depends on your listening/viewing habits. If you don't plan to buy much, or you know specifically what you want, you may save some money by paying for all your files individually. If you're not really sure what you want, or you like a huge variety of music, paying for monthly access might make better sense for you.

Licensing for videos

The two primary licensing options available for videos are:

✔ **Rental:** This option is similar to renting a video from a store. You can view the video as many times as you like within 24 hours from the start of the first play. In addition, the first play must begin within a defined period, such as a week, of your downloading it. Most movies are in the $3 to $5 range.

✔ **Purchase:** You have a license to view the file as frequently as you want, for as long as you want. The purchase cost can be as low as $12, but is more typically in the $15 range.

At the moment, there are no sources for mainstream Hollywood films that allow you to buy a monthly subscription and give you unlimited access to a film library. This can change at any time, so watch for announcements.

Enjoying Basic Multimedia Capabilities

Regardless of the version of your Galaxy S6, some basic multimedia capabilities are common across the different phones. Figure 12-5 shows the Music and Video applications.

Music   Video

Figure 12-5: The multimedia
apps on the Galaxy S6.

Your phone comes with these applications preloaded, and you might have
other multimedia applications as well, depending upon your carrier.

Don't worry about storage capacity for your music. A very rough estimate is
that a gigabyte (GB) of storage will store 120 hours of music. There are limits
on storing videos, however. Roughly, one full-length movie takes up 1GB.

Grooving with the Music Player app

The Music Player app allows you to play music and audio files. The first step
is to obtain music and audio files for your phone.

Some ways to acquire music and/or recordings for your phone are:

✔ Buy and download tracks from an online music store.

✔ Receive them as attachments via e-mail or text message.

✔ Receive them from another device connected with a Bluetooth link.

✔ Record them on your phone.

Buying from an online music store

The most straightforward method of getting music on your phone is from an
online music store. You can download a wide variety of music from dozens
of mainstream online music stores. The Play Store is an option. In addition
to apps, it has music and video. Other well-known sites include Rhapsody,
Amazon MP3, VEVO, and last.fm.

In addition, many more specialty or "boutique" stores provide more differen-
tiated offerings than you can get from the mass-market stores. For example,
MAQAM offers Middle Eastern music (www.maqammp3.com).

The details for acquiring music among the online stores vary from store to
store. Ultimately, there are more similarities than differences. As an example
of when you know what you want, what you really, really want, here's how to

find and download the song "Wannabe" by the Spice Girls. I'm using Amazon MP3. If you don't have Amazon MP3 in your Application list, you would start by loading that app on your phone, as I describe how to do in Chapter 8. When you open it, you see the screen shown in Figure 12-6.

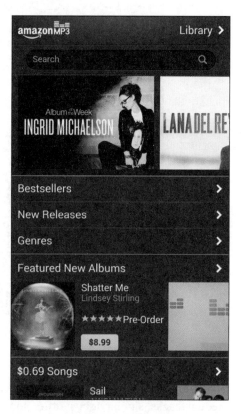

Figure 12-6: The Amazon MP3 Home screen.

From here, you can search for music by album, song, or music genre. Amazon MP3 offers a different free music track and an album at a deep discount every day.

Now to search for the song you want:

1. **Enter the relevant search information in the Amazon MP3 Search field.**

   In this case, I'm searching for "Wannabe" by the Spice Girls. The result of the search for songs looks like Figure 12-7.

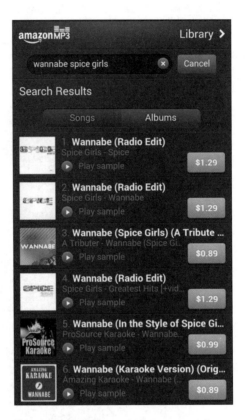

Figure 12-7: Search results for a song at the Amazon MP3 store.

The search results come up with all kinds of options, including albums, individual tracks, similar songs, other songs from the same artist. Be ready for these options.

2. **To purchase the track, tap twice on the price.**

   The left screen in Figure 12-8 shows the price. When you tap once on the price, you get a confirmation message to make sure that you want to buy the download; the price is replaced with a Buy icon, as shown on the right in Figure 12-8. To buy, tap Buy.

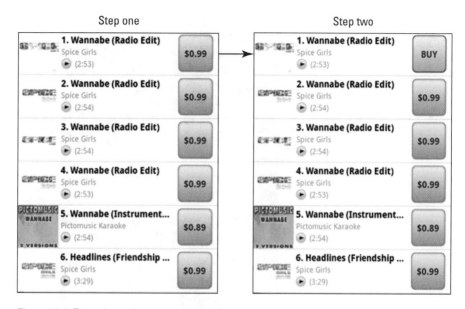

Figure 12-8: Tap twice to buy.

3. Sign in with your account information, as shown in Figure 12-9.

Unless you're going to subsist on the free MP3 files you can get from this site, you need to pay. To pay for files at an online music store, you need an account and a credit card. This process is similar, if not identical, to signing up for the Play Store (see Chapter 8). You need your e-mail account, a password, and in some cases, an account name. In the case of Amazon MP3, you already have an account if you have an account with Amazon. If not, you'll be asked to create an account.

After you enter this information, the file will automatically begin downloading to your phone, and a progress screen (as shown in Figure 12-10) lets you know when you're finished.

The song is now loaded on your phone. When you open the music player, it's ready for you to play.

Receiving music as an attachment

As long as you comply with your license agreement, you can e-mail or text a music file as an attachment. Simply send yourself an e-mail from your PC with the desired music file. You then open the e-mail or text on your phone and save the file in the library of your Music app.

Figure 12-9: The account sign-in screen for the Amazon MP3 store.

Your phone can play music files that come in any of the following formats: FLAC, WAV, Vorbis, MP3, AAC, AAC+, eAAC+, WMA, AMR-NB, AMR-WB, MID, AC3, and XMF.

Recording sounds on your phone

No one else might think your kids' rendition of "Happy Birthday" is anything special, but you probably treasure it. In fact, there is a recording app that comes with your phone. The icon for the Voice Recorder is shown in Figure 12-11.

In general, there is a simple record button that creates a sound file when you stop recording. The sound quality might not be the best, but what you record can be just as important or entertaining as what you buy commercially. Your phone treats all audio files the same and all are playable on your Music Player.

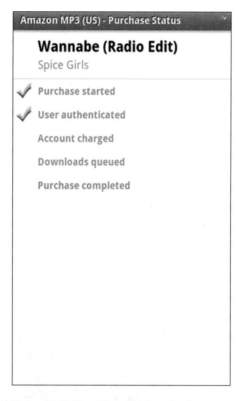

Figure 12-10: The screen for downloading tracks from the Amazon MP3 store.

Figure 12-11: The Voice Recorder icon.

Playing downloaded music

To play your music, tap the Music Player app icon (as shown earlier in
Figure 12-5) to open the Music Player application. The first screen that you
see is shown in Figure 12-12.

The Music Player sorts your music files into a number of categories. You can
select the category you want to use by tapping on the link that says Playlists
at the top of the Home screen. This brings up the pop-up screen seen in
Figure 12-13.

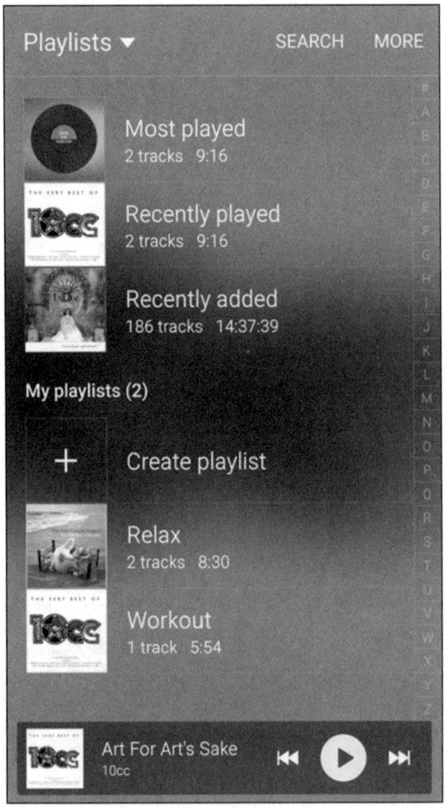

Figure 12-12: Home screen for the Music
Player app.

Figure 12-13: Music categories for the Music Player app.

The categories include:

- ✔ **Playlists:** Some digital music stores bundle songs into playlists, such as Top Hits from the '50s. You can also create your own playlists for groups of songs that are meaningful to you.
- ✔ **Tracks:** This lists all your song files in alphabetic order.
- ✔ **Albums:** Tapping this category places all your songs into an album with which the song is associated. When you tap the album, you see all the songs you've purchased, whether one song or all the songs from that album.
- ✔ **Artists:** This category lists all songs from all the albums from a given artist.
- ✔ **Genres:** This category separates music into music genres, such as country and western or heavy metal.

These categories are useful when you have a large number of files. To play a song, an album, or a genre, open that category and tap the song, playlist, album, artist, or genre, and the song will start playing.

Adding songs as ringtones and alarms

Here's how to add a song as a ringtone or alarm. The first step is to open a contact. A generic contact in Edit mode is seen in Figure 12-14. Refer to Chapter 6 if you have any questions about contacts.

Follow these steps:

1. **Tap the Default Ringtone link.**

   This will bring up a list of ringtones (shown in Figure 12-15).

   A quick scan finds that *Ode to Joy* is not among the options that come with your phone. To use a music file as a ringtone, find the Add button on the bottom.

2. **Tap Add.**

   This brings up a screen of music files on your phone, as shown in Figure 12-16.

3. **Highlight the song you want and tap OK.**

   From now on, when you hear this song, you know it will be your friend Ludwig.

Jamming to Internet radio

If you have not tried Internet radio, you should definitely consider it. The basic idea is that you enter information on your current music favorites, and these services play music that is similar. Pandora and Slacker Radio are

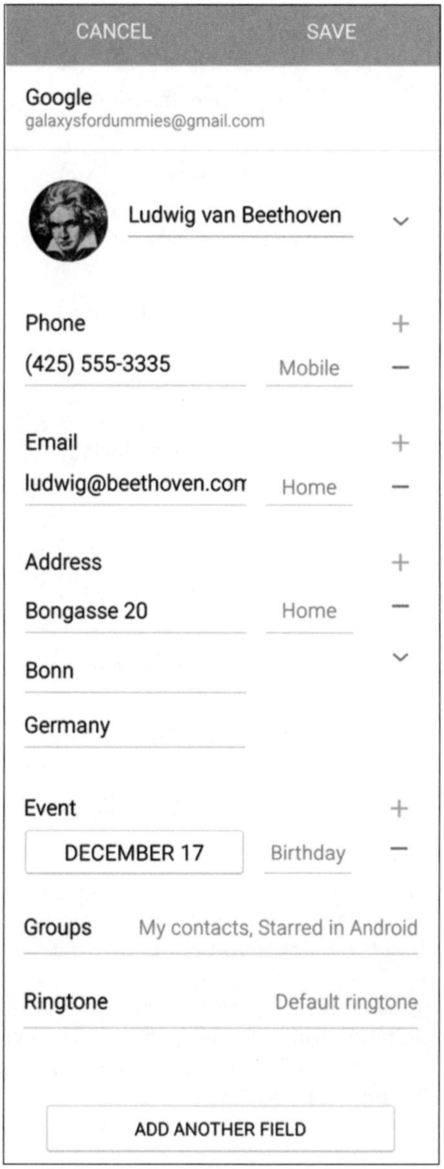

CANCEL   SAVE

Google
galaxysfordummies@gmail.com

Ludwig van Beethoven   ∨

Phone   +

(425) 555-3335   Mobile   —

Email   +

ludwig@beethoven.com   Home   —

Address   +

Bongasse 20   Home   —

Bonn   ∨

Germany

Event   +

DECEMBER 17   Birthday   —

Groups   My contacts, Starred in Android

Ringtone   Default ringtone

ADD ANOTHER FIELD

Figure 12-14: A typical contact for a Baroque composer.

two of the best-known services of this type; one or the other may have been pre-installed on your phone. If not, they're available for download from the Play Store. Figure 12-17 shows some of the 9,000 Internet radio apps in the Play Store.

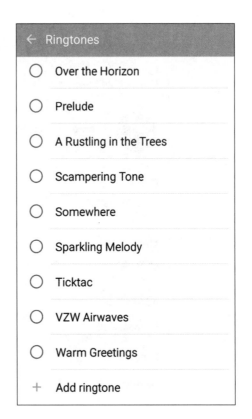

Figure 12-15: Basic ringtones.

These apps are a great way to learn about new songs and groups that may appeal to you. The service streams music to your phone for you to enjoy. You can buy the track if you choose.

Streaming audio files can use a large amount of data over time. This may be no problem if you have an unlimited (or even large) data-service plan. Otherwise your "free" Internet radio service can wind up costing you a lot. You're best off using Wi-Fi.

Looking at your video options

The Music Player app allows you to play music files. Similarly, you use the Video Player app to play video options. The Video Player is in your Application list and might even be on your Home page. In most ways, playing videos is the same as playing audio with a few exceptions:

- ✔ Many people prefer to buy music, but renting is more typical for videos.

- ✔ Video files are usually, but not always, larger.

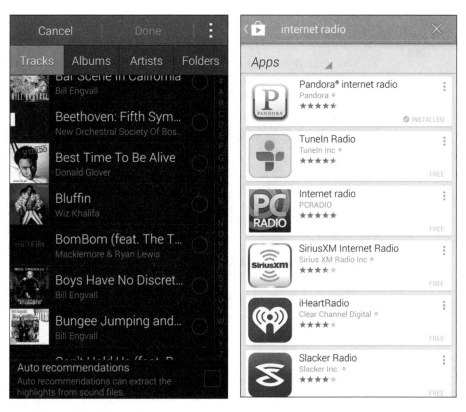

Figure 12-16: The Track selections.

Figure 12-17: Some Internet radio options in the Play Store.

Otherwise, as with music files, you can acquire videos for your phone from an online video store — and you need to have an account and pay for the use. In addition, you can download video files to your phone, and the Video Player will play them like a DVD player.

There are three categories for your videos (which are seen in panorama in Figure 12-18):

- ✓ Movies
- ✓ TV Shows
- ✓ Personal Videos

In Chapter 9, I covered how to use the digital camcorder on your phone. You can watch any video you've shot on your phone: From the Google Play application, scroll over to the Personal Video section.

Your phone can show the following video formats: MPEG-4, WMV, AVI/DivX, MKV, and FLV.

To play your video, simply tap the name of the file. The app begins showing the video in landscape orientation. The controls that pop up when you tap the screen are similar to the controls of DVD player.

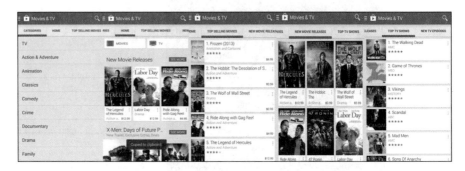

Figure 12-18: Google Play Store Video categories.

Part V
Productivity Applications

In this part. . .

✔ Download your calendars to your phone and upload new events to your electronic calendar

✔ Use mobile Microsoft Office applications from your phone or from the Cloud

✔ Dictate an e-mail or text with S-Voice

✔ Tell your phone to make a call

13

Using the Calendar

In This Chapter

▶ Setting up events

▶ Downloading your calendars to your phone

▶ Uploading events to your PC

Y ou might fall in love with your Galaxy S6 phone so much that you want to ask it out on a date. And speaking of dates, let's talk about your phone's calendar. The Galaxy S6 phone calendar functions are powerful, and they can make your life easier. With just a few taps, you can bring all your electronic calendars together to keep your life synchronized.

In this chapter, I show you how to set up the calendar that comes with your phone, which might be all you need. The odds are, though, that you have calendars elsewhere, such as on your work computer. So I also show you how to combine all your calendars with your Galaxy S6 phone. After you read this chapter, you'll have no excuse for missing a meeting. (Or, okay, a date.)

Some calendars use the term *appointments* for *events*. They are the same idea. I use the term *events*.

Syncing Calendars

Most likely, you already have at least two electronic calendars scattered in different places: a calendar tied to your work computer and a personal calendar. Now you have a third one — the one on your Samsung phone that is synced to your Gmail account.

Bringing together all your electronic calendars to one place, though, is one of the best things about your phone — as long as you're a faithful user of your electronic calendars, that is. To begin this process, you need to provide authorization to the respective places that your calendars are stored in the same way as you authorized access to your e-mail accounts and contacts in Chapters 5 and 6. This authorization is necessary to respect your privacy.

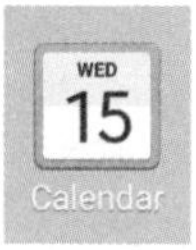

If your phone doesn't have a Calendar icon on the Home page, open the Calendar app from your App list. This same app works with the calendar that's stored on your phone and any digital calendars that you add.

When you first open this app, you see a calendar in monthly format, as shown in Figure 13-1. I discuss other calendar views later in this chapter.

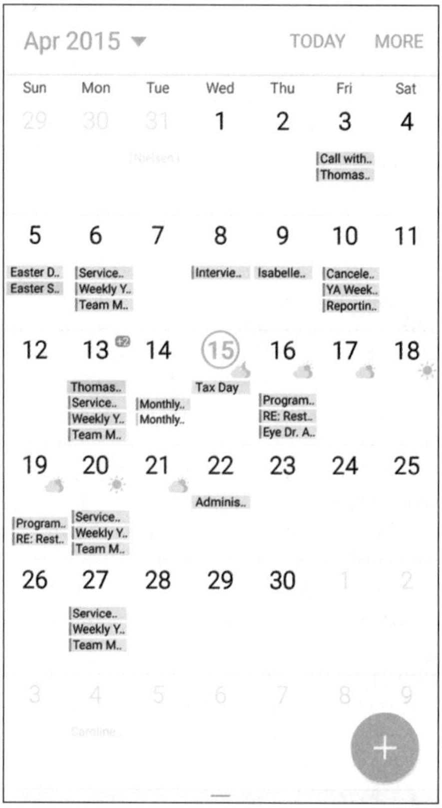

Figure 13-1: The monthly calendar display.

You may already be a winner!

The calendar on your phone might already be populated with events from your work and personal calendars. Don't be concerned — this is good news!

If you've already set up your phone to *sync* (combine) with your e-mail and your calendar (see Chapter 5), your calendars are already synchronizing with your phone.

When you add an account to your phone, such as your personal or work e-mail account, your Facebook account, or Dropbox, you're asked whether you want to sync your calendar. The default setting for syncing is typically every hour.

Unless you get a warning message that alerts you to a communications problem, your phone now has the latest information on appointments and meeting requests. Your phone continues to sync automatically. It does all this syncing in the background; you may not even notice that changes are going on.

You could encounter scheduling conflicts if others can create events for you on your digital calendar. Be aware of this possibility. It can be annoying (or worse) to think you have free time, offer it, and then find that someone else took it.

Setting Calendar Display Preferences

Before you get too far into playing around with your calendar, you'll want to choose how you view it.

If you don't have a lot of events, using the month calendar shown in Figure 13-1 is probably a fine option. On the other hand, if your day is jam-packed with personal and professional events, the daily or weekly schedules might prove more practical. Switching views is easy. For example, just tap the Month link at the top of the calendar, which in this case displays "Apr 2015," to bring up the options. These are shown in Figure 13-2.

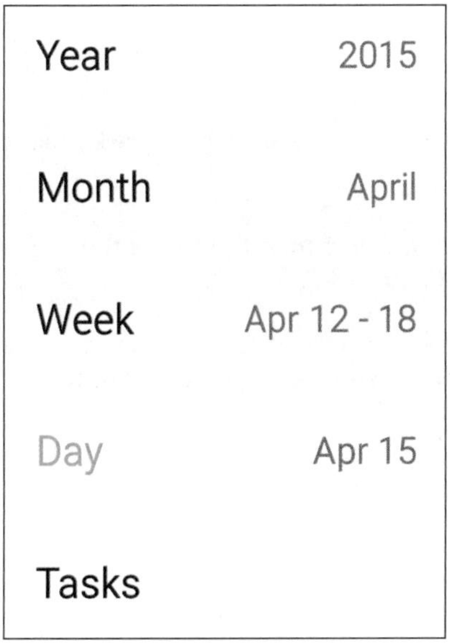

Year	2015
Month	April
Week	Apr 12 - 18
Day	Apr 15
Tasks	

Figure 13-2: The Calendar Display Options pop-up.

If you tap Week, you see the weekly display, as shown in Figure 13-3.

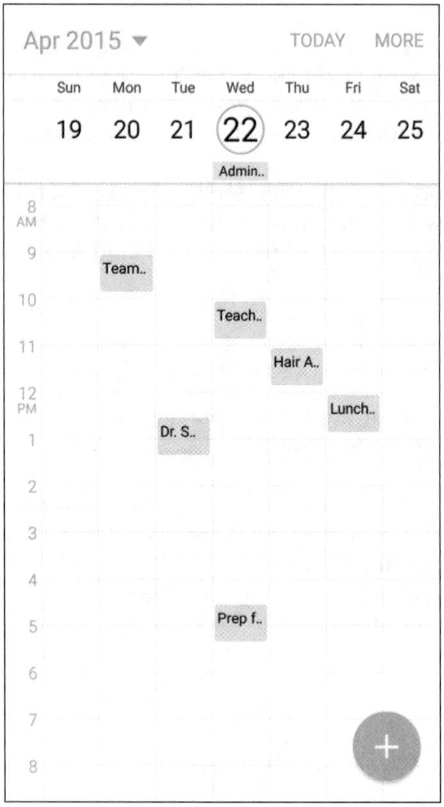

Figure 13-3: The weekly calendar display.

Or tap the Day button at the top of the calendar to show the daily display, as shown in Figure 13-4.

To see what events you have upcoming, regardless of the day they're on, you might prefer List view. Tap the List button at the top of the calendar to see a list of your activities.

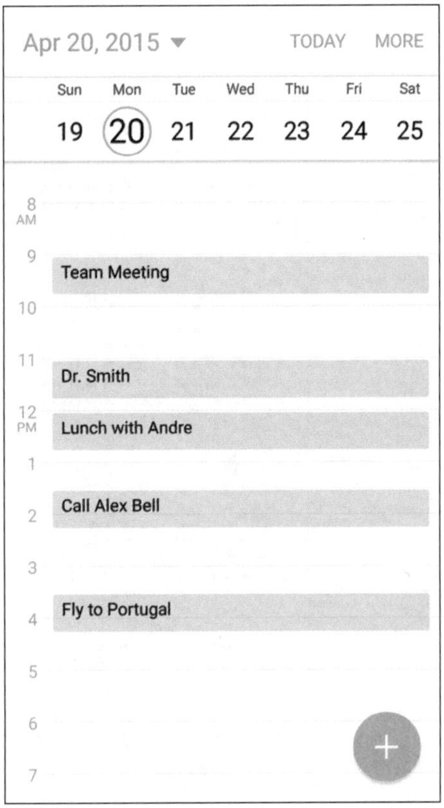

Apr 20, 2015 ▼   TODAY   MORE

Sun	Mon	Tue	Wed	Thu	Fri	Sat
19	(20)	21	22	23	24	25

8 AM

9   **Team Meeting**

10

11   **Dr. Smith**

12 PM   **Lunch with Andre**

1

2   **Call Alex Bell**

3

4   **Fly to Portugal**

5

6

7

Figure 13-4: The daily calendar display.

The weekly and daily calendars only show a portion of the day. You can slide the screen to see the time slots earlier and later. You can also pinch and stretch to seem more or less of the time slots.

There is also an annual calendar as seen in Figure 13-5. This is so busy that it does not allow you to see any appointments. It is primarily useful for setting dates out in the future.

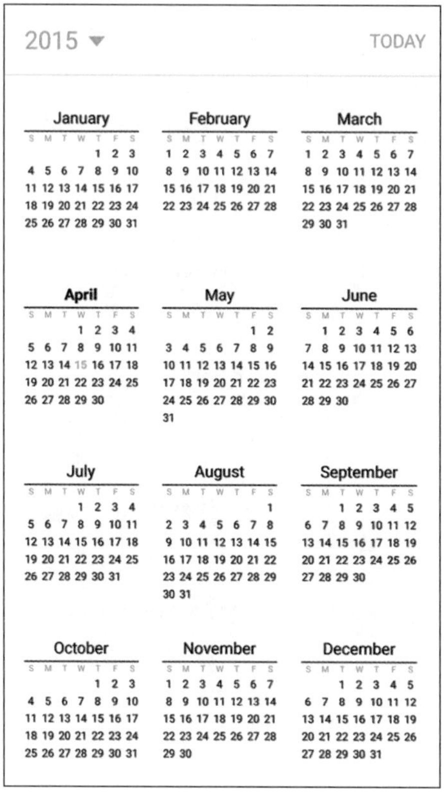

Figure 13-5: The annual calendar display.

Setting Other Display Options

In addition to the default display option, you can set other personal preferences for the calendar on your phone. To get to the settings for the calendar, tap the More link on the daily, weekly, or monthly calendars and tap Settings. Doing so brings up the screen shown in Figure 13-6.

You have the following options:

✓ **First day of week:** The standard in the United States is that a week is displayed from Sunday to Saturday. If you prefer the week to start on Saturday or Monday, you can change it here.

✓ **Show week number:** Some people prefer to see the week number on the weekly calendar. If you count yourself among those, check this option.

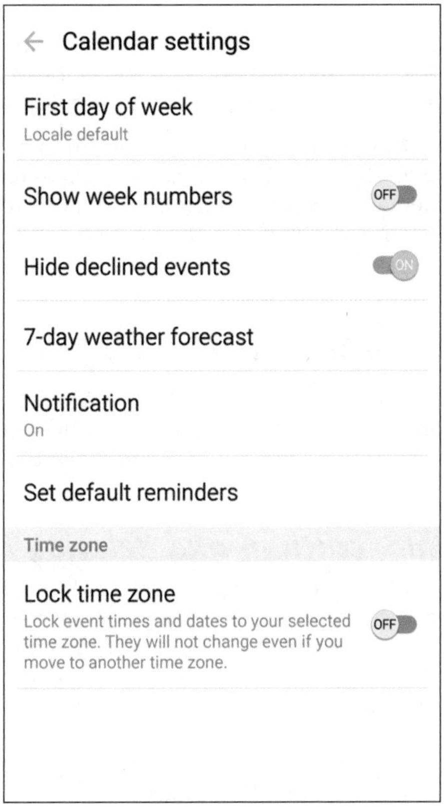

Figure 13-6: The Settings options for the Calendar application.

✔ **Hide declined events:** When some of us decline an event, we don't care to hear about it again. Others may want to keep a reminder of the declined event in case the situation changes (or in case nothing better comes along). The default setting is to hide declined events; if you want to see them, deselect this box.

✔ **7-day weather forecast:** If you look at the monthly calendar shown in Figure 13-1, you can see an image on some of the days representing the weather forecast. If you like seeing this, you can keep this information. If you feel it takes too much real estate on your screen, you can delete it.

✔ **Set notifications:** When an event is approaching, you can have the phone alert you with a pop-up, signal a notification on the status line, or do nothing. The default is to give you a notification, but you can change that option here.

✔ **Set default reminders:** It helps some of us to be reminded about an appointment a few minutes before we are to be somewhere. Others of us find this annoying. This setting lets you choose whether you get a reminder or not and how far in advance you will be reminded.

✔ **Lock time zones:** When you travel to a new time zone, your phone will take on the new time zone. Under most circumstances, this is a nice convenience. However, it may be confusing to some. If you prefer that the calendar remain in your home time zone, check this option.

Creating an Event on the Right Calendar

An important step in using a calendar when mobile is creating an event. It's even more important to make sure that the event ends up on the right calendar. This section covers the steps to make this happen.

Creating, editing, and deleting an event

Here's how to create an event — referred to as (well, yeah) an "event" — on your phone. Start from one of the calendar displays shown in Figures 13-1, 13-3, or 13-4. Tap the bright green circle with the plus (+) sign at the bottom right of the calendar. Doing so brings up the pop-up screen shown in Figure 13-7 (without the keyboard).

The only required information to get things started is a memorable event name and the Start and End times.

You need the following information at hand when making an event:

✔ **Calendar:** Decide on which calendar you want to keep this event. Figure 13-7 shows that this event will be stored on the Gmail calendar. When you tap this selection, the phone presents you with the other calendars you've synced to your phone; you can store an event on any of them.

✔ **Title:** Call it something descriptive so you can remember what it is without having to open it up.

✔ **Start and end:** The two entry fields for the start and end times. Select the All Day toggle if the event is a full-day event.

✔ **Notification:** This field lets you set how soon before an event your phone will alert you that you have an upcoming event. This makes it less likely that you'll be late to an appointment if you set this alert to accommodate your travel time.

✔ **Location:** This setting ties in to the Google Maps app, allowing you to enter an address or a landmark. You can also just enter text.

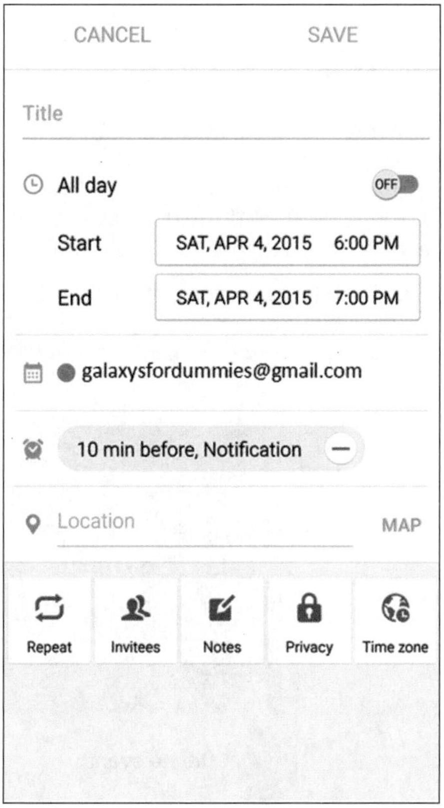

Figure 13-7: The Create Event screen.

If you want, you can enter more details on the meeting by adding:

- ✔ **Repeat:** This option is useful for recurring events, such as weekly meetings.

- ✔ **Invitees:** This allows you to have a group meeting by entering multiple contacts.

- ✔ **Notes:** Add information that you find useful about that meeting.

- ✔ **Privacy:** This is the same idea as the Show Me As option, but for non-Outlook-based calendars.

- ✔ **Time zone:** If you and everyone that is invited will be in the same time zone, you are set. If you happen to be in another time zone or some of the invitees are in other time zones, you can use this option to ensure that you are not setting a meeting off business hours, or worse, in the middle of the night.

After you fill in the obligatory (and any optional) fields and settings, tap the Save link at the top of the page. The event is stored in whichever calendar you selected when you sync.

After you save an event, you can edit or delete it:

- ✓ **Edit:** Open the event by tapping it from within one of the calendar views. This brings up the information as entered. Make your changes and tap Save. It's changed when it syncs.

- ✓ **Delete:** To delete an event, start by tapping the entry on the screen. Tap the green Delete link at the top left. This brings up the pop-up as seen in Figure 13-8 to delete the event. Tap Delete. The event is gone.

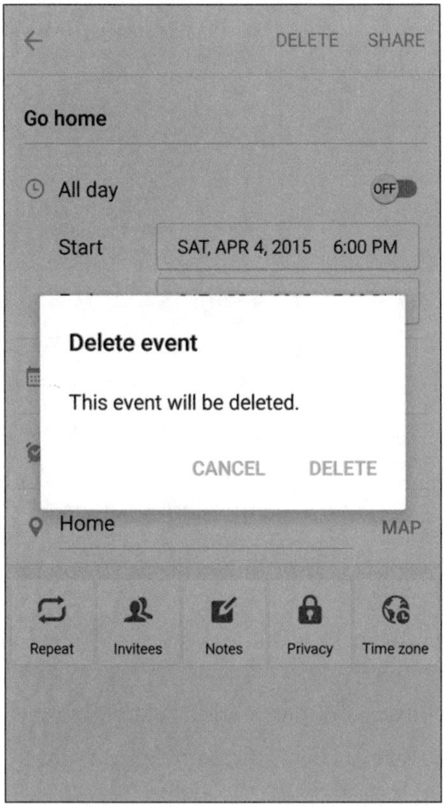

Figure 13-8: The Delete Event pop-up screen.

You can also create an event by tapping the calendar itself twice. Tapping it twice brings up a pop-up where you can enter the event details.

Keeping events separate and private

When you have multiple calendars stored in one place (in this case, your phone), you might get confused when you want to add a new event. It can be even more confusing when you need to add the real event on one calendar and a placeholder on another.

Suppose your boss is a jerk, and to retain your sanity, you need to find a new job. You send your résumé to the arch-rival firm, Plan B, which has offices across town. Plan B is interested and wants to interview you at 1:00 p.m. next Tuesday. All good news.

The problem is that your current boss demands that you track your every move on the company calendaring system. His draconian management style is to berate people if they're not at their desks doing work if they're not at a scheduled meeting. (By the way, I am not making up this scenario.)

You follow my drift. You don't want Snidely Whiplash trudging through your calendar, sniffing out your plans to exit stage left, and making life more miserable if Plan B doesn't work out. Instead, you want to put a reasonable-sounding placeholder on your work calendar, while putting the real event on your personal calendar. You can easily do this from your calendar on your Samsung Galaxy S6. When you're making the event, you simply tell the phone where you want the event stored, making sure to keep each event exactly where it belongs.

The process begins with the Create Event screen. You bring this up by tapping the + sign in the green circle seen at the bottom right-hand corner of any of the calendars seen in Figures 13-1, 13-3, or 13-4. The information for the real event is shown on the left in Figure 13-9. The fake event is shown in the right. This is the one that is saved to your work e-mail. The colored dot by the work address helps you be aware that this is a different calendar.

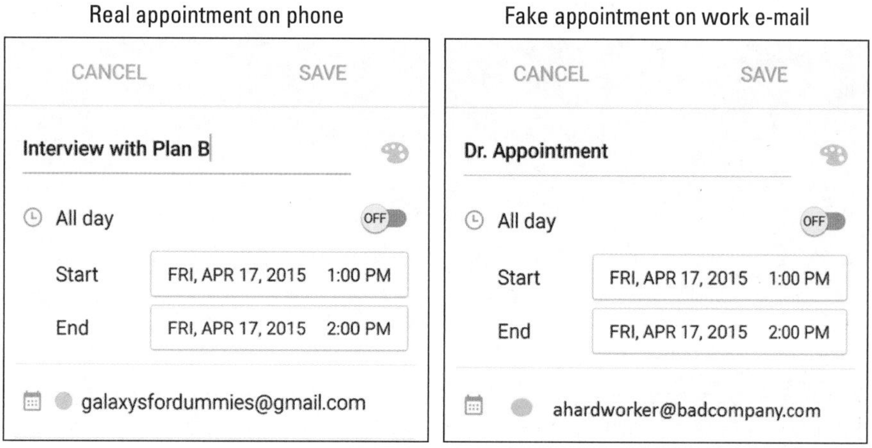

Real appointment on phone	Fake appointment on work e-mail
CANCEL SAVE	CANCEL SAVE
Interview with Plan B	Dr. Appointment
All day OFF	All day OFF
Start FRI, APR 17, 2015 1:00 PM	Start FRI, APR 17, 2015 1:00 PM
End FRI, APR 17, 2015 2:00 PM	End FRI, APR 17, 2015 2:00 PM
galaxysfordummies@gmail.com	ahardworker@badcompany.com

Figure 13-9: The Add an Event screen on your phone.

Now, when you look at your calendar on your phone, you see two events at the same time. (Check it out in Figure 13-10.) The Galaxy S6 doesn't mind if you make two simultaneous events.

Figure 13-10: Two events on the same day on your phone calendar.

Under the circumstances, this is what you wanted to create. As long as your boss doesn't see your phone, you're safe — to try to find more fulfilling employment, that is.

On the Road Again: Taking Your Work with You on Your Phone

In This Chapter
▶ Using mobile Microsoft Office applications
▶ Navigating the Office applications in the Cloud
▶ Sharing files using your phone

*W*hen you pick up your Galaxy S6 phone, you're holding as much computing power as was available in a high-end desktop from a few years ago — and a graphics processor that would have made a hard-core gamer envious. So it's not far-fetched to want to do some work with your Microsoft Office applications, which are relatively modest users of computing power, on your Galaxy S6 while you're away from your desk. Sure. Why not?

The Galaxy S6 phone actually doesn't allow you to leave your computer behind for good, for a few reasons. The most basic is that the sizes of the screen and the keyboard aren't conducive for writing novels and other similarly long documents. What makes the most sense is to use your phone to view Office documents and make minor changes. Leave the hard-core creation and modification efforts to a full-sized PC.

ıle

 Great American Novel.docx
04/20/2015 11:18 AM

 POLARIS Office
Introduction.pptx
06/14/2014 9:09 AM

There are several mobile apps that work on Android phones. This includes Microsoft Office Mobile, WPS Office + PDF from Kingsoft, and Polaris Office + PDF from Infraware. All of these let you be productive on the road without having to pull out your laptop. Depending on what you want to do, you might even be able to leave your heavy laptop at home.

In this chapter, I start with an introduction on the basics, explore the tools on your phone, and explain how you can use them to your best advantage. Then I walk you through the Polaris Office app to show some of its capabilities.

Finally, I fill you in on file sharing, so you can get files on and off your phone and out into the world.

Preparing for Using Office Apps

Before I get too far along, I want to explain the capabilities of this solution and the logic behind working with Microsoft Office applications.

Focusing on the Big Four

Microsoft Office applications are the most popular apps for general purpose business productivity. Virtually every business uses Microsoft Office or applications that can work with Microsoft file formats. As you're probably well aware, the heavy hitters are:

- **Microsoft Word:** For creating and editing documents. These files use the .doc and .docx suffixes.

- **Microsoft Excel:** For managing spreadsheets, performing numerical analysis, and creating charts. These files end in the .xls and .xlsx suffixes.

- **Microsoft PowerPoint:** For creating and viewing presentations. These files end in the .ppt and .pptx suffixes.

- **Adobe Portable Document Format:** This is a format originally specified by Adobe for sharing documents. Called Portable Document Format or PDF for short, these files end in .pdf. Clearly, it is not from Microsoft nor is it a part of the Microsoft Office Suite, but it is widely used by businesses to share documents that are not intended for revision.

For everything Microsoft Office, check out *Office 2013 For Dummies* or *Office 2010 For Dummies,* by Wallace Wang (Wiley).

The newest versions of Microsoft Office files are appended with .docx, .xlsx, and .pptx. Most of the mobile office apps, including Polaris, can work with the older and newer formats. In general, however, more applications work with the older versions. You don't give up much by using the older version, but you do gain more compatibility with other people who aren't as current. Over time, the discrepancies become less of an issue as more people update to the newer format.

If you skip this section and don't have any software on your phone to open Office documents, you won't be able to read any Office documents attached to messages you receive on your phone. On the other hand, you may not want to be able to look at the documents until you're in the office.

Accessing the Office files

The next challenge in working with Office files is keeping track of the most recent version of whatever file you're working on. In the most basic scenario, you're working on a Microsoft Office file yourself. If you have a desktop PC, you're probably accustomed to transferring files among different machines if you want to work on them in different locations, such as home or the office. Here are your traditional options:

- ✔ **Removable media:** You use a thumb drive or disc to move the file from one PC to another.

- ✔ **E-mail:** You e-mail the file from one PC to another.

- ✔ **Server:** You save a copy of your file from the first PC on a server that you can access from both the first and second PC. This includes the ubiquitous Cloud offerings you considered when you were first setting up your phone.

The first option is mostly impractical. Your Galaxy S6 phone doesn't have a disc drive or a USB port for a thumb drive. You can find on the Internet adapters that plug into the micro-USB on the phone on one side and offer a female USB port on the other side for thumb drives. It can work, but this is a hassle for Office files that are changing all the time.

This leaves you with the second two options: using e-mail or using a server. Sending and receiving Microsoft Office files as attachments with text or e-mail messages is probably old hat by now. You receive the e-mail, download the attachment, and work away. When you're done, you save the file to work on later, or you send it back to your PC. I go into more detail about this process later in this chapter.

The server option calls for a little more explanation. By the way, there are two fancy terms for this kind of computing. The first one is *cloud storage*. Cloud storage is a service that is provided, usually for free for basic services, from a number of companies. Hopefully, you took my advice in Chapter 1 and have signed up for at least one of these services.

There is also an idea called a *VPN*, or virtual private network. This is fairly common in businesses. It's similar to cloud computing, but the "cloud" in this case is the company's computer system.

Using Cloud storage

The issue of file sharing is integral to getting the most out of the Office applications on your phone. To make it really work, the more Office files you store on the server, the better. It will do you little good if the files you want to see and change are safely stored on your PC, which you dutifully powered off to save energy.

The principle behind this service is that the server appears to your PC and your phone as if it were a drive or memory card directly connected to your machine. If you know how to copy files from, say, your PC hard drive to a USB thumb drive, you can use a server in the Cloud. You might not know which computer is doing the processing when you open a file. It could be your phone; it could also be a computer on the company network or the server itself. Ultimately, you don't really care as long as it works fast and does what you want.

When you tap a filename that appears on your phone (which is comparable to double-clicking a filename on your PC), the file opens, and you can read and edit it.

When you're done reading or editing, the file gets saved, secure and accessible, until the next time you want to do something to it. This is the essence of the Cloud, and your phone can happily participate.

Your wireless carrier may offer this service to you, but it is also available from Dropbox, Amazon Cloud Drive, Google Drive, and Microsoft OneDrive.

Using a VPN

The idea behind a VPN is that your phone and the company's data network set up a secret password. They know it's you because you entered your password. Any evildoers who see your information exchanges would see gibberish. Only your phone and the company computers know how to unscramble the gibberish.

As with checking your business e-mail on your phone, make sure that your company is okay with you accessing files this way. In many cases, it's okay, but some companies have security policies that simply don't let you (or just anyone) have access to every piece of data that the company has ever had while you could be sitting in a competitor's office.

Reading and Editing Files with Your Phone

Polaris
Office

As I mentioned earlier, there are several mobile apps for Android phones that let you be productive while on the road. Here, I take a look at the Polaris Office app to show you some of its capabilities. You can obtain Polaris Office from the Play Store for free if it's not already installed on your phone, as seen in Figure 14-1.

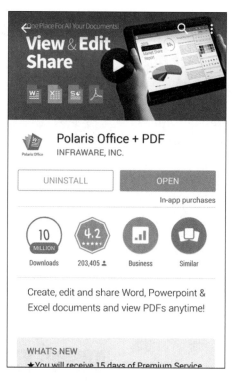

Figure 14-1: The Polaris Office page in the Google Play Store.

Creating a document

To introduce the process, I show you how to create a document on your phone:

1. **On your phone, open the App list and tap the Polaris Office icon.**

   You need to create an account and agree to the End User License Agreement. After you do, the Home screen (shown in Figure 14-2) appears.

   This is the image that you will see first when you open this app.

2. **Tap the icon with the plus sign in the red circle.**

   This is the one with the text balloon that says Create a new document (Hey, this *is* a Dummies book). The options are presented in Figure 14-3.

Figure 14-2: The Polaris Home screen on your phone.

3. **Tap the icon for the file type you wish to create.**

The options are:

- *Text:* Open a blank sheet for a very simple document.
- *Slide:* Open a blank presentation in PowerPoint format (.ppt).
- *Sheet:* Open a blank spreadsheet in Excel spreadsheet format (.xls).
- *Word:* Open a blank sheet in Word format (.doc) or text if it is a very simple document.

Tapping the icon of your choice brings up a screen like that shown in Figure 14-4 — a Word document that describes how to use the app. The details of editing are described in this document.

Figure 14-3: New document options.

4. Tap the Word icon in the upper-left corner to save the document.

Doing so brings up the options shown in Figure 14-5.

In this case, your only option is to save this file in your phone's memory.

5. To save a document, tap the diskette icon in the upper left.

The diskette might indeed be a relic of earlier PC technology, but it's still widely used as an icon to mean Save.

Your phone saves the document on your phone in the format you selected.

You follow the same basic process for files in the other formats. If you want to keep this file on your phone forever, you're set. However, read on if you want to do something more with it.

Word icon
The
I
On
1 2 3 4 5 6 7 8 9 0
Q W E R T Y U I O P
A S D F G H J K L
Z X C V B N M
Sym
English(US)

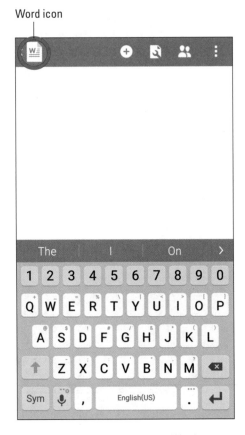

Figure 14-4: Viewing your Polaris Word document on your phone.

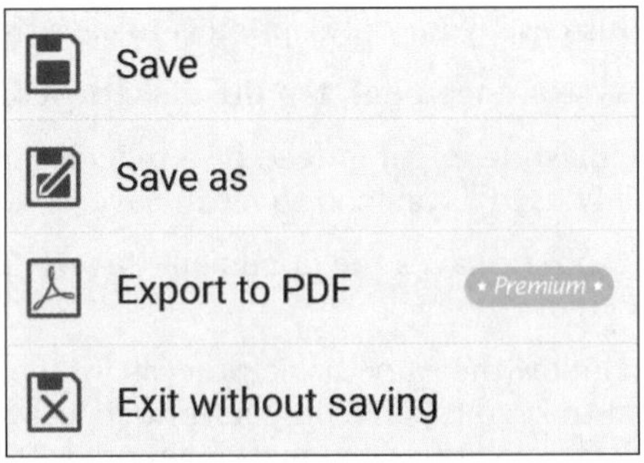
Save
Save as
Export to PDF
Premium
Exit without saving

Figure 14-5: The Save As option on the Polaris My Docs page.

Sending an Office file as an attachment

After a file is saved, it's safe to send it to your home PC or to another PC. When you're ready to e-mail the document to your PC or to another PC, do the following:

1. **Return to the Home page that says My Documents.**

   You see all the documents stored on your phone as seen in Figure 14-6. Here you see my effort to displace *The Great Gatsby* as required reading in the high schools across the country. Imagine I have done some editing, and now it is time to send it to the editor.

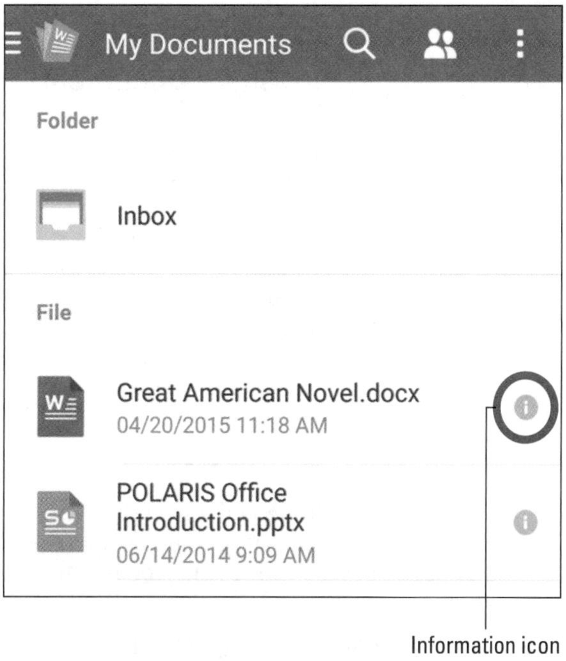

Information icon

Figure 14-6: Office files on my phone.

2. **Tap the information icon to the right of the document.**

   You have several choices from the resulting pop-up screen, as shown in Figure 14-7. In this case, we want to share it.

3. **Tap the Share option.**

   Four options appear, as seen in Figure 14-8.

Figure 14-7: Share pop-up.

Figure 14-8: Share options.

4. **Tap the Attach to E-mail option.**

   If this is the first time you have used e-mail with Polaris, it may ask you which e-mail app you want to use. The next step is to bring up a blank e-mail screen with your document automatically included as an attachment.

5. **Type an e-mail address (probably from your contact list) in the To text box and add a subject and a message if you want.**

   If you want the document on your PC, simply address it to yourself.

6. **Tap Send.**

   The miracle of wireless communication zips the document off to the intended recipient.

The process is the same for Word-, Excel-, and PowerPoint-formatted documents.

The formatting of the document on your phone might not be exactly the same as it is when it reappears on your PC. Save yourself time and don't try to format a document on your Galaxy S6 phone.

Managing Office documents with a server

Regardless of how you send an Office file to or from your phone, the creation and editing steps are the same. The steps in the preceding section cover the basics. You can do basic editing with the simplified icons at the bottom of the screen.

The next step is to work with files stored on a server. As I mention earlier, you can work with any server. The easiest way to describe the process is to start from the server's point of view.

Suppose you're writing the Great American Novel on your PC, but then you want to put it on your phone so you can review it and maybe make some minor edits. The first thing you do is move the file to your Dropbox server from your PC. Figure 14-9 is what it looks like on your desktop PC.

This should look familiar. Here are the steps to view and edit this document on your phone:

1. **Tap the Dropbox icon.**

   Doing so brings up the screen shown in Figure 14-9.

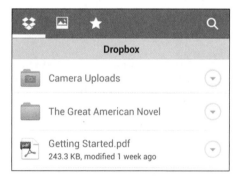

Figure 14-9: Dropbox on a PC.

2. **Tap the folder that represents the folder containing the desired file.**

   In this case, it's the folder titled *Great American Novel.*

3. **Tap the filename to open the file.**

   The image in Figure 14-10 shows my novel so far. (I still have some work to do on this, but I am off to a good start.)

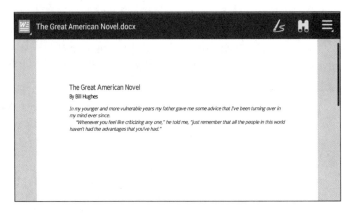

The Great American Novel.docx

The Great American Novel
By Bill Hughes

In my younger and more vulnerable years my father gave me some advice that I've been turning over in my mind ever since.
"Whenever you feel like criticizing any one," he told me, "just remember that all the people in this world haven't had the advantages that you've had."

Figure 14-10: The document open in Polaris.

4. **Read and/or edit the file as desired.**

5. **When you're done, tap the Word icon.**

   Doing so brings up options, including Save.

6. **Tap Save.**

   This saves any changes you've made back to the file — which is stored on DropBox.

This process works with any Microsoft Office file format. It works with cloud servers other than Dropbox too. It can work the same way with your VPN at the office. The tools are there for you to use.

Talking with S-Voice

In This Chapter

▶ Telling your phone to make a call

▶ Dictating an e-mail or text

▶ Doing a web search without typing

▶ Speaking to Facebook

*E*very science fiction movie worth its salt predicts a world where we speak to computers rather than typing in data. Normal conversation is about 150 words per minute, whereas even an expert typist can only type at 90 words per minute. More important, talking is the most basic form of communication. The reality is that there are many technical obstacles to having voice recognition match the ideal of a computer perfectly interpreting the meaning of any user's verbal instructions.

That does not stop us from having some fun in the meantime, however! S-Voice, an app that comes with the Galaxy S6, can handle some basic functions on your phone, including making a phone call, sending an e-mail or a text, searching the Internet, or even updating your Facebook status.

ıl Ludwig.

CANCEL

Hi Ludwig.

You may love this capability, or you may find it to be a gimmick and not very useful. Either way, you can have some fun with this.

Look Ma! No Hands!

To get started, all you need to do is tap the S-Voice icon. After you agree to the terms, including a pinky swear that you will use this app responsibly when you are driving, you get the pop-up screen shown in Figure 15-1.

Figure 15-1: The S-Voice Start screen.

Now ask for what you want. Say you want to call someone.

In the old days, high-end mobile phones would require you to train the voice-recognition software to understand the basics of how you speak. No more. Just tell it who you want to call, by saying, "Call Bill."

Be ready. In just a moment, it calls Bill. It's that easy.

However, if you know several people named Bill, your phone asks you (in a semi-pleasant female voice) which "Bill" you want to call.

You may have heard of "Siri" on the iPhone. Siri responds to questions you ask it. The S-Voice app is the same idea, only it responds to the name "Galaxy."

I refer to the application as S-Voice for the rest of the chapter. Using the name "Galaxy" creates too much confusion between the app and the phone itself.

If you want to call Bill Boyce, a person from your contact list, say "Call Bill Boyce." Within a moment, his phone rings.

A few pointers for using S-Voice. If you hesitate, S-Voice assumes that you are not ready to talk and goes into a sleep mode. To wake it up, just say "Hi, Galaxy." It wakes up, ready to resume listening.

I get to the list of things that work with S-Voice soon. For now, try a few of its simple-yet-valuable capabilities.

Dictating a Text

To send a text, say the words, "Send a text." Done. You see the word appear in the S-Voice box at the bottom of the page as seen in Figure 15-2.

Send a text

Figure 15-2: The S-Voice texting response box.

S-Voice asks you, "Who would you like to message?" Give the name. It looks up their number from your contact list. In Figure 15-3, I have said the name "Ludwig van Beethoven."

Figure 15-3: The S-Voice displays the name.

S-Voice then asks you for your message. Go ahead and say what you would have typed.

S-Voice then converts your words into a message. It displays what it thinks you said in a box similar to the box shown in Figure 15-4.

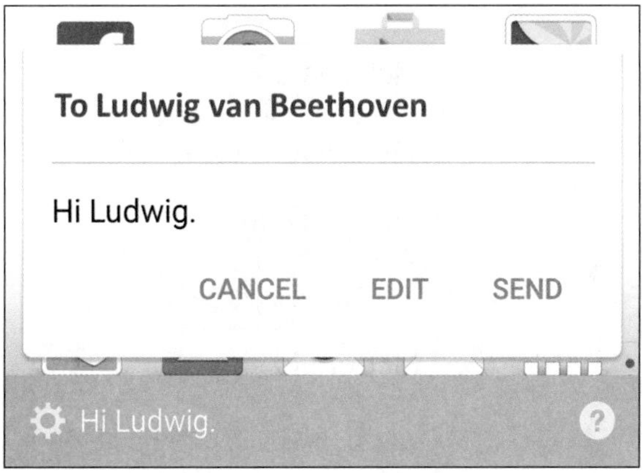

Figure 15-4: The S-Voice text box ready to go.

Read it before you send it. If it is correct, just say "Send" and off it goes. If it's incorrect, you can say "Cancel," and it won't send that message. You can then try again.

Preparing to Work with S-Voice

Texting is a straightforward example, but it is just one of the tasks S-Voice can do for you. You can ask S-Voice to do all kinds of things on your phone. Some examples include:

- Telling you the time
- Setting an alarm

✔ Turning Wi-Fi on or off

✔ Telling you the weather forecast

✔ Setting a countdown timer

✔ Recording your voice

✔ Opening an app

✔ Playing a playlist

✔ Adding an appointment to your schedule

✔ Finding a local restaurant, store, or public location

✔ Navigating to an address or location

All you need to do is ask, and S-Voice does a good job finding what you want. For example, you can ask for a nearby McDonald's, and S-Voice comes back with some options, as shown in Figure 15-5.

Figure 15-5: S-Voice options on a location.

Then you can ask it for directions to the McDonald's you choose. This request causes S-Voice to hand you over to your preferred navigation application, bringing up a screen like the one shown in Figure 15-6.

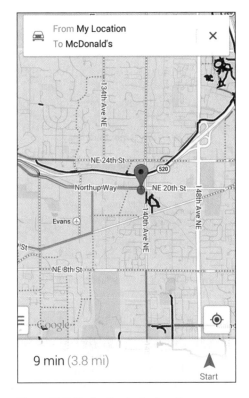

Figure 15-6: Navigation to the location you requested.

Now all you need to do is drive there safely and enjoy!

Searching the Web by Voice

These functions so far are pretty darn cool, but they get better. S-Voice has the ability to do some research on your behalf. For example, say that you have a research project and want to know, "When was the War of 1812?" Ask S-Voice. It comes back with the answer shown in Figure 15-7.

Granted, S-Voice doesn't see the scathingly witty humor in this question. That's not to say that it has no sense of humor. Say to S-Voice, "This is a test." She comes back with the witty retort, "I hope that I do not forget everything I learned."

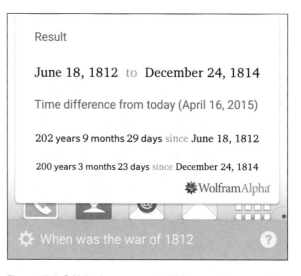

Figure 15-7: S-Voice's response to "When was the war of 1812?"

Changing Settings on S-Voice

As shown in Figure 15-8, you can change many settings on S-Voice. Rather than investigate all of them, I look at a few key ones.

The first of these examples changes the wake-up command. The default is "Hi, Galaxy." Boring. You can change it to any phrase with four or more syllables.

You may as well have some fun with this. S-Voice is your servant. You can name it anything, such as the name of your former gym teacher, a cheating partner, or the love of your life who got away. You get to call it what you want and tell it what to do. There is no one judging you (as long as they do not overhear you!).

Follow the directions in Set Wake-Up Command. It takes you to a new screen and asks you to record your voice saying what you want as your new wake-up command.

Another option you have is to have S-Voice available even when the screen is locked. That's right. The phone can be locked up tighter than Fort Knox, but you can get to everything by asking S-Voice to do it for you. If this worries you that someone could impersonate your voice, toggle "Wake up in secured lock" to the off position.

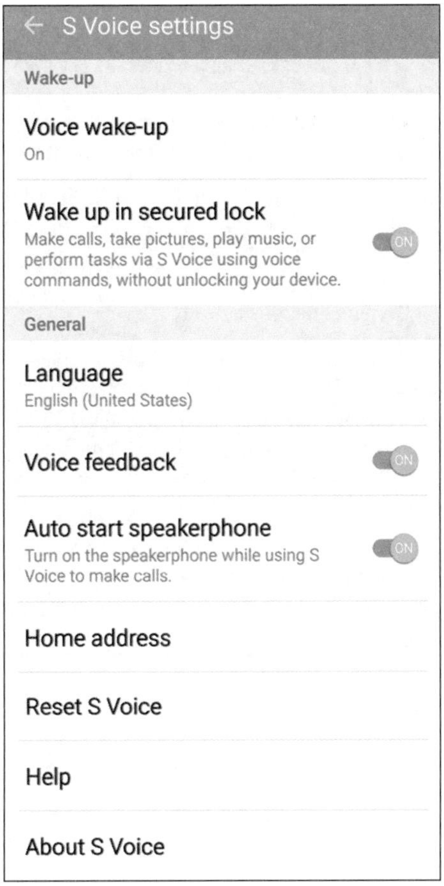

Figure 15-8: S-Voice settings.

Next, you have the choice to have S-Voice feedback from the female voice or not. If you want to get your responses with written pop-ups, toggle this option off.

When you make a call using S-Voice, the default setting is for that call to be conducted via speakerphone. This seems logical. If you are talking with your phone via speakerphone, you probably want to talk to your contact via speakerphone. If you prefer to have the call come up with you holding the phone to your ear, toggle this one off.

Finally, S-Voice would like to know your home address. That allows you to ask, "Navigate me Home." This only works if S-Voice knows where home is. Make sense?

A word about intelligent agents

Among computer scientists, S-Voice is called an *intelligent agent.*

S-Voice is a pretty darn good implementation of intelligent-agent technology. It's about as good as you can get when you're using many of the basic functions of your Galaxy S6. The list of things you can do with S-Voice includes a pretty long list of the primary capabilities.

Even so, the truth is that this technology is not perfected yet. If you don't want to use an intelligent agent until it's perfected, no one could blame you. Before you dismiss this function as a gimmick, however, here are a few things to think about:

- Normal speech communicates ideas at about 150 words per minute.

- A fast typist can type at 90 words per minute.

- In handwriting, most people can write 30 words per minute.

These data show that you and I may be better off if we can adjust our expectations of asking computers to do things for us by speaking to them. If you use S-Voice for standard commands, it performs remarkably fast and accurately. You will get to say to your grandkids that you were among the pioneers who used intelligent agents before it was mainstream.

As long as evil intelligent agent, HAL, from *2001: A Space Odyssey* never comes to pass, it's likely that this technology will become increasingly pervasive.

Part VI
The Part of Tens

Visit www.dummies.com/extras/samsunggalaxys6 for great Dummies content online.

In this part. . .

- Customize your phone to get the most out of it
- Protect your data if you lose your phone
- Avoid losing your phone in the first place
- Discover what features will be coming in future versions

Ten Ways to Make Your Phone Totally Yours

In This Chapter

▶ Getting the most out of your phone

▶ Checking out the extra cool features that make this phone so good

▶ Making a personal statement

A smartphone is a very personal device. From the moment you take it out of the box and strip off the packaging, you begin to make it yours. By the end of the first day, even though millions of your type of phone may have been sold, there's no other phone just like yours.

This is the case because of the phone calls you make, and because of all the options you can set on the phone and all the information you can share over the web. Your contacts, music files, downloaded videos, texts, and favorites make your phone a unique representation of who you are and what's important to you.

Even with all this "you" on your phone, this chapter covers ten ways to further customize your phone beyond what you have already explored. Some of these suggestions involve accessories. Others involve settings and configurations. All are worth considering.

Using a Bluetooth Speaker

In just a matter of a couple of years, Bluetooth speakers have gone from an interesting (and expensive) option to a mainstream one. Prices have come down quickly and the variety of designs for the speakers has grown dramatically. In all cases, you get the benefit of being able to play your music on your phone without the inconvenience of having headphones. You also get a speakerphone, although the quality of the audio can vary dramatically from Bluetooth speaker to Bluetooth speaker.

This accessory is best purchased in a brick and mortar store where you can listen to a variety of choices. Although syncing with a number of speaker choices can be tedious, it's the only way you'll know if a particular Bluetooth speaker meets your needs.

Although sound quality is essential, the folks in the industrial-design department have been having a lot of fun coming up with ways for the Bluetooth speaker to look. Figure 12-3 back in Chapter 12 shows the sleek and sexy Soen Audio Transit.

Figure 16-1 shows another catchy design with the Om/One levitating speaker.

Figure 16-1: Om/One Bluetooth speaker.

Levitating is a great gimmick to catch the attention of the people walking by. The levitating speaker design also has positive implications for sound reproduction. Without contacting anything, there is little chance for interference.

The Audiovox 808 Bluetooth speaker is shaped like a can. (See Figure 16-2).

Figure 16-2: Audiovox 808 Bluetooth speakers.

There is no shortage of imagination when it comes to Bluetooth. Be sure to consider all your options.

Cruising in the Car

You may have gotten the idea that I am concerned about your safety when you're using your phone. True, but I'm also concerned with *my* safety when you're using your phone. I would like you to have a Bluetooth speaker in your car when driving in my neighborhood, if you please.

Some cars have a built-in Bluetooth speaker that connects to a microphone somewhere on the dash as well as to your car speakers. It's smart enough to sense when there's an incoming call and mutes your music in response.

If you don't have such a set-up, there are lots of good options for car speakers. An example is seen in Figure 16-3.

A closely related accessory is a car mount. A car mount will hold your phone in a place you can easily observe as you drive. The mount attaches to an air vent, the dashboard, or the windshield. You could always put your phone on the seat next to you, but that's for amateurs. Instead, offer your phone a place of honor with a car docking station. It makes accessing your phone while you drive safer and easier. Some see getting a car mount as a luxury, but my view is that if you need to upgrade your navigation software, you need a vehicle mount.

Figure 16-3: Bluetooth car speaker.

Be sure to put away the docking station when you park. Even an empty docking station is a lure for a thief.

Figure 16-4 shows the Samsung Vehicle Navigation Mount. It costs about $100, and you can get it at your carrier's store, RadioShack, Best Buy, or online at Amazon.com. This includes a wireless charging pad.

Figure 16-4: The Samsung Vehicle Navigation Mount.

There are also more economical vehicle mounts that are available that do not include a wireless charging pad. An example from Slipgrip is seen in Figure 16-5. It costs closer to $30.

Figure 16-5: A SlipGrip vehicle mount.

This version is special because it is specifically designed to work with larger protective cases. It can be a hassle to have to remove the protective case from your phone to insert it in a vehicle mount. In addition to a car mount, SlipGrip also offers a mount for your bicycle.

When shopping for a car mount or a bike mount, be sure to consider the extra girth associated with a case. If you do not use a case (which is a mistake), you just need to be sure that the mount is compatible with a Galaxy S6. If you have a case on your phone (which is anything but a mistake), be sure the mount will work with the Galaxy S6 *and* the case.

Considering Wireless Charging Mats

Those industrial designers have certainly gone crazy with Bluetooth speakers. They have also been having a field day on wireless charging options. As mentioned, the Samsung Vehicle Navigation Mount seen in Figure 16-4 has a built-in charger.

Most wireless charging mats are designed with the idea that you can place you phone on the mat and the technology will do the rest. You can get a standard Samsung wireless charging pad, as seen in Figure 16-6, for about $50.

They also make them so that the phone can stand upright. The nice folks at Ikea have recently had some good press by building wireless charging capability into their furniture. Look for more options going forward!

Figure 16-6: A Samsung wireless charging pad.

Your Phone Is Watching You

One of the biggest drains on your battery is the backlight on your screen. Older, dumber smartphones have a preset time when they automatically shut off. On those phones, you need to push a button to bring the screen back to life.

You, on the other hand, had the foresight and wisdom to buy a Samsung Galaxy S6 that has Smart Stay. If the front-facing camera recognizes your pretty/handsome face, it keeps the light on as long as you are looking at the screen.

To turn this option on, go to Settings and open up the Display and Wallpaper settings. Turn Smart Stay on and you are ready to rock and roll.

Making a Statement with Wraps

The Samsung Galaxy S6 is attractive, but if you want to spruce it up even more, you can get a wrapping (such as from Skinit; www.skinit.com). There are designs to express more of what is important to you. As a side benefit, they can protect your phone from minor scratches.

Figure 16-7 shows some design options for a skin. It comes with cut-outs for speakers, plugs, microphones, and cameras specifically for the Galaxy S6. Putting the skin on is similar to putting on a decal, although it has a little give in the material to make positioning easier. The skin material and adhesive is super-high-tech and has enough give to allow klutzes like me (who struggle with placing regular decals) to fit the nooks and crannies of the phone like an expert.

If you're not crazy about their designs, you can make your own with images of your own choosing. Just be sure that you have the rights to use the images!

Figure 16-7: Some sample wrap designs.

You Look Mahvelous: Custom Screen Images

In addition to the shortcuts on your extended Home screen, you can also customize the images that are behind the screen. You can change the background to one of three options:

- ✓ Choose a neutral background image (similar to the backgrounds on many PCs) from the Wallpaper Gallery. Figure 16-8 shows a selection of background images that are standard on your phone.

- ✓ Any picture from your Gallery can be virtually stretched across the seven screens of your Home page. (Read more about the Gallery in Chapter 9.)

- ✓ Opt for a "theme" that changes the background and fonts.

The pictures from your Gallery and the Wallpaper Gallery are images that you can set by pressing and holding the Home screen. In a moment, you see icons appear. Select Wallpapers and pick the image you want.

The themes take it to a different level. In addition to the background, the phone will change the fonts and many of the basic icons. We see the default theme in Figure 16-9.

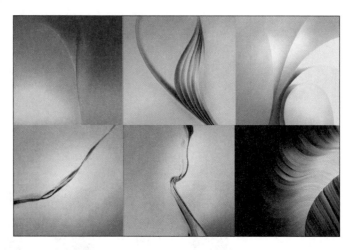

Figure 16-8: Standard wallpaper sample image.

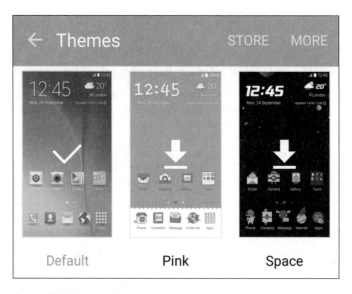

Figure 16-9: Theme options.

There are also a few samples that come on your phone. You may be a "Pink" kind of person or a "Space" nut. If these options are not to your taste, tap the Store link at the top of the page to see a range of options. If you do not see one you like today, be sure to check back as developers are adding new themes all the time.

Empowering Power Savings

Imagine that you are flying on a short hop from Smallville to Littleton. You are about to take off when air traffic control tells you that you need to wait on the tarmac. Unfortunately, you are low on battery. The pilot says that it is OK to use your mobile phone.

Because you do not know how long this will take, you pull out your phone, go to Settings, and tap Battery. From here, you put it in "Power Savings Mode." This slows down a lot of cool features. For example, it dims the screen, slows the processors and mobile data speeds, and kills the vibration mode. This extends the battery life with minor sacrifices to what you can do with your phone. The apps all run, but perhaps not as fast.

Then the pilot says that your plane has a flat tire, the maintenance crew went home, and you could be sitting there for hours.

This time you open Settings, tap Battery, and put your phone in Ultra Power Savings Mode. Your beautiful, powerful smartphone has instantly turned itself into a dumb feature phone. You won't be able to watch a full-length feature film. However, you now have enough battery to make and take phone calls and text messages for hours. This is not an exact science and your mileage may vary, but switching to this mode can multiply the time your smartphone can operate as a phone by eight to ten times.

Setting Do Not Disturb Options

Mobile phones are great. They allow us to be available all the time.

Mobile phones stink. They require us to be available all the time. I never get any downtime.

If you are a member of the second school of thought, your Galaxy S6 has a solution for you. You can go to Settings, select Sounds and Notifications, and tap Do Not Disturb. This turns off the ringer and all notifications until you turn notifications back on. You are in total control.

But what if you are sometimes forgetful and neglect to turn the phone back on? No need to worry. You have a number of options that you can easily program into your phone.

First, you can set a schedule for Do Not Disturb. You could set it so that it will not bother you during sleeping hours. Figure 16-10 shows the set schedule so that this phone will not be disturbed from 10 p.m. to 7 a.m. seven days a week. The phone will not make a peep at night.

Hold on. What if I use my phone as my alarm clock? No problem. Tap the link to Allow exceptions. That takes you to a page as seen in Figure 16-11.

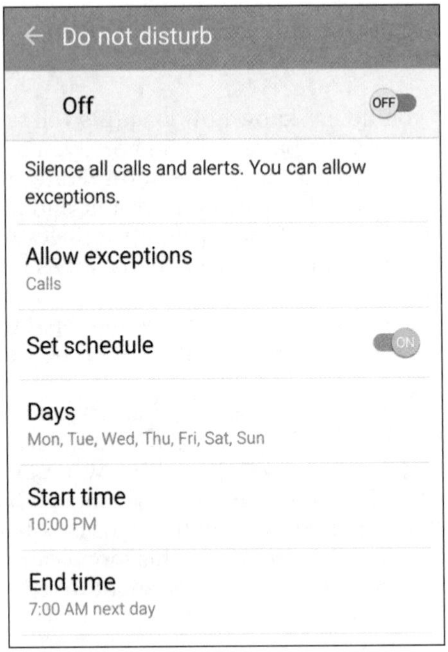

Figure 16-10: Schedule for Do Not Disturb.

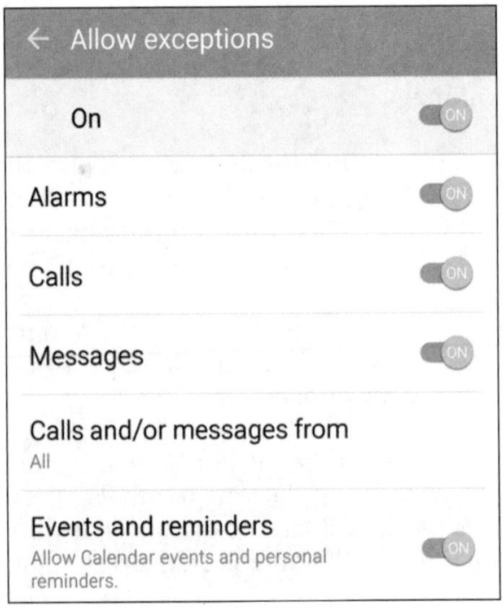

Figure 16-11: Do Not Disturb exceptions.

You have the choice to allow alarms. Toggle that option on and you will get your wakeup alarm. Of course, if you toggle on all the exceptions as is seen in Figure 16-11, you defeat the whole purpose of the Do Not Disturb capability. If you limit your Favorites to a few people, such as close family members, you can let in their calls and keep out any solicitors that have guessed your number. That sounds like a great plan.

Wearing Wearables

Wearables are a class of mobile accessories that have been getting a lot of attention lately. For the most part, they are connected via Bluetooth and typically worn as a watch, although there are some sensors that you can wear in athletic shoes. Samsung offers its wearables under the brand name Gear. These are seen in figure 16-12.

Figure 16-12: Samsung Gear wearables.

In addition to telling the time, these wearables give you notifications, weather, texts, and track some relevant information like the amount of exercise you've done.

Daydreaming While You Work

Readers of a certain age will remember the problem with CRT screens that would have a problem with burn-in. If a screen displayed the same image too long, the phosphor would never fully turn off, showing you a ghost image. This was a particular problem with the first ATMs. The solution was screen-savers that would usually show some image moving around the screen.

Screen burn is less of an issue with modern LCD screens, but we still like screensavers. Besides, this is not an issue with your phone because the screen will shut off. Shutting off saves battery life and gives you an opportunity to require a security code to be entered.

Saving power is good when you are running on the battery, but this is less of an issue if you are recharging the battery and plan to be connected for a lengthy time. Under these circumstances, you can have an old school screensaver by putting your phone into Daydream mode.

You enable Daydream mode by going to Settings, selecting the Display and Wallpaper option, and turning Daydream to the on setting. This will bring up the options seen in Figure 16-13.

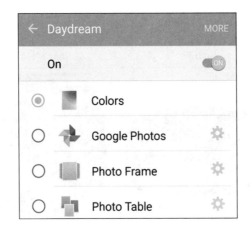

Figure 16-13: Daydream options.

These options allow you to set up a screensaver with bright colors or to randomly display photos. Rather than having a digital photo display that would cost over $100, your phone can do it all when it is being charged. Sweet!

If these options do not thrill you, go to the Play Store and search on Daydreams. You can download apps that display interesting things like the time, motivational quotations, battery charging status, weather forecasts, news, or jokes.

17

Ten Ways to Make Your Phone Secure

In This Chapter

▶ Keeping your phone in one piece

▶ Avoiding losing your phone in the first place

▶ Protecting yourself if you do lose your phone

*B*ack in the "old" days, it sure was frustrating to have your regular-feature phone lost or stolen. You would lose all your contacts, call history, and texts. Even if you backed up all of your contacts, you would have to re-enter them in your new phone. What a hassle.

The good news is that your smartphone saves all your contacts on your e-mail accounts. The bad news is that, unless you take some steps outlined in this chapter, evildoers could conceivably drain your bank account, get you fired, or even have you arrested.

Do I have your attention? Think of what would happen if someone were to get access to your PC at home or at work. He or she could wreak havoc on your life.

A malevolent prankster could send an e-mail from your work e-mail address under your name. It could be a rude note to the head of your company. It could give phony information about a supposedly imminent financial collapse of your company to the local newspaper. It could be a threat to the U.S. president, generating a visit from the Secret Service.

22%

Here's the deal: If you have done anything with your smartphone as described in this book past Chapter 3, I expect you'll want to take steps to protect your smartphone. This is the burden of having a well-connected device. Fortunately, most of the steps are simple and straightforward.

Use a Good Case and Screen Cover

The Samsung Galaxy S6 is sleek and beautiful. The Galaxy S6 Edge has a really cool design that draws attention from people walking by. Plus, the front is made of Gorilla Glass from Corning. This stuff is super-durable and scratch-resistant.

So why am I telling you to cover this all up? It's like buying a fancy dress for a prom or wedding and wearing a coat all night. Yup. It's necessary for safe mobile computing.

Speaking from personal experience, dropping a Galaxy phone on concrete can break the glass and some of the innards. This can happen if you simply keep your phone in a pocket.

There are lots of choices for cases. The most popular are made of silicone, plastic, or leather. There are different styles that meet your needs from many manufacturers. Otterbox is a brand that makes a series of cases for multiple levels of protection. The Defender Series for the Galaxy S6, its highest level of protection, is seen in black in Figure 17-1. You can get other colors if you prefer.

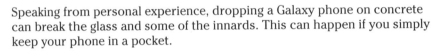

Figure 17-1: Otterbox cases for the Samsung Galaxy S6.

I am told by the cooler members of my clan that wearing the belt clip is the modern equivalent of wearing a pocket protector.

The S6 Edge offers case makers a special challenge to both display the full screen and protect the dickens out of the phone. Spigen offers an attractive and effective solution as seen in Figure 17-2.

Figure 17-2: Spigen case for the Samsung Galaxy S6 Edge.

You don't just use a good case so you can hand off a clean used phone to the next lucky owner. A case makes it a little less likely that you will lose your phone. Your Galaxy S6 in its naked form is shiny glass and metal, which are slippery. Cases tend to have a higher coefficient of friction.

More significantly, a case protects your phone against damage. If your phone is damaged, you have to mail it or bring it to a repair shop. The problem is that many people who bring their phones in for repair don't wipe the personal information off their devices. You really hope that the repair shop can pop off the broken piece, pop on a new one, and send you on your way. It's rarely that easy. Typically, you need to leave your phone in the hands of strangers for some period of time. For the duration of the repair, said strangers have access to the information on your phone.

The good news is that most workers who repair phones are professional and will probably delete any information from the phone before they start fixing it. (And hopefully you recently backed up all your smartphone files.)

However, are you sure that you want to trust the professionalism of a stranger? Also, do you really want the hassle of getting a new phone?

Probably not, so invest in a good case and screen cover. There are many options for different manufacturers of cases. Be sure to shop around to come up with the ideal combination of protection and style right for you.

Put It on Lock Down

The most basic effort you can take to protect your phone is to put some kind of a screen lock on your phone. If you're connected to a corporate network, the company may have a policy that specifies what you must do to access your corporate network. Otherwise you have six choices, listed here in increasing degrees of security:

- Unlock with a simple swipe across the screen
- Unlock with a pattern that you swipe on the screen
- Unlock with a PIN
- Unlock with a password
- Unlock with your fingerprint
- Encrypt everything on your phone and unlock with your fingerprint

You can select any of the first five of these options in the Lock Screen option in Settings. Encrypting everything on your phone (the sixth listed option) has some serious implications, so I describe it in more detail later in the chapter, in the "Encrypt Your Device" section.

If you want to choose one of the first five options, here's what you do:

1. **Tap the Settings icon.**

   This should be old hat by now.

2. **Tap the Lock Screen and Security link.**

   This brings up the options seen in Figure 17-3. You set some of the options mentioned above from this page and others when you follow the next instruction. This can be a little confusing, but bear with me while we explain your options and tell you where to go.

3. **Tap the Screen Lock Type link.**

   This brings up the options seen in Figure 17-4. Each option prompts you through what it needs before establishing your security selection.

 For reasons that sort of make sense, your phone uses some terminology that can be confusing. To clarify, the term *Screen Lock* is an option you can select to prevent unauthorized users from getting into your phone. The term *Lock Screen* is short for the action of locking your screen or enabling the Screen Lock option.

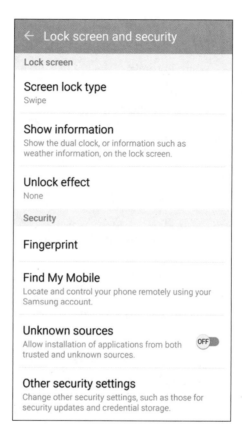

Figure 17-3: The Lock Screen and Security options.

Preparing for your Screen Lock option

Regardless of what screen lock you choose, I recommend that you have ready the following choices at hand:

- A PIN
- A password
- An unlock pattern
- A preference regarding whether you would like to use a PIN, password, or fingerprint

To clarify definitions, a *PIN* is a series of numbers. In this case, the PIN is four digits. A *password* is a series of numbers, upper- and lowercase letters, and sometimes special characters, and is typically longer than four characters. A PIN is pretty secure, but a password is usually more secure. Have them both ready, but decide which one you would prefer to use.

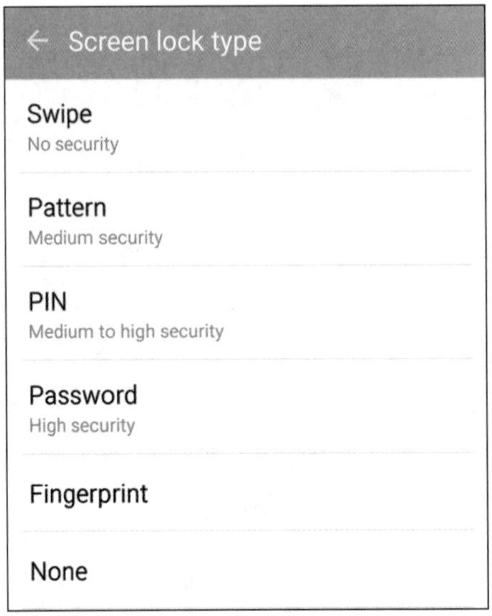

← Screen lock type

Swipe
No security

Pattern
Medium security

PIN
Medium to high security

Password
High security

Fingerprint

None

Figure 17-4: The Screen Lock options.

Selecting among the Screen Lock options

The first option, unlocking your phone with a swipe, fools exactly no one and doesn't slow anyone down. Rather than just having the Home screen appear, your phone tells you to swipe your finger on the screen to get to the Home screen. This is about as secure as waving at an intruder. Let's keep going.

I recommend drawing out a pattern as the minimum screen-lock option. This is quick and easy. Tap the Pattern option on the screen seen in Figure 17-4 to get started. The phone asks you to enter your pattern, and then asks you to enter it again. It then asks you to enter a PIN in case you forget your pattern.

The unlock pattern is a design that you draw with your finger on a nine-dot screen, as shown in Figure 17-5.

The image on the right in Figure 17-5 happens to include all nine dots. You do not need to use all the dots. The minimum number of dots you must touch is four. The upper limit is nine because you can only touch each dot once. As long as you can remember your pattern, feel free to be creative.

Be sure to use a PIN you can remember a long time from now. You only need this PIN if you forget your pattern. That is a very rare situation for most of us.

The next two options on the Screen Lock screen, PIN and Password, are more secure, but only as long as you avoid the obvious choices. If you insist upon using the PIN "0000" or "1111" or the word "password" as your password, don't waste your time. It's standard operating procedure within the typical

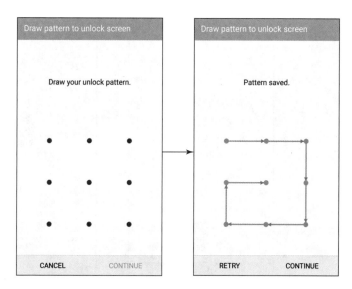

Figure 17-5: The unlock patterns: the blank screen and a sample pattern.

den of thieves to try these sequences first. That's because so many people use these obvious choices.

If, someday, you forget your pattern, your PIN, or your password, the only option is to do a complete reset of your phone back to original factory settings. In such a case, all your texts and stored files will be lost. Try to avoid this fate: Remember your pattern, PIN, or password.

Entering your fingerprint

If you want to access your phone using a fingerprint, here's what you do:

1. **Tap on the Fingerprint link in the Screen Lock Type page (Figure 17-4).**

   Here is a chance for confusion. If you tap Fingerprint on the Lock Screen and Security page (Figure 17-3), you will be taken to a screen that manages the fingerprints stored on the phone. What you want is the Fingerprint link from the Screen Lock Type page, which is shown in Figure 17-4. This will bring up the left image seen in Figure 17-6.

2. **Press and hold lightly the Home button repeatedly.**

   This brings up the screen seen on the right of Figure 17-6. Keep tapping until you reach 100%. The grayed out fingerprint in Figure 17-6 will turn completely blue and then you get a congratulations screen letting you know that you are at 100%.

3. **Enter the password you have ready.**

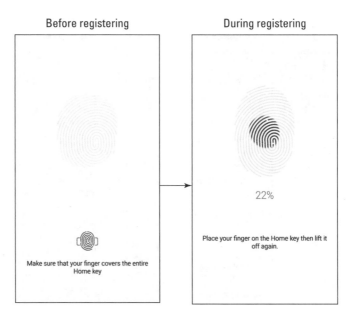

Figure 17-6: The Fingerprint registration screens.

Your fingerprint is now in memory. You can use it to unlock your phone or automatically enter your password for Samsung apps and PayPal. As time goes on, more and more applications will offer you the option of using your fingerprint instead of entering a password.

Even if you use your fingerprint, you must also enter a password. This is in case the phone is unable to recognize your fingerprint for some reason.

Encrypting is serious business, so I describe it in more detail in the next section.

Encrypt Your Device

This is the last options listed earlier for protecting your device. It's an exceptionally secure option: It scrambles every file on your phone into gibberish, which it rapidly descrambles when you need the information. This sounds great; in practice, however, there are some important considerations to think about.

First, all this scrambling and descrambling takes processing power away from other things, such as running the apps. The loss is hardly noticeable in most cases — your phone is awash in processing power — but you never know when it might come back to bite you.

WARNING!

After you encrypt your phone, you can never switch your phone back to non-encrypted use. With the Screen Lock options, you can use a PIN for a while, and then switch back to the pattern if you want. Not so with the encryption option. You will never, ever, ever, ever, get it back together.

If you encrypt your phone and then forget your password, your phone is *bricked*. In effect, its only future use would be in house construction as a brick; you won't be able to use it as a smartphone anymore.

If you're sure you're sure that encryption is for you, here are the steps:

1. **From the Lock Screen and Security screen (Figure 17-3), tap the Other Security Settings link.**

2. **Tap the Encrypt Phone link.**

   Doing so brings up the warning screen as shown in Figure 17-7.

← Encrypt phone

Encrypting your phone will encrypt accounts, settings, downloaded apps and their data, media and other files.

Connect your phone to a charger.

Charge the battery to at least 80% before encrypting your phone.

ABOUT THE ENCRYPTION PROCESS

Encryption may take more than an hour.

Interrupting the encryption process may result in the loss of some or all of your data.

To begin encryption:
- Your phone must be charging. (Keep your phone charging through the entire encryption process.)
- Your phone must be charged to at least 80%.

Once your phone is encrypted, you will need to enter a PIN or password to unlock and decrypt it every time you turn it on. Your unlock password should contain at least 6 characters, including at least 1 number.

ENCRYPT PHONE

Figure 17-7: The encryption warning screen.

As the screen says, have your password ready, the battery at 80 percent or higher, and an hour set aside when you don't need to use your phone. This time, the password must include at least six characters with at least one number. In this case, the password "password1" is also off the table. This is the second-most-common lousy password that thieves routinely try.

3. **Tap the Encrypt Device option.**

    And off it goes. . .

As Secure as Ft. Knox with Knox

It doesn't matter whether you bought the phone at a retail store or whether your company supplied it to you. The fact of the matter is that company data that resides on your phone belongs to your employer. You probably signed a document (now sitting in your HR file) that states that you agree with this arrangement.

This policy is necessary for the company because it has a financial and legal obligation to protect company data, particularly if it pertains to individual customers. Like it or not, this obligation trumps your sense of privacy over the phone you bought and (still) pay for. If this really gets under your skin, you can always carry two smartphones: one for business and one for personal use. This solves the problem, but it's a hassle.

However, there is a better way. Your Samsung Galaxy S6 comes with a capability called *Knox*. Knox logically divides your phone into two modes: one for business use and the other for your personal use. You tap an icon and you're in business mode. You tap another icon and you're in personal mode. Switching between the two is instant and Knox keeps the information from each mode separate.

This is a capability that is only of interest to you if your employer offers support for the service.

Knox comes with three capabilities for the employer:

- Security for the Android OS
- Limitations on the applications that access the business side of your phone
- Remote mobile-device management

This arrangement means that your employer can remotely control the business apps and potentially wipe the data on the business side at its discretion — but it has nothing to do with your personal information. The personal side remains your responsibility.

You may want to suggest to your company's IT department that it look into supporting Knox. Doing so can take a burden off your back.

Put Your Contact Number on the Screensaver

If you've ever found a lost phone, you may recall being faced with a dilemma with multiple choices. Do you:

    a. Take it to the local lost and found?

    b. Take it to a local retail store of the owner's carrier?

    c. Try to track down the rightful owner?

    d. Ignore it and not get involved?

Kudos if you do a, b, or c. If you chose c, you hope that the owner has not locked the screen. If you did option b, the store hopes that the screen isn't locked, in which case someone can look at phone calls and texts so as to contact the owner.

If your phone is the lost one and its screen is locked (as I hope yours is), this plan falls apart — unless you've cleverly put your contact information on the screen. That makes it easy to contact you.

Do not use your mobile phone number as your contact number. I hope I do not have to explain why.

Here are the steps to put your contact information on your Lock Screen:

1. **From the Lock Screen and Security screen (Figure 17-3), tap the Show Information tab.**

2. **Tap the Owner Information screen.**

   This brings up the options shown in Figure 17-8.

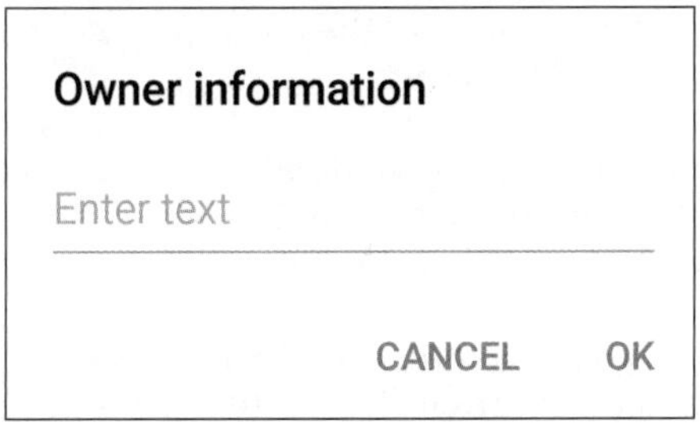

Owner information

Enter text

                CANCEL   OK

Figure 17-8: The Owner information pop-up.

3. **Type in the message of where to contact you if the phone is found.**

   I suggest something like, "Call 425-555-1212 if found." This message will scroll across your lock screen to get the attention of the Good Samaritan.

Now, before you think that you'll never lose your phone, I should point out some research from the firm InStat on this subject. They surveyed a panel of more than 2,000 mobile phone users about how often their phones had been lost or stolen: 64 percent had lost their phones at least once, yet 99 percent of those respondents believed that they were better than average at keeping track of their phones.

These results show that almost all of us think we are pretty good at keeping track of our phones. This same survey found that the respondents lost a phone (on average) every four years. With about 320 million phones in use across the United States, that means more than 200,000 phones "sprout legs and walk away" on a daily basis.

Make it easy to get your phone back by making your contact information accessible, but not so much that you put your privacy at risk.

Be Careful with Bluetooth

Back in Chapter 3, we looked at syncing your phone with Bluetooth devices. We did not mention the potential for security risk at that point. We do it now.

Some people are concerned that people with a radio scanner can listen in on their voice calls. This was possible, but not easy, in the early days of mobile phone use. Your Galaxy S6 can only use digital systems, so picking your conversation out of the air is practically impossible.

Some people are concerned that a radio scanner and a computer can pick up your data connection. It's not that simple. Maybe the NSA could get some of your data that way using complicated supercomputing algorithms, but it's much easier for thieves and pranksters to use wired communications to access the accounts of the folks who use "0000" as their PIN and "password" or "password1" as their password.

Perhaps the greatest vulnerability your phone faces is called *bluejacking*, which involves using some simple tricks to gain access to your phone via Bluetooth.

Do a test: The next time you're in a public place such as a coffee shop, a restaurant, or a train station, turn on Bluetooth. Tap the button that makes you visible to all Bluetooth devices, and then tap Scan. While your Bluetooth device is visible, you'll see all the other Bluetooth devices in your vicinity. You'll probably find lots of them. If not, try this at an airport. Wow!

If you were trying to pair with another Bluetooth device, you'd be prompted to see whether you're willing to accept connection to that device. In this case, you are not.

However, a hacker will see that you are open for pairing, and take this opportunity to use the PIN 0000 to make a connection. When you're actively pairing, your Bluetooth device won't accept an unknown device's offer to pair. But if your device is both unpaired and visible, hackers can fool your Bluetooth device and force a connection.

After a connection is established, all your information is available to the hackers to use as they will. Here are the steps to protect yourself:

- **Don't pair your phone to another Bluetooth device in a public place.** Believe it or not, crooks go to public places to look for phones in pairing mode. When they pair with a phone, they look for interesting data to steal. It would be nice if these people had more productive hobbies, like Parkour or searching for Bigfoot. However, as long as these folks are out there, it is safer to pair your Bluetooth device in a not-so-public place.

- **Make sure that you know the name of the device with which you want to pair.** You should only pair with that device. Decline if you are not sure or if other Bluetooth devices offer to connect.

- **Shorten the default time-out setting.** The default is that you will be visible for two minutes. However, you can go into the menu settings and change the option for Visible Time-out to whatever you want. Make this time shorter than two minutes. *Don't set it to Never Time Out.* This is like leaving the windows open and the keys in the ignition on your Cadillac Escalade. A shorter time of visibility means that you have to be vigilant for less time.

- **From time to time, check the names of the devices that are paired to your device.** If you don't recognize the name of a device, click the Settings icon to the right of the unfamiliar name and "unpair" it. Some damage may have been done by the intruder, but with any luck you've nipped it in the bud.

Here's an important point: When handled properly, Bluetooth is as secure as can be. However, a few mistakes can open you up to human vermin with more technical knowledge than common sense. Don't make those mistakes and you can safely enjoy this capability, knowing that all the data on your phone is safe.

Protect Against Malware

One of the main reasons application developers write apps for Android is that Google doesn't have an onerous pre-approval process for a new app to be placed in the Play Store. This is unlike the Apple App Store or Microsoft Windows Phone Store, where each derivation of an app must be validated.

Many developers prefer to avoid bureaucracy. At least in theory, this attracts more developers to do more stuff for Android phones.

However, this approach does expose users like you and me to the potential for malware that can, inadvertently or intentionally, do things that are not advertised. Some of these "things" may be minor annoyances, or they could really mess up your phone (for openers).

Market forces, in the form of negative feedback, are present to kill apps that are badly written or are meant to steal your private data. However, this informal safeguard works only after some poor soul has experienced problems — such as theft of personal information — and reported it.

Rather than simply avoiding new apps, you can download apps designed to protect the information on your phone. These are available from many of the firms that make antivirus software for your PC. Importantly, many of these antivirus applications are free. If you want a nicer interface and some enhanced features, you can pay a few dollars, but this is not necessary.

Examples include NG Mobile Security and Antivirus, Lookout Security and Antivirus, Kaspersky Mobile Security, and Norton Security Antivirus. If you have inadvertently downloaded an app that includes malicious software, these apps will stop that app.

Don't Download Apps from Just Anywhere

Another way to avoid malware is to download mobile software only from trustworthy websites. This book has focused exclusively on the Google Play Store. You can download Android apps for your phone from a number of other reputable sites, including PocketGear and MobiHand.

Keep in mind that these stores are always on the lookout to withdraw applications that include malicious software. Google uses an internally developed solution they call Bouncer to check for malicious software and remove it from the Play Store. Other mobile software distribution companies have their own approaches to addressing this problem. The problem is that policing malicious software is a hit-or-miss proposition.

As a rule, you should hesitate to download an Android application unless you know where it has been. You are safest if you restrict your app shopping to reputable companies. Be very skeptical of any other source of an Android application.

Rescue Your Phone When It Gets Lost

I talked about putting a message on the Lock Screen of your phone. There are also options that allow you to be more proactive than waiting for a Good Samaritan to reach out to your home phone or e-mail.

There are apps that help you find your phone. Here are a few several "lost it" scenarios and some possible solutions for your quandary:

You know that you lost your phone somewhere in your house. You would try calling your own number, but you had your phone set to Vibrate Only mode.

Remote Ring: By sending a text to your phone with the "right" code that you pre-programmed when you set up this service, your phone will ring on its loudest setting, even if you have the ringer set to Vibrate Only.

If you know that your phone is in your house, the accuracy of GPS isn't savvy enough to tell you whether it's lost between the seat cushions of your couch or in the pocket of your raincoat. That's where the Remote Ring feature comes in handy.

You lost your phone while traveling, and have no idea whether you left it in a taxi or at airport security.

Map Current Location: This feature allows you to track, within the accuracy of the GPS signal, the location of your phone. You need access the website of the company with which you arranged to provide this service, and it will show you (on a map) the rough location of your phone.

Here is where having an account with Samsung comes in handy. Hopefully, you signed up for a Samsung Account when you first got your phone. If you did, you are signed up for the Find My Mobile at `findmymobile.samsung.com`. Figure 17-9 shows the Find My Mobile PC screen.

All you need to do is get to a PC and sign in to your Samsung account. You can tell your phone to ring by clicking on Ring my device. You can have the PC bring up a map by clicking Locate my devices.

I suggest trying these out before you lose your phone the first time.

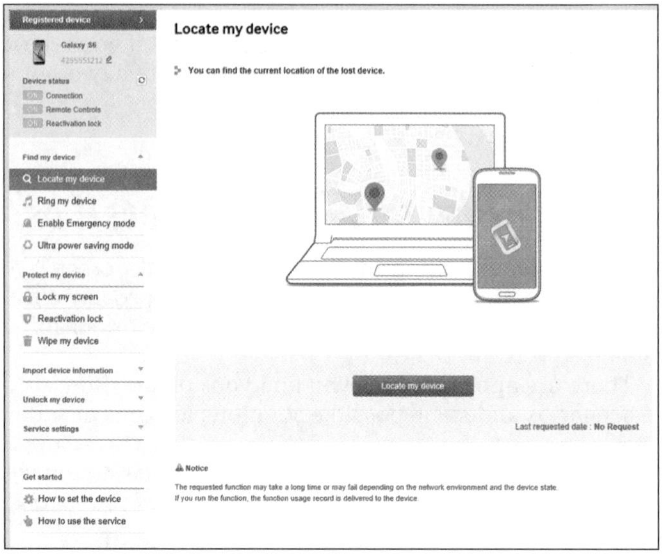

Figure 17-9: The Samsung Find My Mobile PC screen.

Wipe Your Device Clean

As a last-ditch option, you can use Find My Mobile to remotely disable your device or wipe it clean. Here are some of the possible scenarios:

You were robbed, and a thief has your phone.

Remote Lock: After your phone has been taken, this app allows you to create a four-digit PIN that, when sent to your phone from another mobile phone or a web page, locks down your phone. This capability is above and beyond the protection you get from your Screen Lock, and prevents further access to applications, phone, and data.

If you know that your phone was stolen — that is, not just lost — do *not* try to track down the thief yourself. Get the police involved and let them know that you have this service on your phone — and that you know where your phone is.

You are a very important executive or international spy. You stored important plans on your phone, and you have reason to believe that the "other side" has stolen your phone to acquire your secrets.

Remote Erase: Also known as Remote Wipe, this option resets the phone to its factory settings, wiping out all the information and settings on your phone.

You can't add Remote Erase *after* you've lost your phone. You must sign up for your Samsung service beforehand. It's not possible to remotely enable this capability to your phone. You need to have your phone in hand when you download and install either a lock app or a wipe app.

Ten Features to Look for Down the Road

*W*ith the power of your Samsung Galaxy S6 and the flexibility offered in Android applications development, it can be difficult to imagine that even more capabilities could be in the works. In spite of this, the following are ten features that would improve the usability and value of your Galaxy S6 phone.

Smarter Customer Care for Your Phone

You may not realize this, but your cellular carrier lives on pins and needles during the first few weeks after you get your new phone. This is the period when you can return your phone, no questions asked. Once you go past that date, you cannot cancel your contract without a lot of hassle on your part.

This is why, if you bring your phone back to the store reporting a problem, your carrier will tend to swap out your old phone for a brand new one.

Usually you'll just take the new phone and walk out with a big smile on your face. This outcome is good customer care for most products — but not necessarily good customer care for smartphones. The reason? One of the most common sources of trouble has nothing to do with the phone at all. The problem is the customer isn't using it right.

For example, you may have left your Wi-Fi and Bluetooth on all the time, causing your battery to drain too fast. You may have left your phone on your dashboard and "cooked" the battery. Or, through no fault of your own, you may have downloaded two badly written apps that conflict with each other, causing the CPU in the phone to run nonstop as these two apps battle it out for resources. The problem here is that unless someone spends the time to help you with the underlying problem, you'll be back in the store with the same issue.

At that point, however, you cannot return your phone. If you're sympathetic, or very annoying, your carrier may give you a refurbished phone. You walk out of the store, but without the biggest smile on your face. Unfortunately, nobody dealt with the underlying trouble, so you'll be back, once again, with the same problem.

No surprise if you start to think that the problem is with that darn phone. In fact, the store needs to listen to you about how you're using the phone and then help you get the most out of it. This is hard to do in a retail environment where the sales force is under pressure to sell lines of service and gets no concrete reward for helping you with your problem.

This is where smarter customer care comes in. With the proper tools, you can work with a product expert to troubleshoot your phone. Some companies specialize in understanding the underlying problems and coming up with solutions for consumers. This kind of customer care costs the carriers a little more, but it makes for fewer unnecessary returns of perfectly good phones — and for much happier customers.

Control of Your Home Electronics

Traditional home appliances are getting smarter, offering more capabilities for better performance. A problem they have is that adding rows of control buttons (so you can control those new capabilities) complicates manufacture. So the next generation of appliances has begun to add a small LCD screen to the appliance. This can look slick, but it costs a lot and is prone to breakage. Also, the fancy capabilities involve pushing a confusing combination of buttons with cryptic messages displayed on a tiny screen.

The latest idea is to omit the screen altogether, and to give you control of the settings through an application on your smartphone. Your appliance retains the very basic buttons, but allows you to use the fancy capabilities by setting them through your phone. You just download the free application made by the manufacturer from the Google Play Store, and you have your beautiful and logical user interface to control your new product. No strings attached.

For example, your new oven will allow you to turn it on and set the temperature without using a smartphone. However, if you want it to start preheating at 5:30 so you can put the casserole in right when you walk in the door, you set that up through your phone.

Many of us have such capabilities on our ovens. In practice, however, features that aren't used regularly don't become intuitive — and finding the instruction manual is often too much of a hassle.

An application written on your Galaxy S6, on the other hand, can be very intuitive. In just a few clicks, the oven temperature will be ready when you walk in the door.

Even cooler — or is that hotter? — you don't need to be nearby. You could be at the office when you change your oven's settings. The oven will never know the difference.

Before too long, such capabilities will be available on your washing machine, clothes dryer, security system, sprinklers, thermostat, and refrigerator — all coming soon to an appliance store near you!

Entertainment Selector

The traditional view is that we consumers sit in front of our TVs when we want to be entertained and at our PCs when we want to do something productive or communicate electronically. These clear distinctions have blurred since it became possible to watch movies and TV on a PC.

Now that you have HD resolution on your phone, it's not unreasonable to use your phone to do some channel-surfing. When you find what you want, and if it's convenient, you switch to the big-screen TV.

Although such a scenario has been technologically possible in the past, the extreme resolution of your phone makes it convenient and a viable alternative to firing up the big-screen TV in another part of the house.

The technology is present to make this vision a reality. However, it's not nearly as convenient as it could be. Today, you need to open the right applications or select the right channels. It would be convenient if your phone could communicate with the TV and have the TV find the right program, and vice versa. It would be slick if the phone could watch your eyes and detect when you have taken them off the TV screen, just as it can when you take your eyes off the phone screen.

Serving You Better

The smartphone is the mechanism that companies use to find a better way to serve you. This will show up in a few ways.

The first is in much better mobile advertising. There has been talk for a long time that advertisers can tell where you are and then give you ads or coupons based upon your proximity. This is just now starting to become a reality. It's still kinda clumsy. If you have been Googling, say, televisions, you may see ads relating to sales about televisions. In the future, however, your phone may tell you about a sale going on for Samsung televisions when you walk by the Sears store in the mall. That is cool.

Even cooler is to be told that that particular model is on sale at the Sears store and that this particular sale is the best in town by over $20. This can happen if you are doing research at the moment. It may be possible for your app to flag you if you have ever done this kind of research on the Internet.

The second way smartphones are enhancing service is by automating the order-taking process. For example, wherever you see a video kiosk, that company can allow you to interact with the information on the kiosk with your Samsung Galaxy S6. Some fast-food restaurants have installed kiosks so that customers can bypass the line to order from the menu. The items are totaled and paid for by credit card. The customer steps aside and waits for his or her number to be called.

This exact transaction could take place on your smartphone. You don't have to wait while the guy in front of you struggles to decide between a double cheeseburger or two single cheeseburgers . . . and hold the pickles. Instead, you can place your order on your smartphone and wait with eager anticipation to find out what toys are in your kid's meal.

Placing You Indoors

The Global Positioning System (GPS) is great. It can tell you precisely your location on the road and off the road. Chapter 11 covered how it can help you get to where you want to be.

There is a confession to be made. GPS doesn't work so well within buildings. Once you are in a building, your phone only kind of knows where you are. The satellites responsible for sending out signals so your phone can figure out your position are no longer visible, and the GPS in your phone waits patiently until it sees another satellite. Until then, it stops trying to figure where you are.

This is rarely a problem if you are, say, at your home. It is probably only a few thousand square feet. Things are altogether different if you are wandering around the Palazzo Casino in Las Vegas. At 6.95 million square feet, this building has the most floor area of any building in the United States.

You could be anywhere in the 160 acres of luxury resort space. It is unfortunate if the Carnevino Steakhouse sends you a mobile coupon offering a two-for-one meal to your Galaxy S6 while you are already sitting in the Delmonico Steakhouse. It can be a tragedy if you start choking on too big a bite of your porterhouse steak and emergency services cannot find you.

There are some efforts out there to come up with a better way to locate you when you are indoors. One approach has been to estimate your location based upon signal strength of known Wi-Fi access points. A range of companies that hire a large number of smarticles (i.e., smart people), are trying a variety of technologies to address this problem. May the best company win so we may all get better location-based services!

Augmenting Your Reality

You may have seen "augmented reality" in science fiction shows. The idea is that you pull up an application on your smartphone that directs your camera viewfinder to locate and identify via pop-up windows what you're looking at. For example, you hold up your phone while you're walking down the street, and it will tell you the addresses of the buildings that it sees and offer information on the buildings' tenants.

What is happening is that your phone camera is performing image recognition in real time and then doing a look up of information. It all sounds pretty straightforward. Your Galaxy S6 has a high-resolution camera along with massive amounts of processing power and the connectivity to get real-time information. Augmented reality apps are just around the corner.

A word of caution though: Augmented reality has been just around the corner for at least a decade. This is a really cool idea, and it makes for a really interesting demonstration with prototypes. However, we are still waiting for good implementations.

It is likely that the first successful implementations will be on a small scale, such as an art museum offering an app that would allow you to use your camera to tell you the pieces of art you are looking at as you stroll through the galleries.

Other implementations could be augmented shopping. Let's say that it is time to refurnish your living room. You no longer have to imagine how that furniture you see in the store would fit. You take a 360 degree shot of the room you want to redo. You virtually toss out the old sofa and put in the new one you see at the showroom. It is properly sized within your room as you re-arrange the layout. This is far more convenient than having them deliver the sofa in the "meat" world only to find that new furniture does not fit.

More and Better Health Sensors

Currently, you can get health and fitness devices that track a single function, such as heartbeat or the oxygen level in your blood. These are just the beginning. There are prototypes of multifunction devices that track several vital signs.

One factor that helps drive this market is that the number of smartphone users has been growing like gangbusters over the past few years. The number of smartphones sold exceeded the number of dumb phones as of 2014 and shows no sign of slowing. Phones without health sensors are now the exception rather than the rule.

Finally, these devices have the potential to improve your health. It won't be too long before first responders can have the information to render better services faster because they'll know many of the patient's vital signs (via smartphone) before they even leave the station.

Better 911 Services

The 911 system has been keeping the United States safe for more than 45 years. The dirty secret of this service is that the underlying technology used to communicate information on the caller's location hasn't been updated in a long time.

To put this in perspective, your smartphone is designed to work with data at up to 300 million bits per second. When you call 911, the phone that answers your call is designed to work with data at up to 120 bits per second. (Seriously. I am not making this up.)

Many states and regions are trying to address this problem. This effort is called next-generation 911 or NG911. NG911 promises to make the information you already have on your phone available to the people who are sending you help. This new technology is slowly being implemented region by region in different states and counties.

For example, most 911 dispatchers can't access the data from the health sensors described in the previous section. With NG911, you can set up your phone so that first responders receive your vital signs and EKG the moment they get the call to respond to your emergency.

With a larger data pipeline between your smartphone and the first responders, you can send anything that's relevant, including medical history, your emergency contacts, insurance data, and whether you have any protection orders against stalkers. All this information can help you — and it's available right away because regardless of where you happen to be, your phone is typically there with you.

More Body English/Less Tapping

Tapping your screen is not hard, but tilting or twisting your screen can be a more natural motion. For example, Nintendo shook up the gaming world back in 2006 when it launched the Wii gaming console with the Wii remote. The Wii remote added an accelerometer, which opened up a new gaming experience by letting the game player communicate with the game through motion.

Well, guess what: Your Samsung Galaxy S6 has a very accurate accelerometer that can also tell the game what to do with the bowling ball, tennis racket, or whatever.

Up to now, very few applications or games have taken advantage of this capability. All the elements are there in the device to enable it to interpret gestures. The apps just need to take advantage of those elements.

Information Finder

Your smartphone, which is turned on all the time, is very handy if you just need to know the location of the 1994 Winter Olympic Games or the title of Virginia Madsen's first movie. (By the way, it's Lillehammer, Norway, and the 1983 movie *Class*.)

On the other hand, if you want to write a research report on the relative merits of a flat tax compared to a value-added tax, you're probably better off working on a PC. This latter project is best done with a full keyboard and large screen. The time to turn on the PC, watch it boot up, sign in, and connect with the Internet is small when compared to the time spent doing the research and writing.

In between these extremes, your phone is increasingly becoming the preferred tool for accessing information. The ergonomics of the screen, the convenience of the search tools, and the availability of applications all contribute to your phone being the primary source of daily information in lieu of your PC.

What this means to you is that your investment in your next PC should take into account how you use your smartphone. You may need less PC, depending on your information-collection habits.

Index

About the Author

Bill Hughes is an experienced marketing strategy executive with over two decades of experience in sales, strategic marketing, and business development roles at several leading corporations including Xerox, Microsoft, IBM, General Electric, Motorola, and U.S. West Cellular.

Bill has worked with Microsoft to enhance its marketing to mobile applications developers. He also has led initiatives to develop new products and solutions with several high-tech organizations including Sprint Nextel, Motorola, SBC, and Tyco Electronics.

Bill has been a professor of marketing at the Kellogg School of Management at Northwestern University, where he taught Business Marketing to graduate MBA students.

Bill also has written articles on this subject for several wireless-industry trade magazines. He also has contributed to articles in *USA Today* and *Forbes*. These articles were based upon his research reports written for InStat, where he was a principal analyst covering the wireless industry, specializing in smartphones and business applications of wireless devices.

Bill graduated with honors with an MBA degree from the Kellogg School of Management at Northwestern University and earned a Bachelor of Science degree with distinction from the College of Engineering at Cornell University, where he was elected to the Tau Beta Pi Engineering Honor Society.

Dedication

I would like to dedicate this book to my son, Quinlan, as he graduates from high school after having earned his BSA Eagle Scout and being awarded the game ball after the Bellevue High School water polo team won State. It is fun being a proud father.

Author's Acknowledgments

I need to thank a number of people who helped make this book a reality. First, I would like to thank my literary agent, Carole Jelen, of Waterside Publishing, for her support, encouragement, knowledge, and negotiation skills.

I would also like to thank the team at Wiley Publishing: Katie Mohr and Katie Dvorak. Your expertise helped me through the creative process. Thanks for your guidance.

A special thanks to Dee and Russ Tole. We owe you big time.

I also thank Ashley Wimberly and Philip Berne of Samsung Telecommunications America for their ongoing assistance. I would also like to thank Jeanette Park and Lucy Seonhe Park of Infraware, Kristen Tatti of Otterbox, Ryan Monney of Dungeoneers, Hari Seedhar of Soen Audio, Richard Park of Spigen, Yousef Kawar of SlipGrip, and Laura Mignott with Om/One.

I would like to acknowledge all of my family, Susan, Ellis, Arlen, Quinlan, and Indy for trying to keep me grounded (using the positive definition of the word). I would like to thank Lindsey Smith for keeping Ellis semi-grounded.

Publisher's Acknowledgments

Senior Acquisitions Editor: Katie Mohr

Project Editor: Katharine Dvorak

Editorial Assistant: Claire Brock

Sr. Editorial Assistant: Cherie Case

Production Editor: Kumar Chellappan

Cover Image: SkillUp / Shutterstock

Apple & Mac

iPad For Dummies,
6th Edition
978-1-118-72306-7

iPhone For Dummies,
7th Edition
978-1-118-69083-3

Macs All-in-One
For Dummies, 4th Edition
978-1-118-82210-4

OS X Mavericks
For Dummies
978-1-118-69188-5

Blogging & Social Media

Facebook For Dummies,
5th Edition
978-1-118-63312-0

Social Media Engagement
For Dummies
978-1-118-53019-1

WordPress For Dummies,
6th Edition
978-1-118-79161-5

Business

Stock Investing
For Dummies, 4th Edition
978-1-118-37678-2

Investing For Dummies,
6th Edition
978-0-470-90545-6

Personal Finance
For Dummies, 7th Edition
978-1-118-11785-9

QuickBooks 2014
For Dummies
978-1-118-72005-9

Small Business Marketing
Kit For Dummies,
3rd Edition
978-1-118-31183-7

Careers

Job Interviews
For Dummies, 4th Edition
978-1-118-11290-8

Job Searching with Social
Media For Dummies,
2nd Edition
978-1-118-67856-5

Personal Branding
For Dummies
978-1-118-11792-7

Resumes For Dummies,
6th Edition
978-0-470-87361-8

Starting an Etsy Business
For Dummies, 2nd Edition
978-1-118-59024-9

Diet & Nutrition

Belly Fat Diet For Dummies
978-1-118-34585-6

Mediterranean Diet
For Dummies
978-1-118-71525-3

Nutrition For Dummies,
5th Edition
978-0-470-93231-5

Digital Photography

Digital SLR Photography
All-in-One For Dummies,
2nd Edition
978-1-118-59082-9

Digital SLR Video &
Filmmaking For Dummies
978-1-118-36598-4

Photoshop Elements 12
For Dummies
978-1-118-72714-0

Gardening

Herb Gardening
For Dummies, 2nd Edition
978-0-470-61778-6

Gardening with Free-Range
Chickens For Dummies
978-1-118-54754-0

Health

Boosting Your Immunity
For Dummies
978-1-118-40200-9

Diabetes For Dummies,
4th Edition
978-1-118-29447-5

Living Paleo For Dummies
978-1-118-29405-5

Big Data

Big Data For Dummies
978-1-118-50422-2

Data Visualization
For Dummies
978-1-118-50289-1

Hadoop For Dummies
978-1-118-60755-8

Language & Foreign Language

500 Spanish Verbs
For Dummies
978-1-118-02382-2

English Grammar
For Dummies, 2nd Edition
978-0-470-54664-2

French All-in-One
For Dummies
978-1-118-22815-9

German Essentials
For Dummies
978-1-118-18422-6

Italian For Dummies,
2nd Edition
978-1-118-00465-4

Available in print and e-book formats.

Math & Science

Algebra I For Dummies,
2nd Edition
978-0-470-55964-2

Anatomy and Physiology
For Dummies, 2nd Edition
978-0-470-92326-9

Astronomy For Dummies,
3rd Edition
978-1-118-37697-3

Biology For Dummies,
2nd Edition
978-0-470-59875-7

Chemistry For Dummies,
2nd Edition
978-1-118-00730-3

1001 Algebra II Practice
Problems For Dummies
978-1-118-44662-1

Microsoft Office

Excel 2013 For Dummies
978-1-118-51012-4

Office 2013 All-in-One
For Dummies
978-1-118-51636-2

PowerPoint 2013
For Dummies
978-1-118-50253-2

Word 2013 For Dummies
978-1-118-49123-2

Music

Blues Harmonica
For Dummies
978-1-118-25269-7

Guitar For Dummies,
3rd Edition
978-1-118-11554-1

iPod & iTunes
For Dummies, 10th Edition
978-1-118-50864-0

Programming

Beginning Programming
with C For Dummies
978-1-118-73763-7

Excel VBA Programming
For Dummies, 3rd Edition
978-1-118-49037-2

Java For Dummies,
6th Edition
978-1-118-40780-6

Religion & Inspiration

The Bible For Dummies
978-0-7645-5296-0

Buddhism For Dummies,
2nd Edition
978-1-118-02379-2

Catholicism For Dummies,
2nd Edition
978-1-118-07778-8

Self-Help & Relationships

Beating Sugar Addiction
For Dummies
978-1-118-54645-1

Meditation For Dummies,
3rd Edition
978-1-118-29144-3

Seniors

Laptops For Seniors
For Dummies, 3rd Edition
978-1-118-71105-7

Computers For Seniors
For Dummies, 3rd Edition
978-1-118-11553-4

iPad For Seniors
For Dummies, 6th Edition
978-1-118-72826-0

Social Security
For Dummies
978-1-118-20573-0

Smartphones & Tablets

Android Phones
For Dummies, 2nd Edition
978-1-118-72030-1

Nexus Tablets
For Dummies
978-1-118-77243-0

Samsung Galaxy S 4
For Dummies
978-1-118-64222-1

Samsung Galaxy Tabs
For Dummies
978-1-118-77294-2

Test Prep

ACT For Dummies,
5th Edition
978-1-118-01259-8

ASVAB For Dummies,
3rd Edition
978-0-470-63760-9

GRE For Dummies,
7th Edition
978-0-470-88921-3

Officer Candidate Tests
For Dummies
978-0-470-59876-4

Physician's Assistant Exam
For Dummies
978-1-118-11556-5

Series 7 Exam For Dummies
978-0-470-09932-2

Windows 8

Windows 8.1 All-in-One
For Dummies
978-1-118-82087-2

Windows 8.1 For Dummies
978-1-118-82121-3

Windows 8.1 For Dummies,
Book + DVD Bundle
978-1-118-82107-7

 **Available in print and e-book formats.**

Available wherever books are sold. **For more information or to order direct visit www.dummies.com**

Take Dummies with you everywhere you go!

Whether you are excited about e-books, want more from the web, must have your mobile apps, or are swept up in social media, Dummies makes everything easier.

Leverage the Power

For Dummies is the global leader in the reference category and one of the most trusted and highly regarded brands in the world. No longer just focused on books, customers now have access to the For Dummies content they need in the format they want. Let us help you develop a solution that will fit your brand and help you connect with your customers.

Advertising & Sponsorships

Connect with an engaged audience on a powerful multimedia site, and position your message alongside expert how-to content.

Targeted ads • Video • Email marketing • Microsites • Sweepstakes sponsorship

21 Million Monthly Page Views & 13 Million Unique Visitors

# of For Dummies

Custom Publishing

Reach a global audience in any language by creating a solution that will differentiate you from competitors, amplify your message, and encourage customers to make a buying decision.

Apps • Books • eBooks • Video • Audio • Webinars

Brand Licensing & Content

Leverage the strength of the world's most popular reference brand to reach new audiences and channels of distribution.

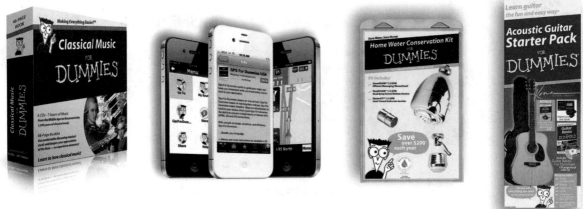

For more information, visit www.Dummies.com/biz

Dummies products make life easier!

- DIY
- Consumer Electronics
- Crafts
- Software
- Cookware
- Hobbies
- Videos
- Music
- Games
- and More!

For more information, go to **Dummies.com** and search the store by category.

FOR
DUMMIES
A Wiley Brand